APPLE SOFTWARE PROTECTION DIGEST

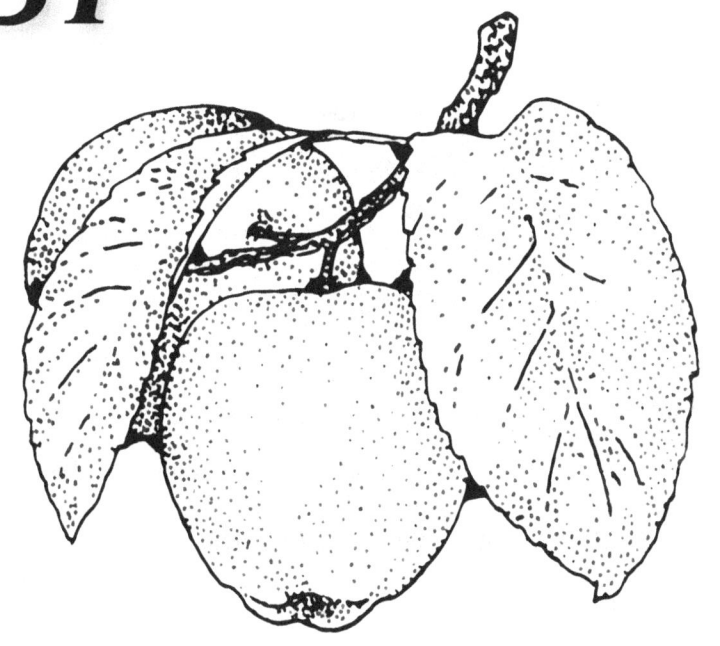

Jules H. Gilder

Produced by
Brian Wiser & Bill Martens

 Apple PugetSound Program Library Exchange

Apple Software Protection Digest

Copyright © 2021 by Apple Pugetsound Program Library Exchange (A.P.P.L.E.). All Rights Reserved.
Published by Apple Pugetsound Program Library Exchange (A.P.P.L.E.)

www.callapple.org

Paperback ISBN: 978-1-6671-0450-8
Hardback ISBN: 978-1-6671-0448-5

ACKNOWLEDGEMENTS

Apple Software Protection Digest was a publication that lasted six issues, originally published in 1985-1986 and copyright by Jules H. Gilder and Redlig Systems, Inc.

This new compilation is copyright by A.P.P.L.E. as the publisher. No claim to copyright over *Apple Software Protection Digest* is created outside of those portions created by A.P.P.L.E..

Special thanks to Alexander Kaltsas for donating the issues.

The Cover and Book were designed by Brian Wiser.

PRODUCTION

Brian Wiser → Cover Design, Apple logo colorizing, Layout, Writing, Editing, Scanning
Bill Martens → Gilder Biography, Production

DISCLAIMER

No part of this book may be reproduced, distributed or transmitted in any form or by any means, including photocopying, scanning, or other electronic or mechanical methods, without prior written permission of the publisher, except in the case of brief quotations contained in articles and reviews, and program listings that may be entered, stored and executed in a computer system, but not reproduced for publication. Thank you for respecting the intellectual property of the authors and publisher.

Disk images are available from the publisher's site: www.callapple.org. No warranty of disk images is made or implied and should be used at your own risk.

Apple Software Protection Digest is an independent publication and has not been authorized, sponsored, or otherwise approved by any institution, public or private.

All images are under copyright and the property of Apple Pugetsound Program Library Exchange, or as otherwise indicated. Use is prohibited without prior permission.

Apple and all Apple hardware and software brand names are trademarks of Apple Inc., registered in the United States and other countries. All other brand names and trademarks are the property of their respective owners.

While all possible steps have been taken to ensure that the information included within is accurate, the publisher, producers, and authors shall have no liability or responsibility for any errors or omissions, or for loss or damages resulting from the use of the information and programs contained herein.

About Jules H. Gilder

Jules H. Gilder is a pioneer in the use of personal computers. He was one of a handful of people to purchase and use the original Apple-1 computer, on which he taught himself 6502 assembly language programming. Since then he has taught hundreds of people both BASIC and assembly language programming in courses at New York University and private seminars.

He has been editor-in-chief of *Personal Computing* magazine, vice president of software for Children's Television Workshop, and editorial director of Hayden Software.

Gilder is the author of eight books covering telephone accessories, integrated software, and science and engineering programs in Pascal and BASIC for the Apple and IBM PC computers:

110 IC Timer Projects

Apple IIc and IIe Assembly Language

BASIC Computer Programs in Science and Engineering

IBM PC Programs in Science and Engineering

More Telephone Accessories You Can Build

Now That You Know Assembly Language

Pascal Programming: Science and Engineering

Telephone Accessories You Can Build

In 1985, Gilder published the first issue of *Apple Software Protection Digest,* dedicated to the subject of protection and how it relates to software for the Apple II series of computers. Six issues were produced by the end of 1986.

About the Producers

Brian Wiser

Brian Wiser is a producer of books, films, games, and events, as well as a long-time consultant, enthusiast and historian of Apple, the Apple II and Macintosh. Steve Wozniak and Steve Jobs, as well as *Creative Computing*, *Nibble*, *InCider*, and *A+* magazines were early influences.

Brian designed, edited, and co-produced dozens of books including: *Nibble Viewpoints: Business Insights From The Computing Revolution*, *Cyber Jack: The Adventures of Robert Clardy and Synergistic Software*, *Synergistic Software: The Early Games*, *The Colossal Computer Cartoon Book: Enhanced Edition*, *All About Applesoft: Enhanced Edition*, *Graphically Speaking: Enhanced Edition*, *What's Where in the Apple: Enhanced Edition*, and *The WOZPAK: Special Edition* – an important Apple II historical book with Steve Wozniak's restored original, technical handwritten notes. Brian is also the author of *The Etch-a-Sketch and Other Fun Programs*.

He passionately preserves and archives all facets of Apple's history, and noteworthy companies such as Beagle Bros and Applied Engineering, featured on AppleArchives.com. His writing, interviews and books are featured on the technology news site CallApple.org and in *Call-A.P.P.L.E.* magazine that he co-produces as an A.P.P.L.E. board member. Brian also co-produced the retro iOS game *Structris*.

In 2005, Brian was cast as an extra in Joss Whedon's movie *Serenity*, leading him to being a producer and director for the documentary film *Done The Impossible: The Fans' Tale of Firefly & Serenity*. He brought some of the *Firefly* cast aboard his Browncoat Cruise and recruited several of the *Firefly* cast to appear in a film for charity. Throughout these experiences, he develops close personal relationships with many actors, authors, and computer industry luminaries. Brian speaks about his adventures to large audiences at conventions around the country.

Bill Martens

Bill Martens is a systems engineer specializing in office infrastructures and has been programming since 1976. The DEC PDP 11/40 with ASR-33 Teletypes and CRT's were his first computing platforms with his first forays in the Apple world coming with the Apple II computer.

Influences in Bill's computing life came from *Byte* magazine, *Creative Computing* magazine, and *Call-A.P.P.L.E.* magazine as well as his mentors Samuel Perkins, Don Williams, Joff Morgan, and Mike Christensen.

Bill is the author of *ApPilot/W1*, *The Anatomy of an EAMON*, and multiple EAMon adventure games, as well as a co-producer of many books including *What's Where in the Apple: Enhanced Edition*, *The WOZPAK: Special Edition*, *Nibble Viewpoints: Business Insights From The Computing Revolution*, and co-programmer for the iOS version of the retro game *Structris*. He has written many articles which have appeared in user group newsletters and magazines such as *Call-A.P.P.L.E.*.

Bill worked for Apple Pugetsound Program Library Exchange (A.P.P.L.E.) under Val Golding and Dick Hubert as a data manager and programmer in the 1980s, and is the current president of the A.P.P.L.E. user group established in 1978. He reorganized A.P.P.L.E. and restarted *Call-A.P.P.L.E.* magazine in 2002. He is the production editor for the A.P.P.L.E. website CallApple.org, writes science fiction novels in his spare time, and is a retired semi-pro football player.

APPLE SOFTWARE PROTECTION DIGEST

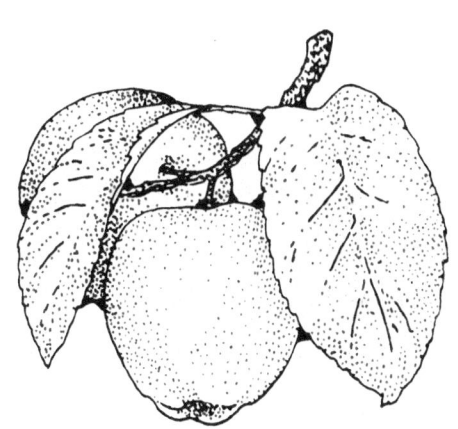

Vol. 1, No. 1 — Premiere Issue   1985

Editorial: Learning to Live with Protection (by Jules H. Gilder) 1
Hiding Applesoft Program Lines 2
Applesoft Line Finder 3
    Applesoft Line Finder (program) 4
Protection Tutorial – Part I 6
    Auto-Running Programs 6
    Making Them Hard to Copy 6
    Skip Track 3 Formatter (program) 6
    Adding Extra Tracks 8
Backing Up *The Print Shop* 10
Print Shop Copy Program 10
Review: *Copy][Plus* 11

Vol. 1, No. 2 — January/February   1986

Editorial: A Little Late, But Better Than Ever (by Jules H. Gilder) 1
Using COPYA to Backup Protected Disks 2
    COPYP Maker (program) 2
How to BRUN Applesoft Programs 4
    BRUN Maker for Applesoft Programs (program) 4
Parameter Files for COPYP 6
    Print Shop Companion (by Stan Kelley) 6
    Sensible Grammar and *Bookends* (by Allen L. Southmayd) 7
    PFS Series – ProDOS Version 7
    Time Is Money 9

| *Homeword* | 9 |

    Homeword 9

    Homeword Speller 9

Change the BLOAD Address of Binary Files 9

Letters 10

Hiding Machine Language Programs in Strings 11

Two Solutions to the Hide-A-Line Problem (by Mark Landwehr) 12

    Applesoft Line-Hide #1 (program) 12

    Applesoft Line-Hide #2 (program) 13

Hiding Program Lines from BASIC (by Eric Wachtenheim) 14

A Handy Decimal/Hexadecimal Converter 15

    Hex/Decimal/Hex Converter (program) 15

Applesoft Line Finder and Vanisher (by Adam Levin) 16

Wipeout: The Ultimate Weapon of Destruction 17

Review: *Locksmith 5.0G* (by J. Scott Barrus) 19

Protection Tutorial – Part II 20

    Formatting a disk 20

    Getting on the track 20

    What a formatted track looks like 20

    What's the address? 20

    Encoding the user data 21

    Hexadecimal to Binary Converter (program) 21

    Making your own protected DOS 22

    4 + 4 Byte Encoder (program) 22

Vol. 1, No. 3 — 1986

Editorial: Some Publishers Dropping Protection (by Jules H. Gilder) 1

Cracks Wanted 2

Crack Index 2

Letters 2

How to Crack a Program 3

Parameter Files for COPYP 6

    Applewriter IIe 6

    Financial Cookbook 6

    Hayes Terminal Program 11

    Microwave 11

Add Undeletable Lines to Your Program 7
    All Line Numbers to 65535 (program) 7
Moving the Catalog to Another Track 9
Review: The quickLoader ROM Card 10

Vol. 1, No. 4 — 1986

Editorial: Help Spread the Word (by Jules H. Gilder) 1
Crack Index 2
Bugs 2
    Print Shop Copier 2
    Print Shop Companion 2
    Tutorial – Part II 2
Letters 2
Protect and Unprotect Programs with *Muffin Plus* and *Demuffin Plus* 3
    6502 Relocator (program by Steve Wozniak, modified by Jules H. Gilder) 4
Protection Tutorial – Part III: All About Self-Sync Bytes 7
Cracks Wanted 8
How to Restore Lost Applesoft Programs 9
    &RESTORE (program) 9

Vol. 1, No. 5 — 1986

Editorial: The Judge Was Wrong (by Jules H. Gilder) 1
Cracks Wanted 2
Bugs: *Print Shop Companion* 2
Letters 2
Crack Index 2
DOS 3.3: In the Back Door, Through the Drive Door 3
    DOS Command Comparer (program) 3
How to Crack "It's the Pits" (by Philip Goetz) 5
The Ultimate Line Hider (by Grant Stevens) 6

Vol. 1, No. 6 — 1986

Editorial: Better Software Warranties (by Jules H. Gilder) 1

Cracks Wanted 2

Next Issue 2

Letters 2

Crack Index 2

How to Crack *Dazzle Draw* (by The Executor & Byte Doc) 3

Five Byte Disk Analyzer (by David Stoll) 6

Unprotecting *Locksmith 5.0* (by Brian A. Troha) 8

COPYP File Parameters — *Karate Champ* (by Brian A. Troha) 9

Review: *Locksmith 6.0* (by Scott Barrus) 10

APPLE SOFTWARE PROTECTION DIGEST

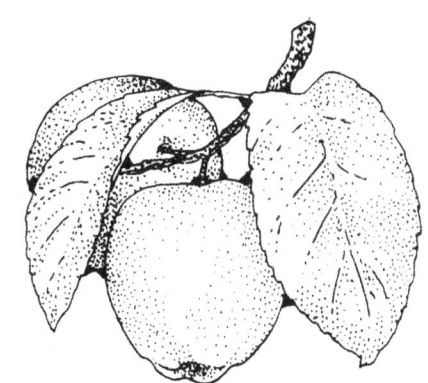

$3.00

Vol. 1, No. 1 — Premiere Issue

Contents

EDITORIAL........................1
HIDING APPLESOFT
    PROGRAM LINES.............2
APPLESOFT LINE FINDER.......3
PROTECTION TUTORIAL – Part 1.6
    Auto-Running Programs........6
    Making Them Hard to Copy....6
    Skip Track 3 Formatter........6
    Adding Extra Tracks...........8
    BACKING UP *PRINT SHOP*...10
    Print Shop Copy Program.....10

REVIEW: Copy][Plus 11

COMING NEXT ISSUE........11

Apple Software Protection Digest: Publisher & Editor, Jules H. Gilder; Contributing Editor, J. Scott Barrus. Copyright © 1985 by Redlig Systems, Inc., 2068 - 79th Street, Brooklyn, NY 11214. All rights reserved. No part of this publication may be reproduced, or electronically transmitted or stored without the publisher's written permission. Published monthly at $24 per year by Redlig Systems, Inc., (718) 232-8429. Reprints of prior issues available for $3 each.

Apple is a registered trademark of Apple Computer, Inc.

LEARNING TO LIVE WITH PROTECTION

Welcome to the Apple Software Protection Digest. This is the first issue of what will be a monthly publication that is dedicated to the subject of protection and how it relates to software for the Apple // series of computers. If you're like me, you've doubtless seen scores of articles in the various computer publications that tackle the subject of software protection. Most of them take a stand for or against it and that's the last you hear of the subject. But more is needed. Software protection is a fact of life and we must learn to live with it.

Too often, purchasers of programs get stuck. They buy a program only to discover that it can't be used with a particular accessory board or disk drive. And, because the program's protected, it can't be modified. Spelling checkers are a good example of this. They're frequently difficult or impossible to use with non-standard or hard disk drives, even though unprotected programs work without difficulty on these drives.

Apple computer owners need a place where they can get more information about software protection. They need a forum where they can exchange ideas with others who face the same or similar problems. They need to know what software protection is, how it's implemented, what are the consequences of it, how it can be overcome if necessary and if there are any comparable unprotected alternatives to particular protected software packages.

Apple Software Protection Digest will provide you with this information and more. It will show you new ways to protect, unprotect and backup your programs. It will teach you how to prevent others from accessing your programs and it will show you how to make them more difficult to copy. In addition, you'll learn how to overcome these and other protection schemes that are in use. You'll learn how to use the powerful, but complicated nibble copy programs. You'll also learn how to *crack* or remove protection entirely from many programs.

With the programs that are included in each issue of the digest, you'll build a valuable library of utility software that will make the job of protecting, unprotecting and backing up software easier. And, on-going tutorials will keep you up-to-date on both simple and sophisticated protection techniques. In addition to all this, every month you will get reviews of hardware, software and books that are of particular importance to the software protection field.

We do not advocate software piracy, because we firmly believe that in the long-run piracy only leads to more expensive and lower quality programs and less user support. Programmers work long, hard hours to get their software working and they deserve to be compensated fairly for it. This cannot happen if software is stolen. On the otherhand, the honest consumer should not be penalized and limited in his or her application of a particular program simply because the publisher decided to protect it. You may have a legitimate need to to back up a program and we hope to supply you with the knowledge you need to do that. Alternatively, you may wish to protect a program that you've written so that others can't copy it. We'll show you how to do that too.

Apple Software Protection Digest welcomes your comments, tips and article contributions. If you have a problem backing up a particular program, let us know, we'll try to help. If you've discovered a way to copy or crack (unprotect) a particular program, let us know about that too. Most likely there are other people who would like to know how to do it also. Finally, if you've come up with an ingenious hardware or software oriented protection scheme, write to us about it so that we can share it with others. If your article is used, you'll receive a free 6-month subscription (or subscription extension) to our publication. Let's hear from you soon.

Jules H. Gilder
Editor & Publisher

HIDING APPLESOFT PROGRAM LINES

Sometimes when you write an Applesoft program, you may find it desirable to make certain sections of it invisible. Maybe you've developed a unique way of solving a problem and you don't want others to copy your algorithm, maybe you want to bury a copyright notice in the code where it won't be easily spotted and deleted, maybe you want to use a machine language subroutine without announcing it to the world, maybe you want to include a password system to prevent unauthorized use of your program or maybe you want to hide the code that implements your copy protection scheme. Whatever the reason, the need to hide one or more Applesoft program lines arises frequently and you should know how to do. I'm going to show three ways to do the job, with the best one being the last one.

Hiding Applesoft lines is an old trick that was used in a lot of early protected software. The most common way to make a line disappear is to end it with a :REM statement and then imbed backspace characters in the REM statement. You'll need one backspace for every character that is going to be hidden plus six additional ones. Remember to include the line number and the spaces that separate it from the text of the line, in the character count. After you've put in the backspace character (and I'll tell you how to do that in a minute) then you'll need an equal amount of additional text that is going to be printed over the text that is to be hidden.

If you try to type the program line: 10 REM and then try to enter backspaces so the line can be erased, you'll quickly find that you have a problem. Go ahead try it. Instead of inserting the backspace character into the REM statement, when you type a backspace (or left arrow) from the keyboard, it moves the cursor back and prevents the line from being stored in memory. This is not what we want. Since backspaces cannot be entered into a program line directly, we're going to have to force it in. To do this, we use a process called *patching*. Patching requires that we place a dummy character in the REM statement every place where there's going to be a backspace. After that's done, we must search the computer's memory for the dummy character and replace it with the code for a backspace.

Since we'd like to automate the search and replace task, a dummy character should be chosen that's not used anywhere else in the program. Several such characters exist on the Apple //e and //c keyboard, but only one exists on the Apple II Plus keyboard, so we'll use that one. The character is the *at sign* (@).

To show you how this works, let's make the following Applesoft program line disappear:

10 PRINT "A"

If we count everything to be hidden (including the line number) we find that we'll need thirteen back spaces. But remember I said you have to add on six to this, so the total is nineteen. Now that we've backspaced to the beginning of the display line, we have to overprint the line to make it disappear. The message you print must be at least as long as the text being hidden. Thus, the new line to be entered should look like this:

10 PRINT "A": REM@@@@@@@@@@@@@@@@@@@NOW THE LINE IS HIDDEN

It's important that you do not leave a space between the REM and the first @. Now, if we wanted to, we could get into the monitor by typing CALL-151 and change all those *at signs* to the backspace character (which is ASCII 8). But that's tedious, so let's make the computer do it. Type in the following line with no line number so that the computer will start executing it the moment you press <RETURN>. If you're going to use this technique a lot, you might prefer to create a TEXT file with this line in it and then EXEC it every time you need it.

D=ASC ("@") : FOR X=2049 TO PEEK (175) + 256*PEEK (176) : POKE X,(PEEK (X) < > D)*PEEK (X) + 8*(PEEK (X)=D) : NEXT

What this line does is set D equal to the ASCII code of the dummy character that is to be replaced. If you decide to use some character other than the @, simply place it between the quotation marks in the line above. Next the computer starts at the beginning of the Applesoft program (location 2049) and checks every byte until the end to see if it's equal to the @ character. If it is, that character is replaced with an 8, which is the backspace character, otherwise it's left alone.

If you look carefully at the one line program that performs the search and replace, you'll notice that there's no IFTHEN statement in it, although from the verbal description it seems as though one is needed. IF...THEN statements cannot be used as easily from the immediate mode, so another way of doing the same thing had to be found. If you haven't already guessed by now, it has to do with the strange statement POKE X, (PEEK (X) < > D)*PEEK (X) + 8*(PEEK (X)=D).

Here we're telling the computer to look at the current location indicated by X. If the value stored there is not equal to D the expression (PEEK (X) < > D) is true and is mathematically equal to a 1, otherwise it's set equal to 0. At the same time, if the contents of location X are not equal to D, the expression 8*(PEEK (X) = D) is not true and evaluates to zero. Thus, whatever was in location X is stored back there again. However, if the contents of location X are equal to D, (PEEK (X) < > D)*PEEK (X) becomes zero and 8*(PEEK (X) = D) becomes 8 (the backspace character), and that's what's stored in memory.

If you've been following so far, and you've typed everything in, you've noticed that when you RUN the program it prints out an A like it's supposed to, but when you try to list it, you get the message "NOW THE LINE IS HIDDEN" printed instead. Good for you. You've just implemented one of several protection techniques that were used on early Apple programs. But don't get too excited, because while this technique works nicely for normal operation of the computer, as early software publishers quickly found out, issuing one simple command overcomes all the hard work you've just done. With your invisible line program still in memory, type in the following two lines in the immediate mode (without a line number):

SPEED=100
LIST

The invisible line lists out to the screen very slowly and you can see it get erased slowly too. And, if you press Control-S before the overprinting starts, you can freeze the line on the screen for as long as you need to copy it down on a piece of paper.

As you can see, this is not a very secure way of hiding Applesoft program lines. In addition, it has a tremendous overhead, and requires a lot of additional memory for each line that is hidden. Surely there must be another way.

Hide a line between two others

If you understand how Applesoft stores a program in memory (and I'll explain that in a minute) you can hide a line between two other lines and make it completely invisible. A line hidden in this manner will function correctly, but will not be visible at all, even if you set SPEED to a very low number. Let's first see how Applesoft stores a program line in memory by looking at the following line:

10 PRINT 123

If we were to look directly into memory, we'd see that the line was stored in the following way:

Address	801	802	803	804	805	806	807	808	809
Contents	0A	08	0A	00	BA	31	32	33	00

Looking at locations $801 and $802 (2049 and 2050 in decimal) we see two hexadecimal numbers stored there: 0A and 08, which comprise the hexadecimal number $080A. In 6502 microprocessor systems, hex numbers are always stored in memory with the low-order byte first. This number represents the location in memory of the start of the next line of the Applesoft program. So if we were to add another line to our program, it would start at location $80A. Thus, the first to bytes of any Applesoft program line are called the *next line pointer*.

The next two bytes at $803 and $804 hold the hex equivalent of the line number. Since our line number is less than 255, only the low-order byte is used (it's set to $0A which equals 10 in decimal). The high-order byte is set to zero. Next, on the fifth byte ($805) we have the start of our line. $805 contains $BA which is the code, or token, that represents the word PRINT and the following locations contain $31, $32 and $33 which are the hex ASCII codes for 1, 2 and 3. Finally, there's a zero, which serves as an end of line marker.

If you're a good detective, by now you may have guessed that this method of hiding lines changes the next line pointer so that the line you want to hide is bypassed. Let's clarify things by using the following three-line program as an example:

10 PRINT
20 PRINT "THIS IS A TEST"
30 PRINT

Let's get into the monitor by typing CALL -151. Then type 801.824. The display you get should look like this:

0801- 07 08 0A 00 BA 00 1D
0808- 08 14 00 BA 22 54 48 49
0810- 53 20 49 53 20 41 20 54
0818- 45 53 54 22 00 23 08 1E
0820- 00 BA 00 00 00

If we want to hide line 20, then all we have to do is change the pointer to it (which is at $801). Let's change the pointer so that instead of pointing to line 20, it points to line 30. If we look at $807, which is where line 20 begins, we see that it points to $81D which is where line 30 begins. Now let's change the pointer to line 20 by typing:

801:1D

Next, get back to Applesoft by typing 3D0G and LIST the program. You should only see line 10 and line 30. Line 20 seems to have disappeared completely. However, if you type RUN, you'll see that line 20 is indeed still there because it prints out the message "THIS IS A TEST". The reason the line is not listed, but is executed is that the *next line pointer* is only used by the LIST, GOTO and GOSUB routines. The routine that executes a program just starts at the beginning of the program and executes everything it finds in consecutive order.

Well, it looks like we found a a good way to hide an Applesoft line. We did, as long as we don't change, add or delete any lines after we've hidden the ones we want, and the lines have to be hidden under program control, after the program has been loaded. The reason is, each time we add, delete or change a line, Applesoft recalculates the next line pointers by calling a routine in the ROMs known as LINKSET ($D4F2) and *corrects* the changes we made. Thus even if we try to delete a non-existing line, our hidden line will immediately re-appear. To verify this, just type 0 and <RETURN> to delete the non-existent line zero. Now list the program. Line 20 has re-appeared again.

Unfortunately, when this version of Applesoft BASIC came out, there was also another version of the language, whose programs started at $3000 instead of $800, being used. In order to insure compatibility between programs written by both versions, DOS was changed to include a call to an automatic pointer resetting routine when a program is loaded from the disk. Thus, once again our protected program will be corrected when it is loaded into place. This is not too bad however, because there are ways to overcome that. We'll talk about automatically loading and running Applesoft programs and bypassing the pointer correction routine next time.

The best way to hide a line

There is still one more way to hide an Applesoft program line and these one has fewer problems and is more effective than the others. This technique takes advantage of a quirk in Applesoft and at the same time allows you to insert invisible identification, such as your initials, into the program as well.

To use this technique, all you do is precede each line that you want to render invisible with 5 colons. Then, we're going to change the code ($3A) for the first colon of each line to a $00. That's all there is to it. When you try to list the line, all you'll get is the line number. Let's try an example. Type in the following 3-line program:

10 PRINT
20 ::::: PRINT "THIS IS A TEST"
30 PRINT

Now get into the monitor by typing CALL -151 and type AF.B0 to get the location of the end of the program + 1. This gives:

AF.B0
00AF- 2A
00B0- 08

Next, display a hex dump of the program by typing 801.829 <RETURN>. You'll get the following:

0801- 07 08 0A 00 BA 00 22
0808- 08 14 00 3A 3A 3A 3A 3A
0810- BA 22 54 48 49 53 20 49
0818- 53 20 41 20 54 45 53 54
0820- 22 00 28 08 1E 00 BA 00
0828- 00 00

Looking at the above hex dump, we see that the first colon ($3A) is located at $80B. Change it to a zero by typing 80B:0 <RETURN>. Now get back to Applesoft by typing 3D0G and list the program. This is what you should get:

10 PRINT
20
30 PRINT

If you run the program it will still print out the "THIS IS A TEST" message. By the way, there's nothing magical about using colons, it's just that you can put them in without effecting the operation of the program in the *unprotected* mode. If you want, however, the second through fifth characters at the beginning of the line can be your initials or anything else. Thus you could have:

20::JHG PRINT "THIS IS A TEST"

However, if you tried to run a program with this line in it without changing the first colon to a zero, you'll get a syntax error. After you make the change however, Applesoft will ignore the remaining four characters so no error message is generated.

It's easy to insert patches into a program line when the line is at the beginning of the program. However, it's a pain in the neck to do it when the line is in the middle of a large program. To make this task easier, the Utility program this month has been designed to make the task easier. It's called Applesoft Line Finder and it will locate any line in the program that you specify, display a hex dump of just that line, and leave you in the monitor mode so you can make any desired changes. Of course, if you want to make all the changes automatically, you can write a short Applesoft program that gets appended to the current program and run that, or you can write a separate machine language program to do it.

To make life interesting, and to give you some incentive, we'll give a free 6 month subscription (or extension) to the best machine language and Applesoft programs that automatically make the required changes. And, if your program automatically changes the remaining four colons to an identification string that the user enters, we'll make it seven months instead of six. Go to it!

APPLESOFT LINE FINDER

Earlier, we had a short discussion on the way a line of an Applesoft program is stored in memory. Without repeating that discussion in detail, let's just review a few pertinent facts. With ROM or language card Applesoft, program storage normally starts at location $801. The first two bytes of an Applesoft line contain a pointer to the location in memory of the next Applesoft line. The next two bytes are reserved for the hex representation of the line number. Then, the actual text of the line is stored with Applesoft keywords replaced by one-byte tokens. Finally, the line is terminated with a zero.

The program APPLESOFT LINE FINDER, takes a line number that is passed to it by the ampersand command and uses some of the routines in the Apple ROMs to first locate the position of the line in memory and then display the line in hex up to and including the terminating zero byte. The program then leaves you in the monitor mode so that you can make any changes desired in the line just displayed.

The program starts at location $2DA, which is the upper part of the input buffer. To use it, the program is loaded and then activated by a CALL 730. Since the program is located in pages 2 and 3 of memory, it can be loaded and run at any time during an Applesoft program's development, without affecting the Applesoft program.

The first part of the program, which starts on line 1360, clears the screen, prints out the program title and sets up the ampersand jump locations on page three to point to a routine that locates the Applesoft line. Immediately following this short routine, is the text that it prints out. The reason the text is placed here up front, is that it is going to be used once, the first time the program is run, and thus is expendable. So we won't have to worry about part of our program, which is stored in the input buffer, being wiped out if a long line of text is entered.

The actual program that finds and displays Applesoft lines starts on line 1660, where an Applesoft routine called LINGET ($DA0C) is called. LINGET is the routine that is used to check get the line number of an Applesoft line that is being entered from the keyboard. It uses TXTPTR, which is the text pointer in the CHRGET routine, and reads the number that TXTPTR is pointing to. It takes this number, converts it to hexadecimal and stores it in LINNUM and LINNUM+1 ($50 and $51). Because this routine is the same one that Applesoft uses to check line numbers, it has the same limitations, namely it is only good for line numbers up to and including 63999.

If you want to display lines greater than that, the JSR LINGET should be replaced by a JSR FRMNUM ($DD67), immediately followed by a JSR GETADR ($E752).

Once the line number has been converted to hex and stored in LINNUM, another Applesoft ROM routine, FNDLIN ($D61A), is called (line 1670). FNDLIN will start at the beginning of the Applesoft program and search for the line number that is currently stored in LINNUM (and of course LINNUM+1). If the line is found, its beginning address is stored in two page zero locations called LOWTR and LOWTR+1 ($9B and $9C). Also, if the number is found the carry bit is set. If the number is not found, the next highest line number, if there is one, is stored in LOWTR and the carry bit is cleared.

Upon returning from FNDLIN, the first thing the program does is to test the carry-bit to see if the line number was found (line 1680). If it was not found, the program branches to line 1940 where a message to the user is printed that rings the bell and tells him that no such line exists in the program. If the line does exist, the Y-register and memory location TEMP are both set to zero (lines 1690 and 1700) and the program jumps to a subroutine that prints out the two-byte address of the data that are going to be displayed on the next line of the video display (line 1710). This subroutine, which is called

```
                    1000  ****************************************
                    1010  ***                                    ***
                    1020  ***        APPLESOFT LINE FINDER       ***
                    1030  ***                                    ***
                    1080  ****************************************
                    1090  *
                    1100  *
                    1110  *
                    1120              .OR  $2DA
                    1130  *
                    1140  *
                    1150  * EQUATES
                    1160  *
0008-               1170  TEMP        .EQ  $8
0018-               1180  TXTPTR      .EQ  $18
003C-               1190  A1L         .EQ  $3C
009B-               1200  LOWTR       .EQ  $9B
03F5-               1210  AMPERSD     .EQ  $3F5
D61A-               1220  FNDLIN      .EQ  $D61A
DA0C-               1230  LINGET      .EQ  $DA0C
F941-               1240  PRNTAX      .EQ  $F941
FC58-               1250  HOME        .EQ  $FC58
FD8E-               1260  CROUT       .EQ  $FD8E
FDDA-               1270  PRBYTE      .EQ  $FDDA
FDED-               1280  COUT        .EQ  $FDED
FF69-               1290  MONZ        .EQ  $FF69
                    1300  *
                    1310  *
                    1320  * This is where the program title is
                    1330  * printed out and the ampersand (&) vector
                    1340  * jump is set up.
                    1350  *
02DA- 20 58 FC      1360              JSR  HOME         Clear the screen.
02DD- A9 F4         1370              LDA  #TEXT1       Get the address of the
02DF- A0 02         1380              LDY  /TEXT1       text to be printed.
02E1- 20 A8 03      1390              JSR  MSGPRT       Print it.
02E4- A2 4C         1400              LDX  #$4C         Get a JMP op code and
02E6- A9 49         1410              LDA  #START       the low and high bytes
02E8- A0 03         1420              LDY  /START       of START's address and
02EA- 8E F5 03      1430              STX  AMPERSD      store them in locations
02ED- 8D F6 03      1440              STA  AMPERSD+1    $3F5, $3F6 and $3F7.
02F0- 8C F7 03      1450              STY  AMPERSD+2
02F3- 60            1460              RTS
                    1470  *
                    1480  *
                    1490  * This is the text for the title and
                    1500  * copyright notice.
                    1510  *
02F4- C1 D0 D0
02F7- CC C5 D3
02FA- CF C6 D4
02FD- A0 CC C9
0300- CE C5 A0
0303- C6 C9 CE
0306- C4 C5 D2      1520  TEXT1       .AS  -"APPLESOFT LINE FINDER"
0309- 8D 8D         1530              .HS  8D8D
030B- C2 D9 A0
030E- CA D5 CC
0311- C5 D3 A0
0314- C8 AE A0
0317- C7 C9 CC
031A- C4 C5 D2      1540              .AS  -"BY JULES H. GILDER"
031D- 8D            1550              .HS  8D
031E- C3 CF D0
0321- D9 D2 C9
0324- C7 C8 D4
0327- A0 A8 C3
032A- A9 A0 B1
032D- B9 B8 B2      1560              .AS  -"COPYRIGHT (C) 1982"
0330- 8D            1570              .HS  8D
0331- C1 CC CC
0334- A0 D2 C9
0337- C7 C8 D4
033A- D3 A0 D2
033D- C5 D3 C5
0340- D2 D6 C5
0343- C4            1580              .AS  -"ALL RIGHTS RESERVED"
0344- 8D 8D 8D
0347- 8D 00        1590              .HS  8D8D8D8D00
                    1600  *
                    1610  *
                    1620  * This part of the program is the main
                    1630  * loop. It gets the line number, finds
                    1640  * it in memory and displays it in hex.
                    1650  *
0349- 20 0C DA     1660  START        JSR  LINGET       Convert number after & to hex.
```

PRTADDR, starts on line 2050 and begins by printing a carriage return and than a space (lines 2050 to 2070). Next, the X-register is set up as a displayed byte counter (line 2080) and is used to permit the display of only eight bytes of data per line. Then the subroutine prints out the address that is stored in LOWTR and LOWTR+1, high-order byte first (lines 2090 to 2120). Finally, a colon is printed out and the program returns to the caller via the RTS in the COUT routine (lines 2130 and 2140).

After printing out the starting memory address of the line of data to be displayed on the screen, a space is printed (lines 1720 and 1730) and eight bytes of data are printed. The byte to be printed is retrieved in line 1740 and checked to see if it is a zero in line 1750. If it is a zero, TEMP is tested to see if five or more bytes have already been printed (lines 1760 and 1770). The reason for this is that for line numbers below 255, the fourth byte, which is the high-order byte of the line number is set to zero. This is not the zero we wish to detect, but rather the zero that terminates the Applesoft program line.

If five or more bytes have been printed already, we know that this zero represents the end of the Applesoft line, so the program jumps to a routine (on line 1850), that prints out the zero, then prints out a carriage return (line 1870) and finally jumps to a routine in the F8 ROM called MONZ ($FF69) which leaves the user in the monitor mode (line 1880). If for some reason you wish to return to the program that called the APPLESOFT LINE FINDER instead of being left in the monitor, it is only necessary to replace the JMP MONZ in line 1880 with an RTS.

If less than five bytes have been printed, we know that this is not the end of the line and we print the zero out just as we would print any other byte (lines 1790 and 1800). Then the program jumps to a routine on line 2210 that increments the two-byte LOWTR pointer and also increments TEMP. After that, the X-register is decremented and tested to see if eight bytes have been printed already (lines 1820 and 1830). If not, the program branches to line 1720 where the next byte is retrieved and printed. Otherwise, it branches to line 1710 where the address of the next byte to be displayed is printed. This process continues until the terminating zero of the Applesoft program line is encountered.

The subroutine located in lines 2300 to 2400 is a message printing routine. Following this routine, on line 2480, is the text for the error message that says the line doesn't exist.

Unlike most programs that use the ampersand, this one is meant to be used primarily from the immediate mode rather than being called from a running program. However, as I indicated earlier, if you want it to return to a program that called it, the change that has to be made is trivial.

continued on page 8

```
034C- 20 1A D6  1670           JSR FNDLIN       Put address of line in LOWTR.
034F- 90 2E     1680           BCC NOLINE       Line doesn't exist.
0351- A0 00     1690           LDY #$0          Zero the Y-register.
0353- 84 08     1700           STY TEMP         and TEMP.
0355- 20 86 03  1710  NXTLIN   JSR PRTADDR      Print address of line.
0358- A9 A0     1720  PRTSPC   LDA #$A0         Print a space.
035A- 20 ED FD  1730           JSR COUT
035D- B1 9B     1740           LDA (LOWTR),Y    Get the next byte in the line.
035F- D0 08     1750           BNE PRINTIT      If it's not zero, print it.
0361- A5 08     1760           LDA TEMP         It is zero, did we pass
0363- C9 05     1770           CMP #$5          the fifth byte?
0365- B0 0D     1780           BCS DONE         Yes, print it and end up.
0367- A9 00     1790           LDA #$0          No, print it and continue.
0369- 20 DA FD  1800  PRINTIT  JSR PRBYTE       Print byte in accumulator.
036C- 20 9F 03  1810           JSR INCR         Increment LOWTR and TEMP.
036F- CA        1820           DEX              Decrease X by one.
0370- F0 E3     1830           BEQ NXTLIN       X=0 start a new line.
0372- D0 E4     1840           BNE PRTSPC       Get and print next byte.
0374- A9 00     1850  DONE     LDA #$0          The last byte is a zero
0376- 20 DA FD  1860           JSR PRBYTE       so print it.
0379- 20 8E FD  1870           JSR CROUT        Print a carriage return.
037C- 4C 69 FF  1880           JMP MONZ         Jump to the monitor.
                1890  *
                1900  *
                1910  * Tell the user the line he requested
                1920  * does not exist.
                1930  *
037F- A9 BE     1940  NOLINE   LDA #TEXT2       Point to text to be
0381- A0 03     1950           LDY /TEXT2       printed.
0383- 4C A8 03  1960           JMP MSGPRT       Print it.
                1970  *
                1980  *
                1990  * This section of the program prints
                2000  * out a carriage return, a space and then
                2010  * the address in memory of the first byte
                2020  * displayed on the line, followed by a
                2030  * colon.
                2040  *
0386- 20 8E FD  2050  PRTADDR  JSR CROUT        Print a carriage return.
0389- A9 A0     2060           LDA #$A0         Print out a space.
038B- 20 ED FD  2070           JSR COUT
038E- A2 08     2080           LDX #$8          Count 8 bytes per line.
0390- A5 9C     2090           LDA LOWTR+1      Print out the address of
0392- 20 DA FD  2100           JSR PRBYTE       the first byte on the
0395- A5 9B     2110           LDA LOWTR        line, high byte first.
0397- 20 DA FD  2120           JSR PRBYTE
039A- A9 BA     2130           LDA #$BA         Then print a colon.
039C- 4C ED FD  2140           JMP COUT
                2150  *
                2160  *
                2170  * Here, the pointer to the contents of
                2180  * the line is incremented.  Location
                2190  * TEMP is incremented too.
                2200  *
039F- E6 9B     2210  INCR     INC LOWTR
03A1- D0 02     2220           BNE INCTEMP
03A3- E6 9C     2230           INC LOWTR+1
03A5- E6 08     2240  INCTEMP  INC TEMP
03A7- 60        2250           RTS
                2260  *
                2270  *
                2280  * This is the message printing routine.
                2290  *
03A8- 85 18     2300  MSGPRT   STA TXTPTR
03AA- 84 19     2310           STY TXTPTR+1
03AC- A0 00     2320           LDY #$0
03AE- B1 18     2330  LOOP     LDA (TXTPTR),Y
03B0- F0 0B     2340           BEQ ENDPRT
03B2- 20 ED FD  2350           JSR COUT
03B5- E6 18     2360           INC TXTPTR
03B7- D0 F5     2370           BNE LOOP
03B9- E6 19     2380           INC TXTPTR+1
03BB- D0 F1     2390           BNE LOOP
03BD- 60        2400  ENDPRT   RTS
                2410  *
                2420  *
                2430  * This is the text that tells the user
                2440  * that the requested line doesn't exist
                2450  * in the program.  A bell is also rung
                2460  * to alert the user to the error.
                2470  *
03BE- 8D        2480  TEXT2    .HS 8D
03BF- CE CF A0
03C2- D3 D5 C3
03C5- C8 A0 CC
03C8- C9 CE C5  2490           .AS -"NO SUCH LINE"
03CB- 87 8D 00  2500           .HS 878D00
```

PROTECTION TUTORIAL — Part I

Copy protection wasn't always a problem for Apple // owners. In the early days of computing (the late 1970s) no programs were copy protected and all could be be easily backed up by using the COPY or COPYA programs provided on the System Master diskette. However, as time went by, some manufacturers discovered that many more copies of of there program were available than they had produced. In addition, they were getting calls from people with questions from people who never bought the program. To combat this, they developed ways to automatically run programs when they were loaded in and made it difficult to copy those programs with the standard copy programs.

Making it run automatically

It's not as difficult as you might think to make machine language programs run automatically as soon as they are loaded. All you have to do is place the address of the start of you machine language program in locations $36 and $37. This should be done by the loading process, so that when the loading is completed and the computer attempts to print out the prompt character, control is automatically transferred to your program. Of course, one of the first things your program should do is restore the proper values to locations $36 and $37. Since it's not possible to make the changes to these two locations and save them out to the disk, you must do it somewhere else in memory, save it out to the disk and then change the loading address on the disk itself or BLOAD the program at $36.

If you have a short machine language program (less than 500 bytes long) you can let it reside in pages 2 and 3 of memory ($200 to $3FF). If it's longer than that, you'll have to place it at $800 and above. In the later case, to retain the auto-run capability, you'll have to save out the screen area as well. Let's see how a program to run automatically. To begin with, we'll first assume that the program will fit in pages 2 and 3 of memory and that its starting address is at $200. We'll use a simple program that clears the screen and prints an "A" as an example.

Since we already said that we can't assemble our auto-run program in the final location it is going to reside in, let's choose another convenient spot. In this case we'll start with $836. At $836 we'll place the address of the start of our program, which we said would be $200. So from the monitor, type in:

836:00 20

Now we have to leave the same amount of space between $836 and the start of our program, as there is between $36 and $200. So, our program which should be assembled to operate at $200, is temporarily stored at $A00 and here it is:

A00:A9 BD 85 36 A9 9E 85 37 20 58 FC
A9 C1 20 ED FD 4C 00 E0

Next, we want to transfer the contents of page 1, which is the stack area for the 6502, to its equivalent higher memory location. In order for the 6502 microprocessor to operate properly, it expects certain values in certain locations on the stack. By transferring the stack to higher memory, we can preserve those locations and load them back in when we load our program. We can do this by typing from the monitor:

900<100.1FFM

Finally, we save the whole thing out to disk as one file by typing:

BSAVE TEST,A$836,L$1DD

where $1DD is the length of memory between $836 and $A12 which is the end of our program. To automatically run our program, we just have to BLOAD TEST,A$36. Try it. If you want to eliminate the need to add the A$36 to the load command, you can use a track and sector editor program to modify the two bytes on the disk that tell DOS where to BLOAD the program. We'll take a look at how to do that next time.

How to make it harder to copy

Until now, we've only talked about auto running machine language programs. While this is an essential part of copy protection, its not enough. If you want to prevent unauthorized copying of a program, you have to prevent copy programs from reading the disk. One of the earliest ways this was done was to leave one or more tracks on a diskette unformatted. Usually this was track 3. When ordinary copy programs copy a diskette, they do it one track at a time. After copying DOS onto the new diskette (DOS is on tracks 0, 1 and 2) the program would attempt to copy track three. Since it was unformatted, the program was unable to read it and an I/O ERROR was caused, crashing the copy program. This was a fairly effective method of preventing copying but eventually copy programs came out that either ignored the I/O ERROR or copied only those sectors that were marked as being used on the Volume Table of Contents — VTOC — which is located on track 17 ($11), sector 0.

Erasing or leaving a track unformatted on a disk is still an effective way to keep people from making casual copies. Although most nibble copy programs (Copy][Plus, Locksmith, Essential Data Duplicator) will easily overcome this obstacle, most Apple // users do not own one of these programs, and rely on COPYA to backup their diskettes.

Those of you who would like to experiment with producing disks with an unformatted track, can do so with the aid of the Applesoft program listed below. This program temporarily modifies DOS 3.3's formatting routine so that it will leave track 3 unformatted. You must use new or erased diskettes because this program simply skips over track three. If you are using a previously formatted diskette, which had track 3 formatted, then it will remain formatted.

A patch to DOS is inserted in line 120 which tells the formatting routine to jump to location $300 (768) where there is a short routine to check and see if track 3 has been reached yet. If it has, the formatter's track counter is incremented by one so that track 3 will be skipped and not formatted. This is followed by the original four bytes that were removed from the formatter code to make room for the jump-to-patch instructions. Finally, this routine jumps back to the formatter which then finishes its job.

Leaving track 3 unformatted is not enough. If you want to prevent any crashes
continued on page 8

```
10  TEXT : HOME
20  A$ = "SKIP TRACK 3 FORMATTER"
30  PRINT  TAB( INT ( LEN (A$) / 2));A$
40  PRINT : PRINT : PRINT : INPUT "ENTER SLOT NUMBER: ";SLT
50  PRINT : INPUT "ENTER DRIVE NUMBER: ";DRV
60  IOB = 47080:TRK = IOB + 4:SCT = IOB + 5
80  FOR X = 768 TO 787
90    READ Y
100   POKE X,Y
110 NEXT X
120 POKE 48891,76: POKE 48892,0: POKE 48893,3
130 PRINT  CHR$ (4);"INITHELLO,S";SLT;",D",DRV
140 POKE 48891,165: POKE 48892,68: POKE 48893,201
150 POKE TRK,17: POKE SCT,0: POKE IOB + 3,0
160 CMD = 47092: POKE CMD,1: CALL 781
170 BUF =  PEEK (47088) + 256 *  PEEK (47089)
180 POKE BUF + 68,0: POKE BUF + 69,0: POKE CMD,2
190 CALL 781: POKE CMD,0
200 PRINT : PRINT : INPUT "DO YOU WANT TO FORMAT ANOTHER DISK? ";A$
210 IF  LEFT$ (A$,1) = "Y" OR  LEFT$ (A$,1) = "y" THEN  RUN
220 DATA 165,68,201,3,208,2,230,68,201,35,76,255,190
230 DATA 160,232,169,183,76,217,3
997 REM
998 REM COPYRIGHT 1985 BY JULES H. GILDER
999 REM ALL RIGHTS RESERVED
```

SOFTWARE PROTECTION TECHNIQUES EXPOSED!

Now, for the first time, owners of Apple // series computers can learn all about the tricks and techniques used to protect Apple software. Apple Software Protection Digest, a new monthly publication, will show you how to protect, unprotect and backup your software.

- Prevent others from accessing your programs
- Make your programs difficult to copy
- Overcome protection schemes on commercial software
- Build a library of protection-oriented utility programs
- Get help with your specific problems
- Learn about the latest advances in protection hardware and software

All this and more can be yours by subscribing to the Apple Software Protection Digest. A one-year subscription is $24, two years is $42.

SUBSCRIBE TODAY!

REDLIG SYSTEMS, INC., Dept. A1357
2068 - 79th St., Brooklyn, NY 11214

Please enter my _____ year subscription to Apple Software Protection Digest.

☐ Enclosed is my check for _____
☐ Please charge my credit card: ☐ VISA ☐ MasterCard ☐ American Express

Card Number _____ Exp. Date _____   Signature _____
Name _____
Address _____
City _____   State _____ Zip _____

Protection Tutorial

continued from page 6

caused by DOS's attempt to store something on track 3, you must tell DOS that track 3 is not available for storage. This can be done by modifying the appropriate bytes ($44 and $45) on track 17 ($11) sector 0. This sector has a special name. It's called the Volume Table of Contents, or VTOC for short and it keeps a record of which tracks are free and which aren't. By changing bytes $44 and $45 on this sector to zeroes, we effectively notify DOS that track 3 cannot be used to store anything. This is done by the code starting at line 150. Line 150 sets up the track and sector, while line 160 sets up the input/output block (IOB) that the next disk operation we do is going to be a read from the disk. The actual disk access is done by a short machine language routine located at 781 ($30D). This program uses DOS's internal read or write a track or sector (RWTS) routine. Once the sector has been read and is stored in memory, line 180 changes the appropriate bytes to zero and sets up the RWTS so that it will write the sector back out to the diskette. This is done in line 190, after which the RWTS command is changed from a write command to a null command.

Add extra tracks to your disks

Another method that is used to prevent people from backing up programs is to add extra tracks to your diskette. While the normal Apple DOS 3.3 diskette is formatted for 35 tracks (numbered 0 through 34) most people are not aware that it is possible to format a diskette with more tracks. In the early days, a single extra track was added and critical information was stored on this track. Since normal copy programs would only copy 35 tracks, the copy wouldn't work because the critical 36th track was missing. However, it didn't take long for the nibble copy programs to incorporate a 36th track capability into their programs. This coupled with the fact that early Apple drives had difficulty accessing the extra track, gradually caused this protection technique to fall out of favor. It is well worth considering again today, however, because drives that are currently available can format a diskette with as many as 40 tracks on them. In addition to giving you extra storage space on the same diskette, you should know that todays nibble copiers still only go up to 36 tracks.

To be safe, and minimize problems with other drives, you ought to consider adding only two tracks to the normal diskette (for a total of 37). This will give you an extra 8K of storage space on the diskette and defeat most copy programs currently available. Making diskettes with the additional tracks is easy. Here's how:

1) First boot DOS 3.3 as usual.
2) Next, enter the monitor by typing CALL -151
3) Change location $AEB5 from $8C to $90 to add one track or 94 to add two tracks
4) Change location $B3EF from $23 to either $24 or $25 (one or two extra tracks)
5) Make the same change to location $BEFE.
6) INIT a blank disk with the newly modified DOS. It will now have 1 or 2 extra tracks on it.

Putting the extra tracks on the disk is not enough. You must now tell DOS that they're available for use. To do this you must change track 17, sector 0 (the VTOC). To do this use a track and sector editor (such as the one found in Copy][Plus) and read in track 17 ($11), sector 0. Next, change byte number $34 from $23 to $24 or $25 — depending on how many tracks you've added. If you've added just one track, change bytes numbered $C4 and $C5 from 0 to $FF. If you've added two tracks, change bytes $C6 and $C7 to $FFs also. Now, just write the sector back out to the disk. That's all there is to it. If you check the disk space on this diskette with FID, you'll find that you now have 32 more sectors available.

Next Issue: All About Modified Disk Formats and RWTS

Applesoft Line Finder

continued from page 5

To use APPLESOFT LINE FINDER, just type in an ampersand, followed by the line number like this, &10. This will cause line 10 of the current Applesoft program to be displayed on the screen in hexadecimal form and leave you in the monitor mode so that changes can be made to it. Since a colon is used to separate the address from the displayed data, it is only necessary to move your cursor up to the line that is going to be changed and copy everything with the right arrow key except those items that are going to be modified. It couldn't be simpler.

Take out a 2-year subscription to Apple Software Protection Digest and save over 12%.

FREE BONUS!

If you subscribe for 2 years before October 1985 we'll send you our Programmer's Number Conversion System FREE.

BECOME AN ASSEMBLY LANGUAGE PROGRAMMING WHIZ

You've spent a lot of time learning Apple assembly language and finally know the difference between BEQ and BCS. Now it's time to put your new-found knowledge to work. Time to throw away your Applesoft programming manual and write programs that make your Apple work like a super-charged, super-fast computer. Time to graduate from the Applesoft BASIC used by beginners, to the 6502 assembly language used by professionals.

To help make this transition, you need an experienced programmer to guide you. You need to develop a library of subroutines that make programming in assembly language as easy as programming in BASIC. You need to learn all the tricks that take experienced assembly language programmers years to acquire. Most important of all, you need the book, *"Now that You Know Apple Assembly Language: What Can You Do With It?"* because it contains all this information *and more.*

It shows you how, step-by-step

"Now That You Know Apple Assembly Language: What Can You Do With It?" will take you step-by-step through the assembly language programming experience. You'll delve into the mysteries of the 6502 stack and learn how to use it to increase the power and versatility of your programs. You'll also learn how to use the Apple's built-in routines to minimize the amount of coding you must do.

Control the output and the input

Frequently it's desirable to gain total control of the computer's output. This book shows you how to *steal control away from the Apple's normal output routines and redirect it to your own program.* Thus if you wanted, you could see the normally invisible control characters, display text on your screen as black on white instead of the normal white on black, format text sent to a printer into pages and much more.

Expand the power of your Apple by *stealing control away from the normal input routines.* Do things like adding a screen print capability, or *convert part of the normal keyboard into a numeric keypad.* It's even possible to *produce self-modifying programs* by EXECing in commands from RAM instead of from the disk drive. Think about the possibilities that offers for protecting your programs. When you want to go back to Applesoft programming, *you'll be able to do it faster with the aid of Applesoft Shorthand,* an assembly language program that types in one or more Applesoft commands at the press of a key, or use another program in the book to *automatically count the number of lines in your Applesoft program.*

With this book you'll also learn about *generating tones and how to figure out the frequency, producing sound effects, teaching your Apple to send Morse code, restoring accidentally erased Applesoft programs, adding new commands to Applesoft and running two Applesoft programs in memory together,* to name a few.

Everything is explained

Unlike other books that merely consist of a collection of programs, this one explains what's happening, where and why. You get detailed descriptions of how the programs work and detailed program listings with virtually every line of code explained. Nothing is left to chance or misinterpretation.

Order now, get 2 FREE gifts

The book costs only $19.95 plus $2 for shipping and handling. Order now and you'll also get a *FREE Programmer's Number Conversion System* that makes it easy to convert between binary, hexadecimal and decimal numbers. No calculators are required. You'll convert numbers almost instantly and wonder how you ever got along without it.

As an extra bonus for prompt ordering, you'll receive a *FREE coupon worth $5 off* the price of a disk with all the assembled programs on it or a disk that contains the source code. These disks normally sell for $15 each. We're offering these FREE gifts for a limited time only, so hurry! *Order today!*

Money-back guarantee*

We're so confident that you'll find this book invaluable and want it in your library, that we're offering a 10-day, no-questions-asked, money-back guarantee. Order the book. Read it and try the programs for ten days. At the end of ten days if you don't think it's worth every penny you paid for it, just send it back in resalable condition and we'll refund your money immediately, no questions asked.

**Redlig Systems, Inc., Dept. A 9783
2068—79th St., Brooklyn, NY 11214**

Please rush me _____ copies of **"Now That You Know Apple Assembly Language: What Can You Do With It?"** at $19.95 each plus $2 shipping and handling. I understand that if I am not delighted with the book I may return it within 10 days for a prompt and courteous refund. In any case, the Programmer's Number Conversion System and $5 coupon are mine to keep.

☐ Enclosed is my check for $ _____

Please charge my credit card:
☐ American Express ☐ MasterCard ☐ Visa

Card No. _____ Exp. _____

Signature _____

Name _____

Address _____

City _____ State _____ Zip _____

*NOTE: Shipping and handling fees are not refundable.

BACKING UP THE PRINT SHOP

One of the more popular programs available for the Apple // is *The Print Shop* from Broderbund Software. This program lets your dot matrix printer produce high quality letterheads, signs and greeting cards with nice high-resolution graphic pictures. Like most software from Broderbund, this program has a copy protection scheme on the diskette that makes it difficult to produce backup copies, although there is provision for producing one backup. This is done if the user presses the ESC key while the program is booting.

In general, most of the diskette is formatted fairly normally, with the exception being that Broderbund has placed the VTOC on track 17,sector 2 instead of sector zero. Also, DOS is stored in slightly different locations on this disk, but that's not really critical. What is critical is that the 35th track (we start from zero so it's labelled track 34) is not written in a standard format and is not copyable by standard copy programs. It turns out, that the major problem that prevents *The Print Shop* from being copyable is a nibble counting routine that is located in a file called MENULIB. If the subroutine jump to the nibble count routine is disabled by replacing the JSR with NOP codes, the rest of the disk is copied, and track 17, sector 2 is stored in sector 0 (where the VTOC should normally be located), the disk will run perfectly.

The Applesoft program that follows should be added on to Apple's COPYA program. This can be done by first loading in COPYA and then typing these lines in, or more conveniently, this program can be entered via a word processor and stored in a text (T) file. From the text file, it can be EXECed into memory once COPYA has been loaded.

As a matter of policy, when copying protected programs, I generally eliminate the disk error routine by using the first two POKEs in line 75. In this case, however, it's not really necessary, because the one track that gives us problems has been eliminated by the third POKE in line 75. Thus the disk with the copy on it will only have the first 34 tracks of the original disk on it. Since the copy program initializes all 35 tracks on the blank, however, the last track will be initialized and will not cause any problems when you want to make a copy of the copy.

Line 80 changes the title of the program that is displayed and line 225, 290 and 295 hook the program additions into the regular COPYA program. Lines 300 and 305 are not needed, so they should be eliminated from COPYA. A call to DOS' RWTS routine is set up in lines 400 to 460, while line 470 reads track 17, sector 2 into memory. Once in memory, one byte in this sector must be changed before it is written back out to the disk on sector 0. The last byte in the sector must be changed from a zero to a one. This is done in line 480 and the sector is then written back out to the disk. Once this operation is complete, DOS' file handler can now access the files on the disk without requiring a modification.

You may recall that I mentioned earlier that if the ESC key is pressed whole the program is booting, that control is passed to The Print Shop's copy routine. Since this routine checks track 34 to see if the one permitted backup copy has already been made, and we have eliminated track 34 from the copy disk, pressing ESC during a boot could cause the program to hang up. To eliminate this, we have to eliminate the code that checks for the ESC key being pressed. Since any check of this sort would require a CMP #$9B instruction, a disk scanning utility (such as the one in Copy][Plus) was used to locate the byte sequence C9 9B on the disk. It turns out that it is in three places: track 0, sector 5; track 0, sector 10 and track 6, sector 14. In lines 490 to 510, these sectors are loaded into memory. If the correct byte sequence is found (it may be located somewhere else on other versions of the program) these two bytes are replaced with two other bytes that prevent the jump to the copy program. If the byte sequence is not located, nothing is done.

Next, the MENULIB file is loaded into memory and a check is made for the presence of the nibble count JSR (lines 530 and 540). If its not where it's supposed to be, the user is notified that this version of the program cannot be copied and execution is terminated. If it is there, however, the JSR is eliminated (line 550) and the modified file is stored back out onto the disk (lines 560 and 570). That's all there is to it. Copies made with this program can be backed up with the normal, unmodified, COPYA program.

```
75   POKE 47426,24: POKE 929,24: POKE 863,34
80   HOME : PRINT "        PRINT SHOP DUPLICATION PROGRAM": PRINT
     : PRINT
225  VTAB 5: HTAB 24: PRINT "        ": IF PEEK (713) = 1
     THEN 295
290  GOTO 600
295  VTAB 19: GOTO 400
300
305
400  IOB = 47080:TRK = IOB + 4:SCT = IOB + 5:CMD = IOB + 12
     :RD = 1:WR = 2
410  BUF =   PEEK (IOB + 8) + 256 *  PEEK (IOB + 9)
420  FOR X = 768 TO 774
430    READ Y: POKE X,Y
440  NEXT X
450  PRINT : PRINT "UNPROTECTING COPY"
460  POKE IOB + 3,0
470  POKE TRK,17: POKE SCT,2: POKE CMD,RD: CALL 768
480  POKE BUF + 255,1: POKE SCT,0: POKE CMD,WR: CALL 768
490  POKE TRK,0: POKE SCT,5: POKE CMD,RD: CALL 768: IF  PEEK
     (BUF + 57) = 201 THEN  POKE BUF + 57,169: POKE BUF + 58,1
     : POKE CMD,WR: CALL 768
500  POKE TRK,0: POKE SCT,10: POKE CMD,RD: CALL 768: IF  PEEK
     (BUF + 55) = 201 THEN  POKE BUF + 55,169: POKE BUF + 56,1
     : POKE CMD,WR: CALL 768
510  POKE TRK,6: POKE SCT,14: POKE CMD,RD: CALL 768: IF  PEEK
     (BUF + 68) = 201 THEN  POKE BUF + 68,169: POKE BUF + 69,1
     : POKE CMD,WR: CALL 768: POKE CMD,0
520  PRINT  CHR$ (4);"BLOAD MENULIB"
530  CK =  PEEK (30727) + 256 *  PEEK (30728)
540  IF CK < > 36311 THEN 590
550  POKE 30726,234: POKE 30727,234: POKE 30728,234
560  S =  PEEK (43634) + 256 *  PEEK (43635):L =  PEEK (43616)
     + 256 *  PEEK (43617)
570  PRINT  CHR$ (4);"BSAVE MENULIB,A";S;",L";L
580  TEXT : HOME : VTAB 5: PRINT "RE-RUN 'PRINT SHOP COPY' TO
     MAKE        ANOTHER COPY OF THE PROGRAM":PRINT CHR$
     (4);"FP"
590  PRINT : PRINT : PRINT  CHR$ (7);"THIS VERSION OF PRINT
     SHOP CANNOT BE    COPIED WITH THIS PROGRAM."
600  PRINT  CHR$ (4);"FP"
610  DATA  160,232,169,183,76,217,3
990  REM
995  REM COPYRIGHT 1985 BY JULES H. GILDER
999  REM ALL RIGHTS RESERVED
```

REVIEW: Copy][Plus

One of the handiest tools that any Apple // owner can possess is this program. Originally designed as just a nibble copy program, over the years, it has developed into a full-blown back-up and disk repair tool with an impressive set of DOS utilities. To give you an idea of just how powerful this program is, here is a list some of the things you can do with it:

- Copy any 16- or 13-sector unprotected disk
- Copy just DOS onto a disk
- Copy individual files
- Catalog a disk
- Show file lengths on the catalog
- Show control characters on the catalog
- Catalog deleted files
- Delete files
- Delete DOS to get more file space
- Lock or unlock files
- Rename files
- Alphabetize the catalog
- Format a disk
- Verify that the disk is good
- Verify that files are good
- Verify whether or not two files are identical
- Check disk drive speed
- View the contents of files
- See a map of what files are stored on the disk and where
- Edit any sector or any file
- Fix file sizes to free up wasted disk space
- Change the boot program on the disk
- Recover files that were accidentally erased by undeleting them

As you can see, the list is a long and impressive one. And the best part of all, is that the program only costs $39.95. While the program is mainly designed to work with DOS 3.3 and DOS 3.2 formatted diskettes, the disk copy and verify functions, as well as the sector editor, can be used with any unprotected 16- or 13-sector diskette, including ProDOS, SOS, CP/M and Pascal formats. While we obviously can't get into a detailed review of every single function of this powerful program, we will take a look at a few of the more interesting features from a software protection point of view.

To begin with, the designers of Copy][Plus Version 5.X (5.5 is the latest current version) did their homework. They realized that people want a powerful tool, but that it also must be easy to operate. It is. Central Point Software has included an Auto Copy feature into the program. When you select the bit copier mode of operation, the Copy][Plus asks you for the name of the program you want to copy. It then searches its internal list of programs and copy parameters to see it it already "knows" how to copy the program. If it does, all you have to do is press RETURN and you're off. Sometimes there are several versions of the same program, each with its own unique copy protection scheme. In that case, the program will list either an alternate, or specify a way of identifying your particular version (e.g. new ProDOS version or old ProDOS version). To choose the one you want, simply use the arrow keys to move the cursor to your choice, and press RETURN.

With over 500 entries on the latest version of the program, the list is fairly substantial. Nevertheless, you'll still find plenty of programs that have not yet made it to the list. But don't worry. Central Point has taken care of that too. About every three months, the company comes out with a parameter update list. If you're a registered owner (you sent your card back) you can get this update for only $5. Believe me, it's worth it. Of course, if the program you wish to copy is not included in the parameter list of Copy][Plus, you can still copy it manually, but this requires a lot more skill.

Another outstanding feature of Copy][Plus is one of the functions that is available from the sector editor operating mode: the disk scanning feature. This function will let you scan the entire diskette, or any part of it, a any series of bytes. You may enter the search text in hexadecimal, or if it is a word or phrase, you can enter the text directly. The search is quick and easy to use and is extremely helpful when you're trying to make back-up copies of disks for which you have no copy parameters. This feature in fact, was used to develop the Print Shop Copy program listed elsewhere in this issue.

While Central Point Software has done an outstanding job in developing the software, they weren't quite as good with the manual. Don't get me wrong, the manual is quite good and comprehensive. It's neatly and conveniently produced as a softcover paperback. The usefulness of the book, however, has been severely limited by the fact that it has no index. With many questions bound to arise during the use of this program, a detailed index would have been an invaluable aid. Without it, the user is forced to frequently thumb through large sections of the book until what he's looking for is found. Let's hope they fix this one major flaw to an otherwise superb product.

Price: $39.95. **Source:** Central Point Software, Inc., 9700 SW Capitol Hwy., #100, Portland, OR 97219. **Call:** (503) 244-5782.

COMING NEXT ISSUE

How to Back-Up Sensible Speller
How to Back-Up The Newsroom
How to Back-Up Wizardry
Using RAM Cards as a Back-Up Tool
Moving the CATALOG to Other Tracks
Protection Tutorial — Part II:
    Modified Disk Formats and RWTS
Using COPYA to Copy Protected Disks
Changing the BLOAD Address of
    Machine Language Programs
A Handy HEX/DEC/HEX Converter
Review: Locksmith 5.0

BECOME AN ASSEMBLY LANGUAGE PROGRAMMING WHIZ

You've spent a lot of time learning Apple assembly language and finally know the difference between BEQ and BCS. Now it's time to put your new-found knowledge to work. Time to throw away your Applesoft programming manual and write programs that make your Apple work like a super-charged, super-fast computer. Time to graduate from the Applesoft BASIC used by beginners, to the 6502 assembly language used by professionals.

To help make this transition, you need an experienced programmer to guide you. You need to develop a library of subroutines that make programming in assembly language as easy as programming in BASIC. You need to learn all the tricks that take experienced assembly language programmers years to acquire. Most important of all, you need the book, *"Now that You Know Apple Assembly Language: What Can You Do With It?"* because it contains all this information *and more*.

It shows you how, step-by-step

"Now That You Know Apple Assembly Language: What Can You Do With It?" will take you step-by-step through the assembly language programming experience. You'll delve into the mysteries of the 6502 stack and learn how to use it to increase the power and versatility of your programs. You'll also learn how to use the Apple's built-in routines to minimize the amount of coding you must do.

Control the output and the input

Frequently it's desirable to gain total control of the computer's output. This book shows you how to *steal control away from the Apple's normal output routines and redirect it to your own program*. Thus if you wanted, you could see the normally invisible control characters, display text on your screen as black on white instead of the normal white on black, format text sent to a printer into pages and much more.

Expand the power of your Apple by *stealing control away from the normal input routines*. Do things like adding a screen print capability, or *convert part of the normal keyboard into a numeric keypad*. It's even possible to *produce self-modifying programs* by EXECing in commands from RAM instead of from the disk drive. Think about the possibilities that offers for protecting your programs. When you want to go back to Applesoft programming, *you'll be able to do it faster with the aid of Applesoft Shorthand,* an assembly language program that types in one or more Applesoft commands at the press of a key, or use another program in the book to *automatically count the number of lines in your Applesoft program.*

With this book you'll also learn about *generating tones and how to figure out the frequency, producing sound effects, teaching your Apple to send Morse code, restoring accidentally erased Applesoft programs, adding new commands to Applesoft and running two Applesoft programs in memory together,* to name a few.

Everything is explained

Unlike other books that merely consist of a collection of programs, this one explains what's happening, where and why. You get detailed descriptions of how the programs work and detailed program listings with virtually every line of code explained. Nothing is left to chance or misinterpretation.

Order now, get 2 FREE gifts

The book costs only $19.95 plus $2 for shipping and handling. Order now and you'll also get a *FREE Programmer's Number Conversion System* that makes it easy to convert between binary, hexadecimal and decimal numbers. No calculators are required. You'll convert numbers almost instantly and wonder how you ever got along without it.

As an extra bonus for prompt ordering, you'll receive a *FREE coupon worth $5 off* the price of a disk with all the assembled programs on it or a disk that contains the source code. These disks normally sell for $15 each. We're offering these FREE gifts for a limited time only, so hurry! *Order today!*

Money-back guarantee*

We're so confident that you'll find this book invaluable and want it in your library, that we're offering a 10-day, no-questions-asked, money-back guarantee. Order the book. Read it and try the programs for ten days. At the end of ten days if you don't think it's worth every penny you paid for it, just send it back in resalable condition and we'll refund your money immediately, no questions asked.

Redlig Systems, Inc., Dept. A 9783
2068—79th St., Brooklyn, NY 11214

Please rush me _____ copies of **"Now That You Know Apple Assembly Language: What Can You Do With It?"** at $19.95 each plus $2 shipping and handling. I understand that if I am not delighted with the book I may return it within 10 days for a prompt and courteous refund. In any case, the Programmer's Number Conversion System and $5 coupon are mine to keep.

☐ Enclosed is my check for $ _____

Please charge my credit card:
☐ American Express   ☐ MasterCard   ☐ Visa

Card No. _____ Exp. _____
Signature _____
Name _____
Address _____
City _____ State _____ Zip _____

---

*NOTE: Shipping and handling fees are not refundable.

APPLE SOFTWARE PROTECTION DIGEST

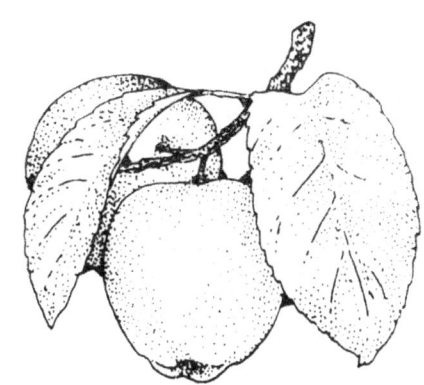

$3.00

Vol. 1, No. 2   January/February 1986

A LITTLE LATE, BUT BETTER THAN EVER

Well, we finally made it. For a while, I suspect that quite a few of you were wondering what happened to us. A couple of you even wrote that you feared your hard-earned bucks went into a black hole, never to be heard from again. Not true! As all of you early subscribers are aware, we sent out notices to each of you explaining that there would be a delay and offered you a complete refund with no questions asked. I'm happy to announce that not one of you requested a refund. I appreciate your confidence.

I think you're all entitled to an explanation of what happened and what you can expect in the future. The first issue of the Digest went together so easily and so quickly, that we really didn't anticipate any problems in getting the second one out. Well, nothing could be further from the truth. Just about everything that could go wrong did. Authors who promised material on cracking some of the more desireable programs, such as Sensible Speller, Newsroom and Wizardry, never came through. Add to that a few hardware problems and some problems with the printer and you wind up with a long delay.

We've finally got everything straightened out however, and we have a big jump on the next issue, so we should be back on schedule. We've also added back-up equipment, so hardware problems shouldn't cause any major delays anymore.

Two bonuses to say thanks

To say thanks to you for bearing with us, we've added two bonuses. Anyone who subscribed to the Digest in 1985 will automatically get an EXTRA FREE ISSUE to compensate them for the long wait. And, all subscribers are getting this double January/February issue, but it will only count as a single issue. Thus, all 1985 subscribers will have their subscriptions expire with the February 1987 issue (that's the last one they'll receive) while the last issue for everyone else who has subscribed up to now, will be January 1987. Everyone who has subscribed to date will have gotten the first issue free. Subscriptions start with the second issue.

Although we've been quite late with this issue, we hope you'll agree that the wait was well worth it.

Program diskettes available

With this issue of the Digest, we are adding a new service. Many of you have asked us to consider coming out with a moderately priced diskette with all the programs on it, so we have. Every month we will make available a diskette with all of the programs (with both source and object code when appropriate) on it. Assembler source files will be saved in text file format to facilitate use with a variety of assemblers. The diskette will be an unprotected DOS 3.3 diskette and will cost only $15.

Cracks wanted list

We've added a new feature to the Digest with this issue, its our Cracks Wanted list. This will list all the programs that readers have expressed an interest in have cracks or back-up procedures for. In addition, starting with the next issue, each issue of the **Apple Software Protection Digest** will contain a list of all the program cracks we've presented during the year so that you'll have a quick and handy reference available at your finger tips.

Another feature we've included with this issue is a Letters column. This is a forum where you, the reader, can ask for information, present short ideas or discuss appropriate topics. It's also the way we get feedback from you one how we're doing.

continued on page 15

Contents

Editorial	1
Using COPYA to Backup Protected Disks	2
How to BRUN Applesoft Programs	4
Parameter Files for COPYP	6
Change the BLOAD Address of Binary Files	9
Letters	10
Hiding Machine Language Programs in Strings	11
Two Solutions to the Hide-A-Line Problem	12
Hiding Program Lines from BASIC	14
A Handy Decimal/Hexel-Decimal Converter	15
Applesoft Line Finder and Vanisher	16
Wipeout: The Ultimate Weapon of Destruction	17
Review: Locksmith 5.0G	19
Protection Tutorial — Part II	20

USING COPYA TO BACKUP PROTECTED DISKS

If you plan on doing a lot of copying of protected diskettes, it would probably pay for you to purchase one of the nibble copy programs. My personal preference is *Copy][Plus*, which we reviewed in the last issue of **ASPD**. By the way, since that review came out, Central Point Software, the producers of *Copy][Plus*, has come out with a new version of the program — Version 6. The program sells for $39.95, but you can purchase it from us for only $30. Anyway, if you'd rather not shell out the $30 dollars, there's an awful lot of protected programs that you can copy with COPYA, as long as you make the appropriate modifications to it, and that's what this article is going to tell you how to do.

We used a slightly modified version of COPYA to duplicate *Print Shop* in our last issue. Comments by **ASPD** readers indicating they like that approach, convinced me to go ahead and develop a general modification to COPYA that could accommodate a wide variety of programs.

Why doesn't COPYA work?

Before we can modify COPYA to copy protected disks (not all of them, but a good number of them) we have to understand why it won't copy them to begin with. The first thing that causes problems for us is the DOS error checking routine. The second thing is COPYA's error checking routine. If either of these routines encounters a diskette with a slightly modified DOS on it, they'll generate an I/O ERROR message and stop. Both of these routines can be easily disabled by executing two POKEs. These are shown in line 75 of the program listing. By the way, the listing consists only of those lines that are to be added to COPYA. I have found that the simplest way to add them is to use an editor or word processor to create a text file that contains these lines. Then you should load COPYA into the Apple's memory and finally, EXEC the text file, which I call COPYP MAKER. Lines 300 and 305 are blank lines and when they're EXECed in, they cause those two lines to be deleted from Apple's original COPYA listing. From now on, I'll be referring to this modified version of COPYA as COPYP, and in fact, this issue already contains some parameters that will allow you to copy some protected programs.

Anyway, let's get back to our program description. The two POKEs that are added in line 75 prevent the I/O ERROR from being generated and will thus permit COPYA to go ahead and duplicate the protected diskette, even though there's something "funny" about it. Sometimes those two POKEs will be all that you'll need to copy a protected diskette. At other times, you may have to change the address and data field bytes to make it possible to copy the diskette. I have provided additional modifications to COPYA to permit you to do this. Lines 85 and 86 read in the address and data field information from data statements. There is a separate data statement for the source (original) diskette and target (copy) diskette. The data listed below is for normal DOS 3.3 diskettes, so you can use this program to copy unprotected software as well.

As you can now see, the tutorial we have in this issue on the data and address fields has not been wasted. At least now you have an idea of why these bytes are being changed. In case you're adventurous and are considering modifying COPYP further to enhance its unprotecting capabilities (and I encourage all of you to do so), a little further explanation of just what is going on here is in order. Line 198 makes the source diskette's address and data field bytes the active ones and inserts them into DOS so that the protected diskette can be read. Line 248 makes the target address and data field bytes the active ones and inserts them into DOS so that the copy diskette can be initialized. Line 258 also uses the bytes for the target diskette, but this time they are inserted into DOS so that the target diskette can be written to.

If you will examine the specific bytes that are changed in lines 395 and 396, you will notice that only the read locations of the address and data field bytes are being changed and might wonder why no write locations are being changed. The answer to that question is simple, the diskette that is being copied, is being transferred from a diskette with a protected DOS on it to a diskette with a normal DOS on it. Since we're only reading the protected diskette, there's no need to change its write locations. And, since the write locations haven't been changed from those normally used, there's no need to adjust them when we want to write data out to the unprotected diskette. Why then do we change the read locations back to normal? The answer to that is easy too. We change them back because after writing to the unprotected diskette, DOS reads what it's written to make sure that it was properly recorded. Not too difficult is it?

COPYP edits sectors too

So far the operation of COPYP has been explained up to line 397. But, just because we can copy a protected program onto an unprotected diskette, doesn't mean that the program will run. It may, but chances are that some routine somewhere in the program checks to make sure that the program is on the protected diskette and the protection scheme is intact. One way of doing this is to incorporate a nibble counting routine (we'll look into nibble counting in more detail in a future issue). To overcome these protection routines, it will be necessary to modify

```
0    REM COPYP MAKER
1    REM
2    TEXT: HOME
65   DIM B(10), S(10), T(10)
75   POKE 47426,24: POKE 929,24
80   PRINT " PROTECTED DISK DUPLICATION PROGRAM": PRINT: PRINT
85   FOR X = 1 TO 10: READ S(X): NEXT X
86   FOR X = 1 TO 10: READ T(X): NEXT X
100  POKE 715, PEEK (110) + 2: REM BUFSTART
198  FOR X = 1 TO 10: B(X) = S(X): NEXT X: GOSUB 395
225  VTAB 5: HTAB 24: PRINT"            ": IF PEEK (713) = 1 THEN 295
248  FOR X = 1 TO 10: B(X) = T(X): NEXT X: GOSUB 395
258  FOR X = 1 TO 10: B(X) = T(X): NEXT X: GOSUB 395
290  GOTO 550
295  VTAB 19: GOTO 400
300
305
395  POKE 47445,B(1): POKE 47455,B(2): POKE 47466,B(3): POKE 47505,B(4):
     POKE 47515,B(5)
396  POKE 47335,B(6): POKE 47345,B(7): POKE 47356,B(8): POKE 47413,B(9):
     POKE 47423,B(10)
397  RETURN
400  IOB = 47080: TRK = IOB + 4: SCT = IOB + 5: CMD = IOB + 12: RWTS =
     768: RD=1: WR = 2
410  BUF = PEEK (IOB + 8) + 256 * PEEK (IOB + 9)
420  FOR X = 768 TO 774
430      READ Y: POKE X,Y
440  NEXT X
450  PRINT: PRINT "DOING SECTOR EDITS NOW": POKE IOB + 3,0
460  READ TK,SE,BYTE,OV,NV
470  IF (TK + SE + BYTE + OV + NV) * 1 = 0 THEN 550
480  POKE TRK,TK: POKE SCT,SE: POKE CMD,RD: CALL RWTS
490  IF PEEK (BUF + BYTE) <> OV THEN 530
500  POKE BUF + BYTE,NV
510  POKE CMD,WR: CALL RWTS
520  GOTO 460
530  PRINT: PRINT: PRINT "THIS VERSION OF THE PROTECTED PROGRAM"
540  PRINT "CANNOT BE UNPROTECTED WITH THE"
```

the code that is stored on the newly copied, unprotected diskette. This is done by reading in the appropriate sector, modifying the bytes of interest, and then writing the sector back out to the diskette. It's possible to do this manually, but it can be time consuming and annoying. It also means you have to have a little bit more of a hacker mentality. With the sector editing modifications I've added to COPYP, however, all you have to do is type in a few data statements, and the program will do the sector edits for you automatically. Here's how it works.

Lines 400 and 410 set up the variable names that will be used in this routine. Descriptive names are used so that it will be a little easier to see what is happening. Lines 420 through 440 read in a short machine language program that uses DOS's RWTS (Read and Write a Track and Sector) routines. Line 450 informs the user that COPYP is now implementing any sector edits that may have been requested. Next, any DATA statements that have been added between lines 999 and 9000 are read and used to specify what specific sector edits should be made (line 460). Line 998 tells you what data and in what order, it should be entered. Because software companies frequently change protection schemes, the COPYP sector editor requires that you enter both the value of the original byte and the value of the new byte that is to replace it. The program then checks to see if the value of the byte to be edited matches the old value of the byte that you entered (line 490). If it does, it proceeds to perform the edit (lines 500 and 510). If it doesn't, it assumes that the protection scheme has changed somewhat and tells the user that the program cannot be unprotected with the parameters that were supplied (lines 530 to 545), and terminates the program.

If no sector edits are requested, the program will read the data in line 9000. It is very important that this line always be present because the zeros it contains signal the program that no more sector edits need to be done and the program should be terminated (line 470).

Determining the parameters

While the COPYP program presented here can be a very useful tool for unprotecting diskettes, that's all it is. As with any other tool, you have to know how to set it up and use it. Setting it up is easy if you have the right information. But getting that information is a little more difficult. How do you know what values are used in the address and data fields? How do you know if any sector edits are required? Mostly its a matter of digging into the protected program and figuring things out. **ASPD** will provide you with parameter files for use with COPYP and hopefully, all of you will contribute your time and expertise as well. Anyone who submits a parameter file or a modification to COPYP that makes it even more useful will get a one-month extension to his or her subscription when we print it. Contribute on a regular basis and you'll wind up getting the Digest for free.

If you're interested in sorting things out by yourself, the first place to start is to either boot the program and then break out of it (you'll need a computer with an old F8 ROM in it or an NMI switch (more about that next issue) to do that. Once you get into the Apple monitor — that's where you get an asterisk (*) as a prompt instead of a square bracket (])), then you can examine the memory locations that hold the data for the data and address fields (see the chart in this month's tutorial). This of course assume that only a slightly modified DOS is used. If that's not the case, then you'll have to use a program that can read in raw data directly from the diskette and display it. From this you'll be able to tell what the various address and data field bytes are.

COPYP is limited

While you'll find COPYP helpful in unprotecting many programs, it can't be used for all of them because it currently lacks the ability to do some of the fancier things such as quarter and half track, nibble insertion, synchronous copying, etc. Over the next few months I hope to be able to add some of these capabilities to the program. Anyone who has ideas on how to improve COPYP is invited to send them in to me, and I'll see to it that the rest of our readers find out about it too. You'll also get a 3 to 6 month extension to your subscription for major, useful, modifications. In the meantime, you have the beginnings of a powerful tool. Let's see what you can do with it.

```
545   PRINT "PARAMETERS YOU'VE SUPPLIED."
550   POKE CMD,0
560   TEXT: HOME: PRINT CHR$(4);"FP"
890   REM
899   REM SOURCE ADDRESS FIELD PROLOGUE BYTES
900   DATA 213,170,150
909   REM SOURCE ADDRESS FILED EPILOGUE BYTES
910   DATA 222,170
919   REM SOURCE DATA FIELD PROLOGUE BYTES
920   DATA 213,170,173
929   REM SOURCE DATA FIELD EPILOGUE BYTES
930   DATA 222,170
935   REM
939   REM TARGET ADDRESS FIELD PROLOGUE BYTES
940   DATA 213,170,150
949   REM TARGET ADDRESS FIELD EPILOGUE BYTES
950   DATA 222,170
959   REM TARGET DATA FIELD PROLOGUE BYTES
960   DATA 213,170,173
969   REM TARGET DATA FIELD EPILOGUE BYTES
970   DATA 222,170
980   REM
981   REM RWTS ROUTINE
982   REM
983   DATA 160,232,169,183,76,217,3
990   REM
995   REM SECTOR EDIT DATA
996   REM
998   REM TRACK,SECTOR,BYTE,OLD VALUE,NEW VALUE
999   REM
9000  DATA 0,0,0,0,0
9993  REM
9994  REM
9995  REM COPYRIGHT (C) 1986 BY
9996  REM
9997  REM JULES H. GILDER
9998  REM
9999  REM ALL RIGHTS RESERVED
```

Don't miss a single issue SUBSCRIBE TODAY!

Apple Software Protection Digest Publisher & Editor, Jules H. Gilder; Contributing Editor, J. Scott Barrus. Copyright © 1986 by Redlig Systems, Inc., 2068-79th Street, Brooklyn, NY 11214. All rights reserved. No part of this publication may be reproduced, or electronically transmitted or stored without the publisher's written permission. Published monthly at $24 per year by Redlig Systems, Inc. (718) 232-8429. Reprints of prior issues available at $3 each. Printed in the U.S.A.

Apple is a resitered trademark of Apple Computer, Inc.

HOW TO BRUN APPLESOFT PROGRAMS

In the last issue we spoke about several different ways that lines in an Applesoft program can be hidden from view. One of the techniques used simply required that the next line pointer of the line before the one to be hidden, be changed so that it points to the line that follows the line or group of lines that are to be hidden. This is an effective technique, but is has some flaws, chief among them being a routine that automatically resets the line pointers to their correct value every time an Applesoft program is loaded.

The other problem with this approach is that if a line is added or deleted from the program, the line links again are automatically re-calculated and corrected. One way to overcome Apple DOS's apparent desire to prevent you from hiding certain program lines is to let DOS BRUN Applesoft programs instead of RUN them. This overcomes DOS's zealous attempts to maintain line link integrity by fooling DOS into thinking that our Applesoft program is actually a binary one. In addition, while we're loading our Applesoft program into memory, we can disable the RESET key and set Applesoft's auto-run flag to prevent anyone from pressing RESET to get out of the program and trying to list it. Finally, if you include an ONERR statement, that checks for someone pressing Control-C, as the first statement in your program, you can also prevent the user from using Control-C to stop the program. The statements you'd have to add to your program would look something like these:

```
0 ONERR GOTO 10000
10000 IF PEEK (222) = 255 THEN RUN
10010 Y = PEEK (222)
10020 PRINT "ERROR = ";Y
10030 RESUME
```

Of course, you can change the line numbers to anything that is convenient for you, but the first line of the program should contain the ONERR statement. These statements will cause the program to re-run itself if a Control-C is attempted and will print out the error number if any other error is encountered. It's best to add these lines only after the rest of the program has been completely debugged.

To make life easy for you, I have written a machine language program that automatically converts any standard Applesoft program into one that can be BRUN. The BRUN MAKER program asks you for the name of the Applesoft program that is to be converted and loads it into memory. At this point, it places a command, **CALL 37876** on the last line of the screen and reduces the active area of the screen by one line so that the information displayed there won't accidentally be erased. You may have noticed that there are several apparent "garbage" characters at the lower right-hand corner of the screen. These "garbage" characters represent

```
              1000 ******************************
              1010 *                              *
              1020 * BRUN MAKER FOR APPLESOFT PROGRAMS *
              1030 *                              *
              1040 *      Copyright (c) 1986 by   *
              1050 *                              *
              1060 *        Jules H. Gilder       *
              1070 *                              *
              1080 *      All Rights Reserved     *
              1090 *                              *
              1100 ******************************
              1110 *
              1120 *
0006-         1130 TXTPTR    .EQ $06
0023-         1140 WNDWBOT   .EQ $23
0025-         1150 CV        .EQ $25
00AF-         1160 PROGEND   .EQ $AF
00D6-         1170 RUNFLAG   .EQ $D6
0200-         1180 INBUFF    .EQ $200
0240-         1190 INBUFF2   .EQ $240
03F2-         1200 RESET     .EQ $3F2
03F4-         1210 POWERUP   .EQ $3F4
07E9-         1220 BRUNSTART .EQ $7E9
D566-         1230 RUN       .EQ $D566
E000-         1240 BASIC     .EQ $E000
FC58-         1250 HOME      .EQ $FC58
FC62-         1260 CRTN      .EQ $FC62
FD6F-         1270 GETLN1    .EQ $FD6F
FDDA-         1280 PRHEX     .EQ $FDDA
FDED-         1290 COUT      .EQ $FDED
              1300 *
              1310 *
              1320           .OR $93A8
              1330           .TA $0800
              1340 *
              1350 * This routine prints the opening screen and asks user
              1360 * for the name of the file that will be converted to a
              1370 * binary file so that it can be BRUN.
              1380 *
93A8- 20 58 FC 1390 START    JSR HOME
93AB- A9 83    1400          LDA #TEXT1
93AD- A0 94    1410          LDY /TEXT1
93AF- 20 52 94 1420          JSR MSGPRT
93B2- 20 6F FD 1430          JSR GETLN1
              1440 *
              1450 * Here the name entered name is transferred to a buffer
              1460 * where it won't be destroyed and the terminating
              1470 * carriage return is converted to a zero.
              1480 *
93B5- A9 00    1490          LDA #$0
93B7- 9D 40 02 1500          STA INBUFF2,X
93BA- CA       1510 LOOP1    DEX
93BB- BD 00 02 1520          LDA INBUFF,X
93BE- 9D 40 02 1530          STA INBUFF2,X
93C1- E8       1540          INX
93C2- CA       1550          DEX
93C3- D0 F5    1560          BNE LOOP1
              1570 *
              1580 * A command that the user must copy with the cursor
              1590 * is printed out on the last line of the display.
              1600 *
93C5- A5 25    1610          LDA CV
93C7- 8D 80 94 1620          STA CV2
93CA- E6 25    1630          INC CV
93CC- A9 1D    1640          LDA #TEXT2
93CE- A0 95    1650          LDY /TEXT2
93D0- 20 52 94 1660          JSR MSGPRT
93D3- A9 17    1670          LDA #$17
93D5- 85 23    1680          STA WNDWBOT
93D7- AD 80 94 1690          LDA CV2
93DA- 85 25    1700          STA CV
              1710 *
              1720 * User is told to type VTAB 24 to continue.
              1730 *
93DC- A9 35    1740          LDA #TEXT3
93DE- A0 95    1750          LDY /TEXT3
93E0- 20 52 94 1760          JSR MSGPRT
              1770 *
              1780 * Now the file is loaded into memory and the user
              1790 * can do intermediate work or VTAB 24 and copy the
              1800 * command that's on the screen.
              1810 *
```

```
93E3- A9 9D      1820           LDA #TEXT4
93E5- A0 95      1830           LDY /TEXT4
93E7- 20 52 94   1840           JSR MSGPRT
93EA- A9 40      1850           LDA #INBUFF2
93EC- A0 02      1860           LDY /INBUFF2
93EE- 20 52 94   1870           JSR MSGPRT
93F1- 20 62 FC   1880           JSR CRTN
                 1890  *
                 1900  * This is where the BRUN code is
                 1910  * copied to its required location.  The command
                 1920  * that is copied with the cursor re-starts program
                 1930  * execution.
                 1940  *
93F4- A2 00      1950           LDX #$0
93F6- BD 68 94   1960  LOOP3    LDA BRUNCODE,X
93F9- 9D E9 07   1970           STA BRUNSTART,X
93FC- F0 03      1980           BEQ FINISHUP
93FE- E8         1990           INX
93FF- D0 F5      2000           BNE LOOP3
                 2010  *
                 2020  * With the binary code in place, the length of the
                 2030  * file that is to be created is calculated and saved
                 2040  * for use with the BSAVE command.
                 2050  *
9401- 38         2060  FINISHUP SEC
9402- A9 E9      2070           LDA #BRUNSTART
9404- E9 01      2080           SBC #$1
9406- 8D 81 94   2090           STA LENGTH
9409- 38         2100           SEC
940A- A5 AF      2110           LDA PROGEND
940C- ED 81 94   2120           SBC LENGTH
940F- 8D 81 94   2130           STA LENGTH
9412- A5 B0      2140           LDA PROGEND+1
9414- E9 07      2150           SBC /BRUNSTART
9416- 8D 82 94   2160           STA LENGTH+1
                 2170  *
                 2180  * The BSAVE command is issued.  The name used is the
                 2190  * same as the original with a B. appended to
                 2200  * it.  The starting address and length are added
                 2210  * to the end of the name.
                 2220  *
9419- A9 A5      2230           LDA #TEXT5
941B- A0 95      2240           LDY /TEXT5
941D- 20 52 94   2250           JSR MSGPRT
9420- A9 40      2260           LDA #INBUFF2
9422- A0 02      2270           LDY /INBUFF2
9424- 20 52 94   2280           JSR MSGPRT
9427- A9 B0      2290           LDA #TEXT6
9429- A0 95      2300           LDY /TEXT6
942B- 20 52 94   2310           JSR MSGPRT
942E- AD 82 94   2320           LDA LENGTH+1
9431- 20 DA FD   2330           JSR PRHEX
9434- AD 81 94   2340           LDA LENGTH
9437- 20 DA FD   2350           JSR PRHEX
943A- 20 62 FC   2360           JSR CRTN
                 2370  *
                 2380  * Here the user is told the name of the binary file
                 2390  * and control is returned to BASIC via the warm
                 2395  * start vector.
                 2400  *
943D- A9 18      2410           LDA #$18
943F- 85 23      2420           STA WNDWBOT
9441- A9 BA      2430           LDA #TEXT7
9443- A0 95      2440           LDY /TEXT7
9445- 20 52 94   2450           JSR MSGPRT
9448- A9 40      2460           LDA #INBUFF2
944A- A0 02      2470           LDY /INBUFF2
944C- 20 52 94   2480           JSR MSGPRT
944F- 4C 03 E0   2490           JMP BASIC+3
                 2500  *
                 2510  * This routine prints out the message pointed to
                 2520  * by the A and Y registers.
                 2530  *
9452- 85 06      2540  MSGPRT   STA TXTPTR
9454- 84 07      2550           STY TXTPTR+1
9456- A0 00      2560           LDY #$0
9458- B1 06      2570  LOOP2    LDA (TXTPTR),Y
945A- F0 0B      2580           BEQ ENDPRT
945C- 20 ED FD   2590           JSR COUT
945F- E6 06      2600           INC TXTPTR
9461- D0 F5      2610           BNE LOOP2
9463- E6 07      2620           INC TXTPTR+1
9465- D0 F1      2630           BNE LOOP2
9467- 60         2640  ENDPRT   RTS
                 2650  *
```

the machine-language code that is being added to your Applesoft program so that it can be BRUN.

At this point, the program returns to Applesoft and allows you to set up your Applesoft program. This is particularly important if you intend to include some hidden lines. Once you've finished preparing your Applesoft program, all you have to do is type **VTAB 24**. This will place the cursor in the protected area of the screen and allow you to copy over the CALL command with the cursor (you do this by repeatedly pressing the right arrow key) and then pressing RETURN. Copy over the CALL 37876 only. Do not copy over the "garbage" characters at the end of the line. You don't have to worry about them being erased when you press RETURN. Since they're located in a protected portion of the screen, nothing will happen to them. After you trace over the CALL command and press return, the new binary file is then saved to the disk drive with a B. appended to the beginning of the program's original name.

The BRUN MAKER program is 570 bytes long and has been incorporated into an Applesoft program to make keying it in and using it simpler. Another advantage of this approach is that it eliminates the need to know assembly language or have an assembler available. For those of you who do know assembly language and want to see how the program was written and what is going on, the well-commented source code listing in should be just the thing you're looking for.

If you take the binary file that is produced by the BRUN MAKER program and convert it to an automatically running program as described on page 6 of the previous issue of **ASPD**, you'll have gone a long way in preventing a user from accessing your program. If you then store it on a 37 track diskette (**ASPD** Vol. 1, No. 1, p. 8) and use a customized DOS (see tutorial in this issue) you'll wind up with a diskette that will be quite difficult to backup.

GET A FREE SUBSCRIPTION

In our first issue, we offered a free six month subscription to anyone who wrote an article that we subsequently published. We had a nice response, but would like to have even more interaction with you, so we're extending that free offer another two months. So hurry up. This offer applies to full-blown articles only. Parameters for use with COPYP or minor modifications of COPYP will entitle you to a one-month extension for each one we use. However, a major revision of COPYP will get you the 6-month prize. So let's see who the lucky winners will be.

PARAMETER FILES FOR COPYP

Listed below are several parameter files for use with COPYP. You can key these lines in directly or you can do what I do and create text files that contain these lines. Then you can load in COPYP and EXEC in the appropriate file for the program you want to copy. You can keep these text files on a disk and re-use them again whenever you want to make another copy. Some of these files have been tested by me and some haven't. It gets to be an expensive proposition to buy each of these programs in order to test out each file. Therefore, if you submit files to us, please make sure you test them thoroughly. Also, please give us the version number of the program you're cracking. Nothing is more discouraging than trying to use a routine that is supposed to work, only to find out that it doesn't. Your reward for doing this will be a one month addition to your subscription.

Print Shop Companion

In the last issue we told you how to make a copy of *Print Shop*. Since that appeared, some of you have asked me to tell you how to back up the *Print Shop Companion*. Now, thanks to Stan Kelley, we can. By the way, Stan is not yet a subscriber and neglected to send us his address so we're having a tough time locating him to give him is complimentary subscription. Stan, if you're reading this, get in touch with us so you can have your own copy of **ASPD**.

Print Shop Companion does not use any special DOS, but has a nibble counter built in Thus, it is not necessary to change any of the Data or Address Field bytes. It will however, be necessary to perform a sector edit. The protection scheme used with this program is identical to the one used with *Print Shop*. The only difference involved is in the actual location on the diskette where the changes should be made.

Stan originally suggested that any copy program could be used to copy the *Print Shop Companion* diskette and that the patch to overcome the protection could then be applied manually with a sector editor. He was only half right. Standard copy programs cannot be used because track $22 (which is the 35th track) is specially formatted and is in fact the track that is used for nibble counting. By adding another modification to our COPYP program however, we can tell it to read and copy only the first 34 tracks (line 72) and forget about the last one, because we're going to disable the nibble count anyway. Thus, the required parameter file to allow COPYP to unprotect the *Print Shop Companion* consists of the following two lines:

continued on page 7

```
                2660 * This is the actual code appended to an Applesoft
                2670 * program to allow it to be BRUN.  The RESET key is
                2680 * programmed to RUN the program when it is pressed and
                2690 * Applesoft's AUTO RUN FLAG is set to make it hard
                2700 * for the user to get control of the computer.
                2710 *
9468- A9 66     2720 BRUNCODE   LDA #RUN
946A- 8D F2 03  2730            STA RESET
946D- A9 D5     2740            LDA /RUN
946F- 8D F3 03  2750            STA RESET+1
9472- 85 D6     2760            STA RUNFLAG
9474- A9 70     2770            LDA #$70
9476- 8D F4 03  2780            STA POWERUP
9479- 20 58 FC  2790            JSR HOME
947C- 4C 66 D5  2800            JMP RUN
947F- 00        2810            .HS 00
9480- 00        2820 CV2        .HS 00
9481- 00 00     2830 LENGTH     .HS 0000
                2840 *
                2850 * Below are all the text messages that are printed out
                2860 * by the BRUN MAKER program.
                2870 *
9483- 8D 8D     2880 TEXT1      .HS 8D8D
9485- A0 A0 A0
9488- C2 D2 D5
948B- CE A0 CD
948E- C1 CB C5
9491- D2 A0 C6
9494- CF D2 A0
9497- C1 D0 D0
949A- CC C5 D3
949D- CF C6 D4
94A0- A0 D0 D2
94A3- CF C7 D2
94A6- C1 CD D3  2890            .AS -"       BRUN MAKER FOR APPLESOFT PROGRAMS"
94A9- 8D 8D     2900            .HS 8D8D
94AB- A0 A0 A0
94AE- A0 A0 A0
94B1- A0 A0 A0
94B4- C3 CF D0
94B7- D9 D2 C9
94BA- C7 C8 D4
94BD- A0 A8 C3
94C0- A9 A0 B1
94C3- B9 B8 B6
94C6- A0 C2 D9  2910            .AS -"               COPYRIGHT (C) 1986 BY"
94C9- 8D        2920            .HS 8D
94CA- A0 A0 A0
94CD- A0 A0 A0
94D0- A0 A0 A0
94D3- A0 A0 A0
94D6- CA D5 CC
94D9- C5 D3 A0
94DC- C8 AE A0
94DF- C7 C9 CC
94E2- C4 C5 D2  2930            .AS -"                 JULES H. GILDER"
94E5- 8D        2940            .HS 8D
94E6- A0 A0 A0
94E9- A0 A0 A0
94EC- A0 A0 A0
94EF- A0 C1 CC
94F2- CC A0 D2
94F5- C9 C7 C8
94F8- D4 D3 A0
94FB- D2 C5 D3
94FE- C5 D2 D6
9501- C5 C4     2950            .AS -"             ALL RIGHTS RESERVED"
9503- 8D 8D 8D
9506- 8D        2960            .HS 8D8D8D8D
9507- C5 CE D4
950A- C5 D2 A0
950D- D4 C8 C5
9510- A0 C6 C9
9513- CC C5 A0
9516- CE C1 CD
9519- C5 BA A0  2970            .AS -"ENTER THE FILE NAME: "
951C- 00        2980            .HS 00
951D- 8D 8D 8D
9520- 8D 8D 8D
9523- 8D 8D 8D
9526- 8D 8D 8D  2990 TEXT2      .HS 8D8D8D8D8D8D8D8D8D8D8D8D
9529- A0 C3 C1
```

```
952C-   CC CC A0
952F-   B3 B7 B8
9532-   B7 B6       3000            .AS -" CALL 37876"
9534-   00          3010            .HS 00
9535-   8D 8D       3020    TEXT3   .HS 8D8D
9537-   D7 C8 C5
953A-   CE A0 D9
953D-   CF D5 A7
9540-   D2 C5 A0
9543-   D2 C5 C1
9546-   C4 D9 A0
9549-   D4 CF A0
954C-   C3 CF CE
954F-   D4 C9 CE
9552-   D5 C5 AC
9555-   A0 D4 D9
9558-   D0 C5       3030            .AS -"WHEN YOU'RE READY TO CONTINUE, TYPE"
955A-   8D          3040            .HS 8D
955B-   A7 D6 D4
955E-   C1 C2 A0
9561-   B2 B4 A7
9564-   A0 C1 CE
9567-   C4 A0 D4
956A-   C8 C5 CE
956D-   A0 D4 D2
9570-   C1 C3 C5
9573-   A0 CF D6
9576-   C5 D2 A0
9579-   D4 C8 C5
957C-   A0 C3 C1
957F-   CC CC       3050            .AS -"'VTAB 24' AND THEN TRACE OVER THE CALL"
9581-   8D          3060            .HS 8D
9582-   D3 D4 C1
9585-   D4 C5 CD
9588-   C5 CE D4
958B-   A0 D7 C9
958E-   D4 C8 A0
9591-   D4 C8 C5
9594-   A0 C3 D5
9597-   D2 D3 CF
959A-   D2 AE       3070            .AS -"STATEMENT WITH THE CURSOR."
959C-   00          3080            .HS 00
959D-   8D 84       3090    TEXT4   .HS 8D84
959F-   CC CF C1
95A2-   C4 A0       3100            .AS -"LOAD "
95A4-   00          3110            .HS 00
95A5-   8D 84       3120    TEXT5   .HS 8D84
95A7-   C2 D3 C1
95AA-   D6 C5 A0
95AD-   C2 AE       3130            .AS -"BSAVE B."
95AF-   00          3140            .HS 00
95B0-   AC C1 A4
95B3-   B7 C5 B9
95B6-   AC CC A4    3150    TEXT6   .AS -",A$7E9,L$"
95B9-   00          3160            .HS 00
95BA-   8D 8D       3170    TEXT7   .HS 8D8D
95BC-   D4 C8 C5
95BF-   A0 C2 C9
95C2-   CE C1 D2
95C5-   D9 A0 C6
95C8-   C9 CC C5
95CB-   A0 C8 C1
95CE-   D3 A0 C2
95D1-   C5 C5 CE
95D4-   A0 D3 C1
95D7-   D6 C5 C4
95DA-   A0 C1 D3
95DD-   BA          3180            .AS -"THE BINARY FILE HAS BEEN SAVED AS:"
95DE-   8D          3190            .HS 8D
95DF-   C2 AE       3200            .AS -"B."
95E1-   00          3210            .HS 00
95E2-   00          3220            .HS 00
```

```
10 TEXT : HOME
20 PRINT "   BRUN MAKER FOR APPLESOFT PROGRAMS"
30 PRINT : PRINT : PRINT
40 PRINT "NOW LOADING MACHINE LANGUAGE PROGRAM"
50 PRINT "INTO MEMORY.  PLEASE WAIT."
60 VTAB 9
```

continued from page 6

72 POKE 834,34
1000 DATA 3,12,224,169,96

Line 1000 puts a machine-language return code right at the beginning of the call to the nibble counting routine, totally bypassing it. By the way, if you're interested in examining the nibble counting code directly, break out of the program and get into the monitor. Then type **B619L**. This is the nibble counting routine. If you have an Apple //e or //c and can't break out of the program without it rebooting, then you can use a sector editor that disassembles code directly from the diskette (*Copy][Plus* has this feature). The nibble counting routine is located on track 3, sector 6 and starts with the 25th byte (in hex that's 19). That's all there is to it. See, that wasn't so hard.

Sensible Grammar and Bookends

Here's some tips on how to unprotect *Sensible Grammar* and *Bookends* (both of which are published by Sensible Software) from Allen L. Southmayd of San Antonio, TX. Allen says that this procedure is based on information published in Computist by Don G. Grande, who used it to unprotect version 2.06 of Bookends. It can be used for other versions as well, he points out, but you'll have to locate the right track and sector. The same technique is used on Sensible Grammar, says Allen. I converted the information Allen sent in to DATA statements for use with COPYP. Here they are:

1000 DATA 5,0,56,247,86 : REM BOOKENDS VERSION 2.0

1000 DATA 1,13,56,247,86 : REM BOOKENDS VERSION 2.06

1000 DATA 4,4,17,247,56 : REM SENSIBLE GRAMMAR VERSION 1A

Allen notes that if you have the program *Essential Data Duplicator III (EDD)* that you can use that to make a backup copy of *Sensible Grammar*. To do that you copy tracks $0 to $22 (remember the $ indicates hexadecimal numbers) using option 2. Then, he says, change parm 28 to $02 or $03 and recopy track $00 until the program boots properly. Thanks for the advice Allen. We're adding one month onto your **ASPD** subscription. Keep the contributions coming.

PFS Series - PRODOS Version

The new PRODOS versions of *PFS WRITE, GRAPH, REPORT* and *FILE* all use the same copy protection scheme. To disable it, all you have to do is copy the disk, and then perform a single sector edit.

continued on page 9

Tutorial

continued from page 22

line 1 or you can type in line 2 from Applesoft. Line 2 can be entered either from the direct execution mode (without a line number) or in the deferred execution mode (with a line number).

1. B955:AA N B95F:D5 N BC7A:AA N BC7F:D5

2. POKE 47445,170 : POKE 47455,213 : POKE 48250,170 : POKE 48255,213

The first two locations that are modified by these lines are the READ locations and the last two are the WRITE locations. To switch back to normal DOS 3.3, simply enter either of the following lines:

1. B955:D5 N B95F:AA N BC7A:AA N BC7F:D5

2. POKE 47445,213 : POKE 47455,170 : POKE 48250,213 : POKE 48255,170

You could just as easily change the bytes in the prologue of the data field instead of the address field. Or, you can change the first two epilogue bytes in either field. You can use a combination of techniques. The possibilities are almost endless, and each change you make results in a unique protected DOS.

Try your hand at making up some diskettes with a modified version of DOS. You'll be pleased to see how easy it really is. If you are going to use a modified DOS as described here, bear in mind that the level of protection afforded is limited since most nibble copy programs that are currently available can easily copy diskettes created with modified versions of DOS 3.3. However, it will prevent standard copy programs, such as COPYA, from duplicating your diskette.

continued on page 13

Table 3
Data Field DOS Locations

Location	Byte	Address Hex	Decimal
Prologue Read	D5	B8E7	47335
	AA	B8F1	47345
	AD	B8FC	47356
Prologue Write	D5	B853	47187
	AA	B858	47192
	AD	B85D	47197
Epilogue Read	DE	B935	47413
	AA	B93F	47423
Epilogue Write	DE	B89E	47262
	AA	B8A3	47267

```
70  PRINT TAB( 14);: FLASH : PRINT "LOADING...": NORMAL
80  FOR X = 1 TO 570
90    READ Y
100   POKE 37799 + X,Y
110 NEXT X
120 VTAB 7
130 PRINT : PRINT
140 PRINT "THE PROGRAM IS NOW READY TO USE."
150 PRINT "TYPE 'CALL 37800' TO ACTIVATE IT."
160 DATA 32,88,252,169,131,160,148,32
170 DATA 82,148,32,111,253,169,0,157
180 DATA 64,2,202,189,0,2,157,64
190 DATA 2,232,202,208,245,165,37,141
200 DATA 128,148,230,37,169,29,160,149
210 DATA 32,82,148,169,23,133,35,173
220 DATA 128,148,133,37,169,53,160,149
230 DATA 32,82,148,169,157,160,149,32
240 DATA 82,148,169,64,160,2,32,82
250 DATA 148,32,98,252,162,0,189,104
260 DATA 148,157,233,7,240,3,232,208
270 DATA 245,56,169,233,233,1,141,129
280 DATA 148,56,165,175,237,129,148,141
290 DATA 129,148,165,176,233,7,141,130
300 DATA 148,169,165,160,149,32,82,148
310 DATA 169,64,160,2,32,82,148,169
320 DATA 176,160,149,32,82,148,173,130
330 DATA 148,32,218,253,173,129,148,32
340 DATA 218,253,32,98,252,169,24,133
350 DATA 35,169,186,160,149,32,82,148
360 DATA 169,64,160,2,32,82,148,76
370 DATA 3,224,133,6,132,7,160,0
380 DATA 177,6,240,11,32,237,253,230
390 DATA 6,208,245,230,7,208,241,96
400 DATA 169,102,141,242,3,169,213,141
410 DATA 243,3,133,214,169,112,141,244
420 DATA 3,32,88,252,76,102,213,0
430 DATA 0,0,0,141,141,160,160,160
440 DATA 194,210,213,206,160,205,193,203
450 DATA 197,210,160,198,207,210,160,193
460 DATA 208,208,204,197,211,207,198,212
470 DATA 160,208,210,207,199,210,193,205
480 DATA 211,141,141,160,160,160,160,160
490 DATA 160,160,160,160,195,207,208,217
500 DATA 210,201,199,200,212,160,168,195
510 DATA 169,160,177,185,184,182,160,194
520 DATA 217,141,160,160,160,160,160,160
530 DATA 160,160,160,160,160,202,213
540 DATA 204,197,211,160,200,174,160,199
550 DATA 201,204,196,197,210,141,160,160
560 DATA 160,160,160,160,160,160,160,160
570 DATA 193,204,204,160,210,201,199,200
580 DATA 212,211,160,210,197,211,197,210
590 DATA 214,197,196,141,141,141,141,197
600 DATA 206,212,197,210,160,212,200,197
610 DATA 160,198,201,204,197,160,206,193
620 DATA 205,197,186,160,0,141,141,141
630 DATA 141,141,141,141,141,141,141,141
640 DATA 141,160,195,193,204,204,160,179
650 DATA 183,184,183,182,0,141,141,215
660 DATA 200,197,206,160,217,207,213,167
670 DATA 210,197,160,210,197,193,196,217
680 DATA 160,212,207,160,195,207,206,212
690 DATA 201,206,213,197,172,160,212,217
700 DATA 208,197,141,167,214,212,193,194
710 DATA 160,178,180,167,160,193,206,196
720 DATA 160,212,200,197,206,160,212,210
730 DATA 193,195,197,160,207,214,197,210
740 DATA 160,212,200,197,160,195,193,204
750 DATA 204,141,211,212,193,212,197,205
760 DATA 197,206,212,160,215,201,212,200
770 DATA 160,212,200,197,160,195,213,210
780 DATA 211,207,210,174,0,141,132,204
790 DATA 207,193,196,160,0,141,132,194
800 DATA 211,193,214,197,160,194,174,0
810 DATA 172,193,164,183,197,185,172,204
820 DATA 164,0,141,141,212,200,197,160
830 DATA 194,201,206,193,210,217,160,198
840 DATA 201,204,197,160,200,193,211,160
850 DATA 194,197,197,206,160,211,193,214
860 DATA 197,196,160,193,211,186,141,194
870 DATA 174,0
880 REM
890 REM  COPYRIGHT (C) 1986 BY
900 REM  JULES H. GILDER
910 REM  ALL RIGHTS RESERVED
```

CHANGE THE BLOAD ADDRESS OF BINARY FILES

When binary files are saved out to diskette under DOS 3.3 it is necessary to specify not only the length of the file to be saved, but also the address of the start of the file. When the file is loaded back into memory at a latter time, it is this starting address that is used to properly place the program where it belongs. The designer's of Apple's DOS however, realized that sometimes, you might like to have the ability to save a file out from one location in memory and load it back in to another. This is particularly important when you're putting together protection schemes or when you want to modify a program that it will automatically run when it's loaded in (see **ASPD** Vol. 1, No. 1, p. 6).

To accommodate such situations, Apple made it possible to use the A or A$ option (e.g. BLOAD FILE,A$300) to BLOAD a file into a different address than the one it was saved from. While this technique is better than not being able to do anything at all, it nevertheless is awkward. A much more reasonable solution would have been for Apple to include a DOS command that would automatically change the information on the diskette that tells DOS where to start loading the file in.

Since Apple did not have the foresight to include such a versatile command, we'll just have to do it ourselves. To make the job simple, I've decided to use the standard DOS command parser (command interpreter). In order to do this however, it will be necessary to get rid of one of DOS's already existing commands. In the eight years that I've owned my Apple, I've never used the CHAIN command, so I think it's fairly safe to convert that command into one that will change the BLOAD address of a binary file.

Change it to CHADR

The first thing we must do is change the actual command to something that is more mnemonic (connected with the operation that's going to be performed and therefore easy to remember). Since we're going to change the address, why not change the command to CHADR? To do that, all we have to do is change the the last two letters of the CHAIN command from IN to DR. DOS has a table of all the commands stored in RAM starting at 43140 ($A884). By POKEing new values into these locations, it is therefore possible to change the commands that DOS recognizes (we'll talk more about this in the next issue of **ASPD**). The changing of the CHAIN command name is actually done by two simple POKEs in line 30 of the program listing.

Next, to keep the program out of the way, we'll store it in high memory starting at 38320 ($95B1 in hex). Once we know where the program is going to reside in memory, we have to notify DOS so that it will know how to access it. Just as DOS held a table of com-

```
10  HIMEM: 38320
20  POKE 40230,176: POKE 40231,149
30  POKE 43158,68: POKE 43159,210
40  POKE 43281,32: POKE 43282,113
50  FOR X = 1 TO 67
60    READ Y
70    POKE 38320 + X,Y
80  NEXT X
90  PRINT : PRINT : PRINT
100 PRINT "THE 'CHAIN' COMMAND HAS BEEN CHANGED TO"
110 PRINT "'CHADR'. TO USE IT SPECIFY THE FILENAME"
120 PRINT "AND THE NEW ADDRESS.  THE ADDRESS CAN"
130 PRINT "BE IN DECIMAL, OR IF PRECEDED BY A"
140 PRINT "DOLLAR SIGN ($), HEXADECIMAL."
200 DATA 173,101,170,41,15,201,1,240
210 DATA 3,76,196,166,173,114,170,141
220 DATA 244,149,173,115,170,141,245,149
230 DATA 32,168,162,173,194,181,201,127
240 DATA 144,11,169,10,141,92,170,32
250 DATA 252,162,76,213,166,41,15,201
260 DATA 4,240,4,169,13,208,237,172
270 DATA 244,149,173,245,149,32,224,163
280 DATA 76,252,162
```

mand names in RAM, it also holds a table of addresses of where each routine begins. This table starts at 40222 ($9D1E). The jump address for the CHAIN command is located at 40236 ($9D26). If we POKE the address of our machine language program into 40236 and 40237, then whenever the CHADR command is issued, it will jump to our program instead of the CHAIN routine. That's exactly what is done in line 20 of the program.

Before actually loading the program that implements the CHADR command into memory, we have one more job to do. We must now tell DOS which of the optional features of DOS are valid with our command. For example, we want to require a file name and address and also let the user specify an optional volume number, slot number and drive number. Once again, we have a table in memory that holds this information (at 43281 for the CHAIN command) and once again we have two POKEs that will set the command up the way we want it to be. This is done in line 40 of the program.

Load the routine into memory

Now that we've set up the DOS command to do exactly what we want, the only thing left to do is load in a short machine language routine that will do the actual work for us. This is done in line 50 through 80 in the BASIC listing.

Just as with the BSAVE command, the new CHADR command that we've implemented will permit you to use either an A or an A$. To change the BLOAD address of a file to 2048 (the text screen for example), you would issue the following command:

CHADR FILENAME,A2048 or CHADR FILENAME,A$800

That's all there is to it. I'm sure you'll find, as I did, that this will be one of your most useful DOS modifications and a big help in implementing software protection schemes.

COPYP Parameters
continued from page 7

COPYP can do the job by simply adding the line below:

1000 DATA 4,1,170,25,3

PFS PLAN uses a similar protection scheme, but it is located on a different track than the others. To make a usable unprotected copy of it type in the following line:

1000 DATA 1,13,170,25,3

Time Is Money

To make an unprotected copy of *Time Is Money*, use the following data:

1000 DATA 5,15,25,189,96

Homeword

This word processing program from Sierra On-Line can be copied by typing in the following line into the COPYP program:

1000 DATA 16,10,0,206,96

Homeword Speller

This is a companion spelling checker that works with *Homeword*. Unprotecting it is almost as simple as unprotecting *Homeword*, except instead of changing one byte, you'll have to change two. The following lines, when added to COPYP will make the unprotected copy for you.

1000 DATA 1,7,200,32,76
1010 DATA 1,7,201,18,220

Letters

Dear Editor:

Congratulations on your new publication. The quality of the material in the premier issue was excellent. If it remains that way you should have a winner. I'm rooting for you.

For the past year I've wished that I could deprotect a BASIC checkbook program (Disk-O-Check) which no longer is being sold. As a matter of fact, the company that produced it has gone out of business. My aim is to put the program onto my Sider disk where file access would be considerably more rapid. Is it your plan to consider such problems and to provide information that would enable me to accomplish this feat?

Regardless of your answer, please accept my check for a one year subscription. I am also purchasing your Assembly Language book for my library.

Sandy Mossberg
Rye Brook, NY

Your complaint is a common one Sandy. Many good programs would be much more useful if they could be put on a hard disk drive. Also, it is unfortunately too common that software companies that were here yesterday, are gone today. I am currently working on cracking Disk-O-Check for you and when it's done, I will describe how it was done in the digest so that others in a similar situation, even though the program may be different, can do it too.

Dear Editor:

In the past few months I have been searching wildly for cracking and copying information. I just read about your publication and would like you to send me a sample copy. I have been searching for something like this for months. I am interested in the challenge, fun and usefulness of hacking and cracking and I hope you can help me.

Matt St. Jean
New Milford, CT

Matt, your sample copy is in the mail. I hope you enjoy it and will become a regular reader of ours.

Dear Editor:

I have read the first issue of the Digest from cover to cover several times and find it unusually interesting and helpful. I look forward to many learning sessions and I anxiously await its delivery. Some things I would enjoy seeing in the Digest would be a letters or readers column, checksums for the program listings and available diskettes of the programs on a periodic basis at a nominal cost.

I have a problem with the print shop program that maybe one of your readers can help me with. My system is an Apple //e, Rev. B, Apple Extended 80 Col. card, Enhanced except I replaced the new character generator ROM with the old one because I didn't like those mouse characters. I replaced the CD ROM with a 2764 EPROM burned with Don Lancaster's patch to give absolute reset capability. I have an Apple DuoDisk drive in slot 6, a Microtek RV-611c parallel card in slot 1 with an Apple DMP and an Epson RX-100, and an Applied Engineering Z-80 card in slot 7. When I run the *Print Shop* printer test I get 2 or 3 garbage characters (not always the same) and then the printer is deselected. The same thing happens when I design something with the *Print Shop* and try to print it out. My daughter runs the same disk on her //c with an Apple Scribe printer with no problems. Help!

Virgil Flint
Poway, CA

Well Virgil, here's the Letters column. A diskette with all the programs from this issue and the previous one is now available from us for only $15, so you don't have to key all the data in yourself. We'll have a diskette available with every issue. We haven't implemented a checksum technique yet, but we're working on it. It should be in the next issue or at the latest the one after that. As far as your problems with Print Shop are concerned, I don't know what to say. We've gotten lots of letters and so have other publications, concerning the problem of printing out with the program. From all the responses I've seen, Broderbund doesn't seem to be very responsive to its customers' needs. I've printed your problem here and hopefully one of our readers will be able to help you.

Decimal/Hexadecimal Converter

continued from page 15

```
10   TEXT : HOME
20   A$ = "HEX/DECIMAL/HEX CONVERTER": GOSUB 420
30   PRINT :A$ = "COPYRIGHT (C) 1986 BY": GOSUB 420
40   A$ = "JULES H. GILDER": GOSUB 420
50   A$ = "ALL RIGHTS RESERVED": GOSUB 420
60   FOR X = 1 TO 84
70     READ NUM
80     POKE 767 + X,NUM
90   NEXT X
95   CALL 768
100  PRINT : PRINT : PRINT : PRINT
110  PRINT "THE HEXADECIMAL TO DECIMAL CONVERTER IS"
120  PRINT "NOW ACTIVE.  TO USE IT, TYPE AN"
130  PRINT "AMPERSAND (&) AND THE NUMBER TO BE"
140  PRINT "CONVERTED.  TO CONVERT FROM HEXADECIMAL"
150  PRINT "TO DECIMAL, PRECEDE THE NUMBER WITH A"
160  PRINT "DOLLAR SIGN ($)."
165  PRINT : PRINT "         &768 RETURNS $0300 WHILE"
170  PRINT "         &$300 RETURNS 768"
190  END
200  DATA 162,76,169,16,160,3,142,245
210  DATA 3,141,246,3,140,247,3,96
220  DATA 201,36,240,23,32,103,221,32
230  DATA 82,231,169,164,32,237,253,165
240  DATA 81,240,3,32,218,253,165,80
250  DATA 76,218,253,160,0,32,177,0
260  DATA 240,8,73,128,153,0,2,200
270  DATA 208,243,153,0,2,168,32,167
280  DATA 255,166,62,165,63,192,6,144
290  DATA 3,76,153,225,192,3,176,2
300  DATA 169,0,76,36,237
420  L = LEN (A$)
430  PRINT TAB( (40 - L) / 2);A$
440  RETURN
```

Dear Editor:

Thank you for the complementary copy of your premier issue of **Apple Software Protection Digest**. I tried to use your *Print Shop* copy program and got an UNABLE TO WRITE error. I checked the drive and the diskette and everything seemed fine. Then I tried eliminating line 277 in Apple's COPYA program, which is the error-trapping routine for the UNABLE TO WRITE error, and the program worked perfectly. I would appreciate your entering a subscription for me. By the way, if you have any suggestions for backing up Word Handler or for eliminating the non-standard file formats, which have a tendency to garbage disks containing other programs, I'd be grateful to hear of them.

Paul Dunseath
Ottawa, Ontario

Glad you liked our first issue Paul. I think you'll like our second one even better. I'm adding your request to our Wanted list and hopefully we'll be able to accommodate you real soon.

HIDING MACHINE LANGUAGE PROGRAMS IN STRINGS

One of the key elements involved in producing protected software is making it difficult for the software cracker to not only access your program code, but to also make it difficult for him or her to understand what's going on. Finally, you want to make it easy for the would be cracker to overlook some important code.

A technique that I have found very handy in this last regard, is to hide short machine language programs in either strings or REM statements within your BASIC program. If, after doing that, you go one step further and hide the particular line that the REM or string appears in, using any of the line hiding techniques we've already discussed, then you'll make your program significantly more difficult to crack.

The basic technique of hiding a machine language program in REMs or strings merely requires that you set the string or REM statement up to have at least the same number of characters as you have bytes in your machine-language program. You could set aside more than you need, but obviously less just won't do. To show you how it's done, let's take a simple example. I'm going to take the WIPEOUT 1 program that's described elsewhere in this issue, and hide that in a string. If you go back and look at that program, you notice that the code is position dependent (that means it was designed and assembled to work in only one specific location in the computer and thus it is not relocatable). Because of that, the specific position dependent reference, which occurs on line 1150 of the program, will have to be changed once we know the new location where the program is going to reside in memory. To avoid this sort of problem, it is best to use relocatable, or position independent programs when possible. They take a little more time and effort to produce, but they're much more flexible.

Here's how to do it step by step

To begin the step-by-step description of how to hide machine language programs in strings, let's first produce a short Applesoft BASIC program, such as the one listed below.

```
10  PRINT "THIS IS A TEST"
20  GOTO 40
30  A$ = "12345678901234567
    89012345678901234567890"
40  CALL XXXX
50  PRINT "THAT'S ALL FOLKS!"
```

You'll notice that in line 30, I've defined A$ as a series of digits from 1 through 0 (for 10). I've found this to be very convenient, because it makes it very easy to count the number of bytes used. Another advantage of this approach is that it stores an easily distinguishable pattern of bytes in RAM memory.

When this program is run, it should print out **THIS IS A TEST** execute a machine language program that is located at XXXX and then print **THAT'S ALL FOLKS!** If the machine language program that we have it call is WIPEOUT 1, however, memory will be cleared to all zeros and the last line of the program will never be executed.

Locate the string in memory

Now we have two things to do. We must first determine where our string begins in memory so we know where to store our machine language program, and second, we must change the Xs in the CALL statement to the appropriate number. The easiest way to locate the string in memory is to use the Applesoft Line Finder program that was published in the last issue of **ASPD** (you can also use the Applesoft Line Finder and Vanisher program from this issue) and simply enter the number of the line that the string is located on. By doing that and typing an &30, you'll get the following display on your computer screen.

```
]&30

081F: 51 08 1E 00 41 24 D0 22
0827: 31 32 33 34 35 36 37 38
082F: 39 30 31 32 33 34 35 36
0837: 37 38 39 30 31 32 33 34
083F: 35 36 37 38 39 30 31 32
0847: 33 34 35 36 37 38 39 30
084F: 22 00
```

As you can easily see from this display (even if you didn't know that the 1 was stored as a 31 in hexadecimal), the string itself begins at memory location $0827 (remember that's a hexadecimal number). The decimal equivalent of $827 is 2087. This is the location of the start of our machine-language program and line 40 can now be changed from CALL XXXX to CALL 2087.

If you counted the number of digits we placed in A$, you'd find that it's 40, so that is the maximum size we should allow our machine language program to be. If we have a longer program, just make the string longer. You can go up to about 230 characters. Those of you who know that strings can be as long as 255 characters may question this discrepancy. The limit is due to the fact that Applesoft limits the length of a line that can be typed in to 239 characters. If you take away what you need for the line number and the A$= you're left with about 230 (actually 233).

Load the program into the string

To load the machine language program into the string you can key it in directly as it's real short. The best thing, however is to BLOAD it in from a diskette, using the destination (A$) parameter. If for example, I had my program stored on a diskette as WIPEOUT 1, then to load it where it belongs in my BASIC program I would have to type BLOAD WIPEOUT 1,A$827. This would load my machine language program right into the string in my Applesoft BASIC program. Alternatively, I could have typed in (from the monitor mode) the following to load the program in:

```
*827:A0 00 84 D6 B9 E2 02 99
 00 02 C8 C9 82 D0 F5 4C 70 FF
 B8<RETURN>

*:B0 B0 BA B0 A0 CE A0 B8 B0
 B1 BC B8 B0 B0 AE B9 B5 C6 C6
 CD 82<RETURN>
```

Once we have the machine code in its proper location, if it's not relocatable, we'll have to patch it so that it can run there. For WIPEOUT 1, that means we'll have to change the two bytes located at $82C. We do this by typing **CALL -151** to get into the monitor mode if we're not already in it, and then type:

```
* 82C:39 08 <RETURN>
```

Now type **3D0G** to get back to Applesoft and then type **LIST**. Your program should look like this:

```
10  PRINT "THIS IS A TEST"
20  GOTO 40
30  A$ = "  COLOR=
40  CALL 2087
50  PRINT "THAT'S ALL FOLKS!"
```

Notice that line 30 has changed and now has a strange looking statement in it. Don't worry about it. It may look strange, but it works fine. At this point, it's very important to tell you that absolutely no changes should be made to your Applesoft program from now on. Don't add any lines and don't delete any lines. If you do, you will mess up your program irretrievably. This, by the way, is another plus for hiding critical machine language routines in strings, because it makes changing a program virtually impossible without destroying it.

Ordinary saves won't work

Another thing you should be aware is that you shouldn't count on being able to save your program to a diskette this way, because it will be destroyed after it's loaded back into memory. The reason for this is that there are some zeros in the assembly language program, and Applesoft interprets them as end of line markers with faulty links to the next line of the Applesoft program. When Applesoft tries to correctly link the program (which occurs when a program is loaded or

continued on page 14

TWO SOLUTIONS TO THE HIDE-A-LINE PROBLEM

by Mark Landwehr

After seeing the challenge offered in the first issue regarding hidden program lines, I put together two machine-language programs that will hide any Applesoft program lines that are desired. The programs use two of the different techniques that were described in the first issue of **Apple Software Protection Digest**.

In the first program, Applesoft Line-Hide #1, all the lines that are to be hidden must begin with 5 colons, as was described in the original article. The program has two modes of operation. In one, you can specify individual lines that should be hidden, while in the second, all lines that have five colons in front of them will be hidden.

The program makes use of several Applesoft ROM routines and also uses the **&** to both jump to the machine language routine and pass parameters (in this case the line number) to it.

Set up the ampersand jump

The program is activated by typing **CALL 768**. It immediately returns you to Applesoft and it appears as if nothing has happened. In fact, however, the program set up the ampersand (&) jump parameters (this is done by the code marked INIT in the listing) so that the working part of the program (labelled START) will be jumped to every time the & key is entered.

The first thing that the program does once it's called via the &, is a subroutine jump to Applesoft's CHRGOT routine. This is a very short routine that is located on page zero and is used everytime an Applesoft command is entered. Applesoft used it to recognize that the ampersand was entered, and it left an internal pointer set to the next character after the &. If there was nothing else entered, the pointer will be pointing to a zero. If, however, a line number was entered too, the pointer will be pointing to it.

A jump to the CHRGOT routine will cause the accumulator to be loaded with whatever is being pointed to. If it turns out that the accumulator contains a value other than zero, we know a line number was entered too, and the program branches to the code that handles individual lines (the section marked ONE in the listing). If a zero was loaded into the accumulator, then the program assumes that the user wants all lines that have five colons in front of them to be hidden and falls into the subroutine, called ALL, that does this.

Whether the ONE or ALL subroutines are used, both of them make use of the CHECK subroutine, which inspects the line being processed to see if it has five colons in front of it. If it does, the first colon is replaced with a zero to implement the hiding, otherwise, the line is ignored.

```
              1000 ******************************************
              1010 *                                        *
              1020 *   A P P L E S O F T   L I N E - H I D E  # 1  *
              1030 *                                        *
              1040 * Will make any or all program lines that begin *
              1050 * with 5 colons disappear. Line numbers will    *
              1060 * remain visible, but with no program data...   *
              1070 *                                        *
              1080 *            COMMAND SYNTAX              *
              1090 *                                        *
              1100 *        & = all lines with 5 colons     *
              1110 *        &<line#> = desired line only    *
              1120 *                                        *
              1130 ******************************************
              1140 *
              1150 *
              1160 *
0000-         1170 PTR      .EQ $00        storage pointer
0067-         1180 TXTTAB   .EQ $67        start of BASIC program
009B-         1190 LOWTR    .EQ $9B        pointer used by FNDLIN
00B7-         1200 CHRGOT   .EQ $B7        fetch data routine
03F6-         1210 AMPER    .EQ $3F6       ampersand vector
D61A-         1220 FNDLIN   .EQ $D61A      search for line number
DA0C-         1230 LINGET   .EQ $DA0C      put line number in zero page
              1240 *
              1250 *
              1260          .OR $300
              1270 *
              1280 * This routine initializes the ampersand jump vector.
              1290 *
0300- A9 0B   1300 INIT     LDA #START
0302- A0 03   1310          LDY /START
0304- 8D F6 03 1320         STA AMPER
0307- 8C F7 03 1330         STY AMPER+1
030A- 60      1340          RTS
              1350 *
              1360 * Check entry after the "&". If nothing, do all lines.
              1370 * If there's a number, then execute only on that line.
              1380 *
030B- 20 B7 00 1390 START   JSR CHRGOT     Get entry.
030E- D0 1F   1400          BNE ONE        Handle a single line.
              1410 *
              1420 * Hide all lines in program that begin with 5 colons.
              1430 *
0310- A5 67   1440 ALL      LDA TXTTAB     Load start of program
0312- A4 68   1450          LDY TXTTAB+1   pointers.
0314- 85 00   1460          STA PTR        Save pointers to zero
0316- 84 01   1470          STY PTR+1      page locations.
0318- A0 00   1480 LOOP1    LDY #$0        Initialize index.
031A- B1 00   1490          LDA (PTR),Y    Get lo-byte link
031C- 48      1500          PHA            and save it.
031D- C8      1510          INY
031E- B1 00   1520          LDA (PTR),Y    Get hi-byte link
0320- 48      1530          PHA            and save it too.
0321- F0 35   1540          BEQ DONE       If it is 0, end prgrm
0323- 20 44 03 1550         JSR CHECK      Check for 5 colons.
0326- 68      1560          PLA            Retrieve hi-byte link.
0327- 85 01   1570          STA PTR+1      Store it.
0329- 68      1580          PLA            Retrieve lo-byte link.
032A- 85 00   1590          STA PTR        Store it.
032C- B8      1600          CLV            Always go and look at
032D- 50 E9   1610          BVC LOOP1      the next line.
              1620 *
              1630 * Hide only the line that was specified by the user.
              1640 *
032F- 20 0C DA 1650 ONE     JSR LINGET     Put line# in LINNUM.
0332- 20 1A D6 1660         JSR FNDLIN     Find line in program.
0335- 90 23   1670          BCC DONE2      Clear carry, no line.
0337- A5 9B   1680          LDA LOWTR      Load address of the
0339- A4 9C   1690          LDY LOWTR+1    desired line.
033B- 85 00   1700          STA PTR        Store it in zero
033D- 84 01   1710          STY PTR+1      page locations.
033F- 20 44 03 1720         JSR CHECK      Check for 5 colons.
0342- F0 16   1730          BEQ DONE2      Return to caller.
              1740 *
              1750 * Check for 5 colons at the start of the line, and, if
              1760 * found, put a zero in place of first colon.
              1770 *
0344- A0 04   1780 CHECK    LDY #$4        Initialize index.
0346- B1 00   1790 LOOP2    LDA (PTR),Y    Get line data byte.
0348- C9 3A   1800          CMP #':        Is it a colon?
```

Hide lines without colons too

If you have already written a program and don't want to go back through it to add colons to it, you can use the second program, Applesoft Line-Hide #2. This program will hide any line or group of lines, regardless of whether there are five colons at the beginning or not. In fact, you might want to use both programs together to hide your program lines.

This program is somewhat similar to the first one in that it too uses the ampersand (&) to activate the program. In this case however, entering just the & by itself will give you a SYNTAX ERROR. This program requires that you enter two line numbers, the numbers of the lines that surround the one(s) you wish to hide. These two line numbers must be separated by a comma. Thus, in a program with lines numbered 10, 20 and 30, to hide line 20, you would type & 10,30. To hide several lines, just chose your first and last lines so that they surround the range to be hidden. The last line in you program can be hidden too, by simply specifying a larger, nonexistent line number for the second parameter in the ampersand command.

Since the command syntax for both of these programs is different, it would not be difficult to combine both of them into one program. Personally, I think that this may be a little confusing, which is why I left them as separate programs.

Thanks for your entry Mark. You won the best program award and will get an extra 6 months of ASPD.

Tutorial *continued from page 8*

After going through all of this article and reaching this point, you just might be asking yourself, "If this copy protection scheme can be copied with a nibble copier, what good is it?" The answer is simple. Knowledge is power. If you understand how this scheme works, you can incorporate it with a variety of other techniques that we'll discuss in the coming months and be able to produce a diskette that will be awfully difficult to copy. I say awfully difficult, because nothing can be 100% impossible to copy (although recently I've seen some programs that sure seem like it). More importantly, if you're trying to unprotect or back up a disk that you've purchased, you'll want to know what to look for. Now at least you have the basic knowledge that you need.

Next time we'll look at a special type of byte that is used on diskettes and causes a lot of problems for those interested in overcoming copy protection. This is known as the sync byte. In the mean time, try experimenting with what you've learned so far. If you come up with any interesting cracking or protecting techniques, let us know about them. If we publish yours, you'll get a free six-month extension to your current subscription.

```
034A- D0 0E      1810            BNE  DONE2       No, then forget it.
034C- C8         1820            INY
034D- C0 09      1830            CPY  #$9         Done 5 checks yet?
034F- 90 F5      1840            BCC  LOOP2       No, do more.
0351- A0 04      1850            LDY  #$4         Yes, back to 1st byte.
0353- A9 00      1860            LDA  #$0         Get ready to store
0355- 91 00      1870            STA  (PTR),Y     a zero there.
0357- 60         1880            RTS
                 1890  *
                 1900  * Exit routine. If entered from ALL routine, link bytes
                 1910  * must be pulled off of the stack. If from the ONE
                 1920  * routine, just return to the calling routine.
                 1930  *
0358- 68         1940  DONE      PLA
0359- 68         1950            PLA
035A- 60         1960  DONE2     RTS
```

```
                 1000  ***********************************************
                 1010  *                                             *
                 1020  *   A P P L E S O F T   L I N E - H I D E  #2 *
                 1030  *                                             *
                 1040  * Will hide any program line that user desires. *
                 1050  * User must enter line preceding hidden line. *
                 1060  * and line immediately following hidden line. *
                 1070  *     (Also works for a group of lines)       *
                 1080  *                                             *
                 1090  *              COMMAND SYNTAX                 *
                 1100  *                                             *
                 1110  *     &<line# preceding>,<line# following>    *
                 1120  *                                             *
                 1130  ***********************************************
                 1140  *
                 1150  *
                 1160  *
0000-            1170  PTR        .EQ $00        pointer for first byte
0002-            1180  PTR2       .EQ $02        pointer for second byte
009B-            1190  LOWTR      .EQ $9B        pointer used by FNDLIN
03F6-            1200  AMPER      .EQ $3F6       ampersand vector
D61A-            1210  FNDLIN     .EQ $D61A      search for line number
DA0C-            1220  LINGET     .EQ $DA0C      put line number in zero page
DEBE-            1230  CHKCOM     .EQ $DEBE      check for comma
                 1250
                 1260             .OR $300
                 1270  *
                 1280  * This routine initializes the ampersand jump vector.
                 1290  *
0300- A9 0B      1300  INIT       LDA #BEGIN
0302- A0 03      1310             LDY /BEGIN
0304- 8D F6 03   1320             STA AMPER
0307- 8C F7 03   1330             STY AMPER+1
030A- 60         1340             RTS
                 1350  *
                 1360  * Get the first (preceding) line number and store
                 1365  * pointers.
                 1370  *
030B- 20 0C DA   1380  BEGIN      JSR LINGET     Get the line number.
030E- 20 1A D6   1390             JSR FNDLIN     Find it in memory.
0311- A5 9B      1400             LDA LOWTR      Load pointers to the
0313- A4 9C      1410             LDY LOWTR+1    desired line.
0315- 85 00      1420             STA PTR        Save to zero page
0317- 84 01      1430             STY PTR+1      locations.
0319- 20 BE DE   1440             JSR CHKCOM     Check for a comma.
                 1450  *
                 1460  * Get the second (following) line number and store
                 1465  * pointers.
                 1470  *
031C- 20 0C DA   1480             JSR LINGET     Get the line number.
031F- 20 1A D6   1490             JSR FNDLIN     Find it in memory.
0322- A5 9B      1500             LDA LOWTR      Load pointers to the
0324- A4 9C      1510             LDY LOWTR+1    desired line.
0326- 85 02      1520             STA PTR2       Save to zero page
0328- 84 03      1530             STY PTR2+1     locations.
                 1540  *
                 1550  * Take the address of the link bytes of the second
                 1560  * (following) line and store them as the link bytes
                 1570  * in the first (preceding) line.
                 1580  *
032A- A0 00      1590             LDY #$0        Initialize the index.
032C- A5 02      1600             LDA PTR2       Lo-byte link of second line
032E- 91 00      1610             STA (PTR),Y    stored in first line number.
0330- C8         1620             INY
0331- A5 03      1630             LDA PTR2+1     Hi-byte link of 2nd line number
0333- 91 00      1640             STA (PTR),Y    stored in first line number.
0335- 60         1650             RTS
```

HIDING PROGRAM LINES FROM BASIC

by Eric Wachtenheim

I recently bought your assembly language book, *Now That You Know Apple Assembly Language: What Can You Do With It?* With it I got a free copy of your **Apple Software Protection Digest** and read the article on finding Applesoft program lines. I also saw the challenge of making a program that automatically hides the lines and saw the 6 free issue bonus for completing this program and set at it.

My first step towards making this program was analyzing the format in which the Apple stores its Applesoft programs. I learned by looking through memory that the first two bytes of a line point in Lo/Hi byte format to the next line. After that was two bytes for the line number, also in Lo/Hi byte format, and then the tokens that represent the various BASIC keywords (e.g. PRINT, REM, GOTO, etc.) I saw for each line with five colons at the beginning that there were five "3A"s right after the line number. Seeing this I decided to check if the first five characters of each line were "3A"s and if they were, I change the first 3A to a 00. I proceeded to do this using the next-line pointer to find out where the next line began. The result is the program below. It must be appended to the program on which you wish to hide the lines. It can be activated by typing **RUN 63000**.

This magazine reminds me of the very beginning of another protection oriented magazine which has grown to be very informative and popular. This rapid growth is in my opinion do to the contributions of the readers. So come on all you **ASPD** readers, contribute!!

Thanks for your contribution Eric. Since you were the only one to submit a BASIC program to hide lines, the 6-month subscription prize is yours. Keep the contributions coming.

```
63000  REM ************************
63010  REM *      LINE HIDER      *
63020  REM * BY ERIK WACHTENHEIM  *
63030  REM ************************
63040  REM
63050  REM LINES TO BE HIDDEN MUST
63060  REM BE PRECEDED BY 5 COLONS
63070  REM THIS SUBROUTINE MUST BE
63080  REM APPENDED TO  THE TARGET
63090  REM PROGRAM AND CALLED FROM
63100  REM THERE WITHIN. GOOD LUCK
63110  REM
63120  BASE = 2049
63130  IF PEEK (BASE) = 0 AND PEEK (BASE + 1) = 0 THEN 63170
63140  IF PEEK (BASE + 4) = 58 AND PEEK (BASE + 5) = 58 AND
       PEEK (BASE + 6) = 58 AND PEEK (BASE + 7) = 58 AND PEEK
       (BASE + 8) = 58 THEN POKE BASE + 4,0
63150  BASE = PEEK (BASE) + 256 * PEEK (BASE + 1)
63160  GOTO 63130
63170  END : REM IF USING AS A SUBROUTINE PLACE A RETURN HERE
       INSTEAD OF AN END.
```

Hiding Machine Language

continued from page 11

a line is added or deleted), your machine-language program will get clobbered.

The only way you can save this program out to a diskette is to use the BRUN MAKER program. To do this, RUN BRUN MAKER and have it load in your Applesoft program. When BRUN MAKER returns you to the Applesoft mode, BLOAD your machine language program where it belongs and then from the immediate mode (with no line number) type **VTAB 24** and trace over the CALL statement. Your Applesoft program with the machine language program in the string will now be safely recorded on a diskette.

To check out the program, just type **RUN**. The computer will type out the message in line 10, delay for a few seconds, and then return with the Applesoft prompt (]). It never got to the last line of the program, because the call to the machine language routine erased all of memory. Go ahead, try to list the program. It's not there. Unlike the NEW or FP commands which only erase pointers to the program (allowing it to be reconstructed by an ambitious cracker), WIPEOUT 1, erased every memory location from the beginning of BASIC to the beginning of DOS. There's no way that the program can be resurrected.

While the example that I have given was for storing programs in strings, the identical technique can be used to store machine language program in REM statements.

continued from page 13

```
10   REM BASIC PROGRAM TO INSTALL
20   REM APPLESOFT LINE-HIDE #1
30   REM
40   TEXT : HOME
50   PRINT "APPLESOFT LINE-HIDE #1": VTAB 5
60   FOR X = 1 TO 90
70     READ Y
80     POKE 767 + X,Y
90   NEXT X
100  PRINT : PRINT : PRINT "INSTALLATION COMPLETE."
110  CALL 768
120  DATA 169,11,160,3,141,246,3,140
130  DATA 247,3,96,32,183,0,208,31
140  DATA 165,103,164,104,133,0,132,1
150  DATA 160,0,177,0,72,200,177,0
160  DATA 72,240,53,32,68,3,104,133
170  DATA 1,104,133,0,184,80,233,32
180  DATA 12,218,32,26,214,144,35,165
190  DATA 155,164,156,133,0,132,1,32
200  DATA 68,3,240,22,160,4,177,0
210  DATA 201,58,208,14,200,192,9,144
220  DATA 245,160,4,169,0,145,0,96
230  DATA 104,104,96
```

```
10   REM BASIC PROGRAM TO INSTALL
20   REM APPLESOFT LINE-HIDE #2
30   REM
40   TEXT : HOME
50   PRINT "APPLESOFT LINE-HIDE #2": VTAB 5
60   FOR X = 1 TO 53
70     READ Y
80     POKE 767 + X,Y
90   NEXT X
100  PRINT : PRINT : PRINT "INSTALLATION COMPLETE."
110  CALL 768
120  DATA 169,11,160,3,141,246,3,140
130  DATA 247,3,96,32,12,218,32,26
140  DATA 214,165,155,164,156,133,0,132
150  DATA 1,32,190,222,32,12,218,32
160  DATA 26,214,165,155,164,156,133,2
170  DATA 132,3,160,0,165,2,145,0
180  DATA 200,165,3,145,0,96
```

A HANDY DECIMAL/HEXADECIMAL CONVERTER

As you get more and more involved in protecting and unprotecting programs you'll find yourself using hexadecimal numbers more frequently. You'll find that having a quick and easy way of converting numbers back and forth between decimal and hexadecimal will become essential. If you've got a *Texas Instruments Programmer* calculator or a pad of our *Programmer's Number Conversion System* forms, then you've got the problem licked. If not, you'll probably find this short utility program to be extremely useful. It can reside in memory while you're working on other programs and be instantly called up by using the ampersand (&) character.

Of course, you can write a BASIC program to do the conversion, but that would mean it couldn't be conveniently available for use while you're working on other BASIC programs. The alternative is to use a machine-language program to do the conversions for you. That's where the HEX/DECIMAL/HEX CONVERTER program comes in. This program will allow you to convert numbers in either direction. An added advantage of the program is that it does not have to be used in an Applesoft program only, but can also be used in the immediate mode. A fully-commented assembly listing of the program and an Applesoft program to load and activate the converter are provided.

continued on page 10

Editorial
continued from page 1

Free unclassified ads

Starting with the next issue, we're going to add an Unclassified Ad section to the Digest. Subscribers are each entitled to one free unclassified ad. Ads must be typed double spaced, contain no more than 50 words and include full name and address. Ads are printed on a first-come, first-served, space available basis.

Protection consultants wanted

Frequently we get requests from people who are interested in hiring a consultant to implement a copy protection scheme. If you're knowledgeable in this area and are available for consulting work, please write us a letter stating your experience in this area, and what your consulting fee is. Be sure to include your name, address and phone number. We will place you on a list that will go out to all those who inquire. While our Digest deals only with the Apple computer, several of the requests we've had deal with other computers as well, so please list all the computers that you offer protection consulting for.

Jules H. Gilder
Publisher & Editor

```
         1000 *******************************
         1010 ***                         ***
         1020 ***  HEX/DECIMAL/HEX CONVERTER ***
         1030 ***                         ***
         1040 ***    COPYRIGHT (C) 1982 BY   ***
         1050 ***       JULES H. GILDER     ***
         1060 ***     ALL RIGHTS RESERVED   ***
         1070 ***                         ***
         1080 *******************************
         1090 *
         1120           .OR $300
         1140 *
         1150 * EQUATES
         1160 *
003E-    1170 A2L      .EQ $3E
0050-    1180 LINNUM   .EQ $50
00B1-    1190 CHRGET   .EQ $B1
0200-    1200 IN       .EQ $200
03F5-    1210 AMPERSD  .EQ $3F5
DD67-    1220 FRMNUM   .EQ $DD67
E199-    1230 IQERR    .EQ $E199
E752-    1240 GETADR   .EQ $E752
ED24-    1250 LINPRT   .EQ $ED24
F941-    1260 PRNTAX   .EQ $F941
FDDA-    1270 PRBYTE   .EQ $FDDA
FDED-    1280 COUT     .EQ $FDED
FFA7-    1290 GETNUM   .EQ $FFA7
         1300 *
         1320 * This is where the ampersand (&) vector
         1330 * jump is set up.
         1340 *
0300- A2 4C     1350        LDX #$4C       Get JMP op code and
0302- A9 10     1360        LDA #START     the low and high bytes
0304- A0 03     1370        LDY /START     of START's address and
0306- 8E F5 03  1380        STX AMPERSD    store them in locations
0309- 8D F6 03  1390        STA AMPERSD+1  $3F5, $3F6 and $3F7.
030C- 8C F7 03  1400        STY AMPERSD+2
030F- 60        1410        RTS
         1430 *
         1440 * This part of the program checks to
         1450 * see if the character immediately following
         1460 * the ampersand (&) was a dollar sign.
         1470 * If it was, control is passed to the
         1480 * routine that converts from hexadecimal
         1490 * to decimal.  Otherwise the number is
         1500 * decimal and converted to hexadecimal.
         1510 *
0310- C9 24     1520 START  CMP #$24       Is it a dollar sign ($)?
0312- F0 17     1530        BEQ HEXIN      Yes, convert hex to decimal.
0314- 20 67 DD  1540        JSR FRMNUM     No, evaluate number or formula
0317- 20 52 E7  1550        JSR GETADR     Convert to integer form.
031A- A9 A4     1560        LDA #$A4       Output a dollar sign ($).
031C- 20 ED FD  1570        JSR COUT
031F- A5 51     1580        LDA LINNUM+1   Get most high byte.
0321- F0 03     1590        BEQ PRINTLO    If zero, get low byte.
0323- 20 DA FD  1600        JSR PRBYTE     Otherwise print high byte.
0326- A5 50     1610 PRINTLO LDA LINNUM    Get low byte.
0328- 4C DA FD  1620        JMP PRBYTE     Print it.
         1630 *
         1640 *
         1650 * This routine handles the hexadecimal
         1660 * to decimal conversion.
         1670 *
032B- A0 00     1680 HEXIN  LDY #$0        Zero offset index.
032D- 20 B1 00  1690 HEXIN2 JSR CHRGET     Get the next character.
0330- F0 08     1700        BEQ PUTBUF     Store in buffer and convert.
0332- 09 80     1710        EOR #$80       Set high bit.
0334- 99 00 02  1720        STA IN,Y       Store in input buffer.
0337- C8        1730        INY            Increment offset index.
0338- D0 F3     1740        BNE HEXIN2     Get next character.
033A- 99 00 02  1750 PUTBUF STA IN,Y       Store zero in buffer.
033D- A8        1760        TAY            Zero offset index.
033E- 20 A7 FF  1770        JSR GETNUM     Convert ASCII to hex.
0341- A6 3E     1780        LDX A2L        Store low byte in X-register.
0343- A5 3F     1790        LDA A2L+1      Store high byte in Y-register.
0345- C0 06     1800        CPY #$6        Check if number too large.
0347- 90 03     1810        BCC INRANGE    No, it's okay.
0349- 4C 99 E1  1820        JMP IQERR      Yes, print error message.
034C- C0 03     1830 INRANGE CPY #$3       Converting only 1 byte?
034E- B0 02     1840        BCS PRINTIT    No, do both.
0350- A9 00     1850        LDA #$0        Yes, do just one.
0352- 4C 24 ED  1860 PRINTIT JMP LINPRT    Convert and print number.
```

APPLESOFT LINE FINDER AND VANISHER

by Adam Levin

I'll take a shot at seven free issues of your fine magazine! I have written written a routine to automatically hide BASIC program lines that have five colons in front of them. The routine is short, sweet and simple, and it even overwrites those four pesky 3As (the hex code for a colon).

To save time and effort, the program has been written as an addition to the Applesoft Line Finder program that was published in the last issue. All you have to do is add the lines listed below to that file and the resulting program will not only display the BASIC line as it's stored in memory, but it will also prevent it from being listed out from BASIC.

As an extra added bonus, my routine will add from one to four characters in place of from one to four 3As. The characters to be substituted for the 3As, are typed directly in from the keyboard. If you don't want to change the 3As, just press RETURN. Also note, that my additions will never alter a line which doesn't begin with a colon (which no normal line needs to do).

You did a nice job Adam, but one thing you forgot to do was to check that all five colons were present. If they're not (let's say only four are present) the modifications that your program makes will cause the BASIC program to crash. This is not the best program submitted, but we will reward your effort by giving you a free three month subscription. Let's see what else you can do. For those of you who missed the last issue, I've included a BASIC program listing that implements the Applesoft Line Finder with Adam Levine's modification to it.

CRACKS WANTED

Every month we will devote one section of the magazine to listing programs that you, our readers would like to see cracked (unprotected). Anyone submitting a technique for unprotecting any of these programs will receive 2 months of the Digest for free. Below is a short list of program cracks requested so far, so let's see you get to work on these.

1. Sensible Speller – DOS 3.3
2. Sensible Speller – ProDOS
3. Newsroom
4. Disk-O-Check
5. Dazzle Draw
6. Crush, Crumble and Chomp
7. Wizardry
8. Word Handler

```
1120            .OR $2C0
1255  RDKEY     .EQ $FD0C           Monitor read routine.
1660  START     JSR LINGET          These 3 lines are from your
1670            JSR FNDLIN          original program, just to show
1680            BCC NOLINE          where my lines get inserted.
1681            LDY #$4             Offset to skip next line pointer & number.
1682            LDA (LOWTR),Y       Is 1st character a colon?
1683            EOR #$3A            If it is, make it zero.
1684            BNE .1              It's not continue Jules' routine.
1685  .0        STA (LOWTR),Y       Store zero in line, and
1686            INY                 get ready to index to next byte.
1687            CPY #$9             Past all possible colons?
1688            BCS .1              Yes, continue Jules' routine.
1689            STY TEMP            No, save index for later.
1690            JSR RDKEY           Get a character to put in place
1691            JSR COUT            of colon and echo it to screen.
1692            LDY TEMP            Restore the index.
1693            CMP #$8D            <RETURN> key?
1694            BNE .0              No, put it into line & repeat.
1695  .1        LDY #0              This is your line with local label.
1880            RTS                 Return to BASIC instead of monitor.
```

```
10  TEXT : HOME : PRINT "APPLESOFT LINE VANISHING PROGRAM": VTAB 5
20  FLASH : PRINT "INSTALLING MACHINE LANGUAGE PROGRAM."
25  NORMAL
30  FOR X = 1 TO 272
40    READ Y
50    POKE 703 + X,Y
60  NEXT
70  VTAB 5: PRINT "INSTALLATION HAS BEEN COMPLETED. TO USE"
75  PRINT "THE PROGRAM, TYPE '& LINENUMBER'. IF THE";
80  PRINT "LINE IS PRECEDED BY 5 COLONS, IT WILL BE";
85  PRINT "HIDDEN AND A HEX DUMP OF THE LINE WILL"
90  PRINT "BE DISPLAYED.   IF THE 5 COLONS ARE NOT"
92  PRINT "PRESENT, JUST THE HEX DUMP WILL BE"
93  PRINT "DISPLAYED."
94  PRINT : PRINT "PRESS ANY KEY TO CONTINUE";: GET A$: PRINT
96  CALL 704
100 DATA 32,88,252,169,218,160,2,32
110 DATA 169,3,162,76,169,47,160,3
120 DATA 142,245,3,141,246,3,140,247
130 DATA 3,96,193,208,208,204,197,211
140 DATA 207,198,212,160,204,201,206,197
150 DATA 160,198,201,206,196,197,210,141
160 DATA 141,194,217,160,202,213,204,197
170 DATA 211,160,200,174,160,199,201,204
180 DATA 196,197,210,141,195,207,208,217
190 DATA 210,201,199,200,212,160,168,195
200 DATA 169,160,177,185,184,178,141,193
210 DATA 204,204,160,210,201,199,200,212
220 DATA 211,160,210,197,211,197,210,214
230 DATA 197,196,141,141,141,141,0,32
240 DATA 12,218,32,26,214,144,73,160
250 DATA 4,177,155,73,58,208,21,145
260 DATA 155,200,192,9,176,14,132,8
270 DATA 32,12,253,32,237,253,164,8
280 DATA 201,141,208,235,160,0,132,8
290 DATA 32,135,3,169,160,32,237,253
300 DATA 177,155,208,8,165,8,201,5
310 DATA 176,13,169,0,32,218,253,32
320 DATA 160,3,202,240,227,208,228,169
330 DATA 0,32,218,253,32,142,253,96
340 DATA 169,191,160,3,76,169,3,32
350 DATA 142,253,169,160,32,237,253,162
360 DATA 8,165,156,32,218,253,165,155
370 DATA 32,218,253,169,186,76,237,253
380 DATA 230,155,208,2,230,156,230,8
390 DATA 96,133,24,132,25,160,0,177
400 DATA 24,240,11,32,237,253,230,24
410 DATA 208,245,230,25,208,241,96,141
420 DATA 206,207,160,211,213,195,200,160
430 DATA 204,201,206,197,135,141,0,0
```

WIPEOUT: THE ULTIMATE WEAPON OF DESTRUCTION

The ultimate method of preventing unauthorized access to your program is to completely wipe it out of memory. I don't mean you should implement a NEW or even an FP command, if the program is in BASIC. That only changes the program pointers, and leaves the bulk of the program intact in memory, ready for the would be cracker to resurrect it. And if you did take that approach, how would you handle machine code programs? No, the ultimate answer to getting rid of your program is to totally obliterate it by filling all of memory with zeros, or some other byte if you've a mind to.

Drastic as this may sound, implementing the actual task is really quite simple and requires only very short and simple machine language programs. Of course, a BASIC routine could be used to do most of the job, but that would be easily detectable, and would take quite a bit of time too. No, machine language is definitely the right choice for this job, and here's how to do it.

Two different approaches

Since the task is really quite simple to implement, I will show you two different ways to do it. Both have their advantages and disadvantages. The first program is called, appropriately enough, WIPEOUT 1, and while it is the longer one of the two, it is also more flexible and harder to detect.

WIPEOUT 1 makes use of the fact that if we stuff the input buffer, which starts at location 512 ($200), with a valid string of monitor commands and then jump to the appropriate place in the F8 ROM, that series of commands will be implemented. This approach to wiping out memory is quite unconventional from a programming point of view, which is one of the reasons it's harder to detect (people don't know what they're looking at). For those of you who have done some work while in the Apple's monitor mode however, you'll recognize this as being a quite common approach to the situation.

Looking at the assembly language source listing you'll notice that the first thing the routine does is to store a zero in the autorun flag. I've included that just in case your program set it, so that you don't have to remember to reset it. The rest of the code simply moves the command string from its current location into the input buffer. And finally, line 1200 jumps to the ROM routine that causes the command in the input buffer to be executed.

If you look at line 1220, you notice that the command string ends with a hex $82. This is the code for a Control-C, and it cause the computer, which would normally return to the asterisk prompt in the monitor mode, to instead return to the Applesoft mode. As long as this short program resides somewhere in the $800 to $95FF memory range, the pro-

```
                        1000  *****************************
                        1010  ***                        ***
                        1020  ***      WIPEOUT 1         ***
                        1030  ***                        ***
                        1040  *****************************
                        1050  *
                        1060  *
                        1070           .OR  $2D0
                        1080  *
00D6-                   1090  RUNFLAG  .EQ  $D6
FF70-                   1100  EXECUTE  .EQ  $FF70
                        1110  *
                        1120  *
02D0- A0 00             1130           LDY  #$0
02D2- 84 D6             1140           STY  RUNFLAG
02D4- B9 E2 02          1150  LOOP     LDA  STRING,Y
02D7- 99 00 02          1160           STA  $200,Y
02DA- C8                1170           INY
02DB- C9 82             1180           CMP  #$82
02DD- D0 F5             1190           BNE  LOOP
02DF- 4C 70 FF          1200           JMP  EXECUTE
02E2- B8 B0 B0
02E5- BA B0 A0
02E8- CE A0 B8
02EB- B0 B1 BC
02EE- B8 B0 B0
02F1- AE B9 B5
02F4- C6 C6 CD          1210  STRING   .AS  -"800:0 N 801<8C0.95FFM"
02F7- 82                1220           .HS  82
```

```
1    REM BASIC PROGRAM TO INSTALL
2    REM WIPEOUT 2 PROGRAM
3    REM
30   TEXT : HOME
40   FOR X = 1 TO 26
50     READ Y
60     POKE 543 + X,Y
70   NEXT X
80   PRINT : PRINT : PRINT "INSTALLATION COMPLETE."
90   PRINT : PRINT "CALL 544 TO USE WIPEOUT 2"
100  DATA 169,8,133,7,169,0,168,133
110  DATA 6,133,214,145,6,200,208,251
120  DATA 230,7,165,7,201,150,208,236
130  DATA 96,82
```

```
                        1000  *****************************
                        1010  ***                        ***
                        1020  ***      WIPEOUT 2         ***
                        1030  ***                        ***
                        1040  *****************************
                        1050  *
                        1060  *
                        1070           .OR  $220
                        1080  *
0006-                   1090  POINTER  .EQ  $06
00D6-                   1100  RUNFLAG  .EQ  $D6
9600-                   1110  STARTDOS .EQ  $9600
                        1120  *
                        1130  *
0220- A9 08             1140           LDA  #$8
0222- 85 07             1150           STA  POINTER+1
0224- A9 00             1160  LOOP1    LDA  #$0
0226- A8                1170           TAY
0227- 85 06             1180           STA  POINTER
0229- 85 D6             1190           STA  RUNFLAG
022B- 91 06             1200  LOOP2    STA  (POINTER),Y
022D- C8                1210           INY
022E- D0 FB             1220           BNE  LOOP2
0230- E6 07             1230           INC  POINTER+1
0232- A5 07             1240           LDA  POINTER+1
0234- C9 96             1250           CMP  /STARTDOS
0236- D0 EC             1260           BNE  LOOP1
0238- 60                1270           RTS
```

gram will not only wipe out the program you want to protect, but itself as well. To make it easy for you to key in and use the program, it has been converted to a short Applesoft BASIC program.

More conventional destruction

A more conventional way of wiping out memory is shown in the program. This is probably the way most programmers would approach the task if asked to implement it. The advantage of this approach is that it is much shorter than the other one. It takes only 26 bytes instead of the 40 required by the other routine. This might be an important factor if memory space is of the essence, as it so often is. Again, before the actual memory wipeout begins, the autorun flag is reset to zero.

Once again for your convenience, the machine language program has been converted to a BASIC one. By using either one of these techniques, you can make it much harder for prying eyes to find out what you're doing.

```
1    REM BASIC PROGRAM TO INSTALL
2    REM WIPEOUT 1 PROGRAM
3    REM
30   TEXT : HOME
40   FOR X = 1 TO 40
50      READ Y
60      POKE 719 + X,Y
70   NEXT X
80   PRINT : PRINT : PRINT "INSTALLATION COMPLETE."
90   PRINT : PRINT "CALL 720 TO USE WIPEOUT 1"
100  DATA 160,0,132,214,185,226,2,153
110  DATA 0,2,200,201,130,208,245,76
120  DATA 112,255,184,176,176,186,176,160
130  DATA 206,160,184,176,177,188,184,176
140  DATA 176,174,185,181,198,198,205,130
```

BECOME AN ASSEMBLY LANGUAGE PROGRAMMING WHIZ

"Now That You Know Apple Assembly Language: What Can You Do With It?" will take you step-by-step through the assembly language programming experience. You'll delve into the mysteries of the 6502 stack and learn how to use it to increase the power and versatility of your programs. You'll also learn how to use the Apple's built-in routines to minimize the amount of coding you must do.

Control the output and the input

Frequently it's desirable to gain total control of the computer's output. This book shows you how to *steal control away from the Apple's normal output routines and redirect it to your own pro-*

*NOTE: Shipping and handling fees are not refundable.

Redlig Systems, Inc., Dept. A 9783
2068—79th St., Brooklyn, NY 11214

Please rush me _____ copies of "**Now That You Know Apple Assembly Language: What Can You Do With It?**" at $19.95 each plus $2 shipping and handling. I understand that if I am not delighted with the book I may return it within 10 days for a prompt and courteous refund. In any case, the Programmer's Number Conversion System and $5 coupon are mine to keep.

☐ Enclosed is my check for $ _____
Please charge my credit card:
☐ American Express ☐ MasterCard ☐ Visa
Card No. _____ Exp. _____
Signature _____
Name _____
Address _____
City _____ State _____ Zip _____

---

gram. Thus if you wanted, you could see the normally invisible control characters, display text on your screen as black on white instead of the normal white on black, format text sent to a printer into pages and much more.

Expand the power of your Apple by *stealing control away from the normal input routines.* Do things like adding a screen print capability, or *convert part of the normal keyboard into a numeric keypad.* It's even possible to *produce self-modifying programs* by EXECing in commands from RAM instead of from the disk drive. Think about the possibilities that offers for protecting your programs. When you want to go back to Applesoft programming, *you'll be able to do it faster with the aid of Applesoft Shorthand,* an assembly language program that types in one or more Applesoft commands at the press of a key, or use another program in the book to *automatically count the number of lines in your Applesoft program.*

With this book you'll also learn about *generating tones and how to figure out the frequency, producing sound effects, teaching your Apple to send Morse code, restoring accidentally erased Applesoft programs, adding new commands to Applesoft and running two Applesoft programs in memory together,* to name a few.

As an extra bonus for prompt ordering, you'll receive a *FREE coupon worth $5 off* the price of a disk with all the assembled programs on it or a disk that contains the source code. These disks normally sell for $15 each. We're offering these FREE gifts for a limited time only, so hurry! *Order today!*

Money-back guarantee*

We're so confident that you'll find this book invaluable and want it in your library, that we're offering a 10-day, no-questions-asked, money-back guarantee. Order the book. Read it and try the programs for ten days. At the end of ten days if you don't think it's worth every penny you paid for it, just send it back in resalable condition and we'll refund your money immediately, no questions asked.

REVIEW: Locksmith 5.0 Level G

by J. Scott Barrus

First let me preface my review with the comment that I really wanted to review the much publicized *Locksmith 6.0*, but as late as February 17th, Alpha Logic Business Systems was still not shipping the program. They have my order, and money, for over a month and say that it should be shipping any day now, but I've heard that before. With this in mind, I'll therefore go ahead with a review of the latest, currently available version of *Locksmith*.

Locksmith was one of the first anti-copy protection programs out on the market and was originally produced and marketed by Omega MicroWare. The original *Locksmith* could copy programs with almost any protection scheme that was in use when it first came out. Naturally, upon hearing this, software manufacturers rushed to change their schemes so that they would be *Locksmith* resistant. As they changed, so did *Locksmith*. The race was on. Over the years, a total of seven different revisions have come and gone, with the last currently available one being 5.0 level G.

It has an impressive manual

The program comes with an impressive 139 page manual that discusses everything from the history of *Locksmith* and protection schemes, to how to use the program. To supplement the manual, Omega MicroWare decided to come out with a *Locksmith Newsletter*. They came out with one issue. *(Editor's note: Alpha Logic Business Systems decided to pick up on that idea too, but in spite of the fact that they collected money for it, no further issues were ever produced.)* The issue of the newsletter that did come out gives suggestions on how to use some of the harder to understand functions of *Locksmith*.

The *Locksmith* manual is very technical, and most people will find it hard to read and use. Alpha Logic Business Systems has said however, that they are in the process of re-writing the manual. They claim that this will be available to all former *Locksmith* owners, but I suspect that it will really only be pertinent to the next release, *Version 6.0 of Locksmith*, and that it would be of limited value to *Version 5.0* owners. Nevertheless, the company says that it is being written with the average user in mind. This contrasts with the former manual which assumed you were an expert, or at least an advanced user.

When the program is booted up, the user is asked if he wants to load the language card. Upon further investigation of the manual, I found out that this is how *The Inspector* is loaded into memory. The next thing that the user sees is the main menu. There are many options available to the user from this menu. The program always goes to an option and then returns to this main menu. The utilities that come with the program, as well as the copier, are:

- Backup/copy disk
- Parameter changes
- Text editor
- Quick scan disk
- 16 sector utilities (fast disk verify, backup, format, compare, sync signature)
- Inspector/Watson
- Erase diskette
- Nibble editor
- Disk speed
- Certify disk

One of the important aspects of *Locksmith* is that there is built into it a *Locksmith Programming Language*. Files (called LPL files), produced by the editor for use with this language, allow the user to change different algorithms, parameters and send special instructions to the screen. The manufacturer makes available a file of parameters for a variety of programs, or if you wish, you can key the file in yourself from the newsletter. There is also a default file that comes on the *Locksmith* diskette.

It's not easy to use

The *Locksmith Programming Language* is not easy and it takes some time and effort to study and master it. The language is not needed however, because the user can change parameters and algorithms manually. The problem with the manual approach, however, is that if at a later date you want to use the same changes, you must again enter them manually. Nevertheless, I have found that for occasional copying of a diskette, the manual approach is fine.

Locksmith comes with a text editor that can be used to change the LPL file. There's nothing special about the editor and it can in fact be used to edit any DOS 3.3 text files. Due to the slow loading nature of *Locksmith*, however, I'd really recommend other text editors for non-Locksmith applications. After loading in an LPL file with the text editor, you can then copy a disk using this parameter file by selecting the Backup option from the main selection menu.

Many options are available

There are many other options available with *Locksmith* as well. There is a Disk Scan option which lets the user visually (through hi-res graphics) check a diskette to see what the sync byte format is. A Disk Speed option can be used to check, and if necessary adjust, your disk drive speed for best copying results. Another handy tool is the nibble editor. With it, the user can access any nibbles on the diskette to try and figure out what protection scheme is being used. With it, a test of the different algorithms and parameters can be made to see what is necessary to make the diskette readable. It can also be used to find specific byte patterns. This searching capability comes in very handy when you're trying to locate nibble counting code.

It's a powerful copy program

Locksmith is a very powerful copy program. It can copy almost anything. The biggest drawback that I have found with it is that the algorithms, although briefly described in the manual, are still difficult to understand. There are not enough examples provided to make their functions crystal clear. I have been using *Locksmith* for quite a while now, and am still not overly comfortable using it and the manual to make backups. Also, it would be very helpful if the manual had an index in it so that pertinent information could be easily located. Another shortcoming of the program and its documentation is that it is not clear why one would want to use a particular algorithm. What's the selection process? Why should algorithm A be used and not B? The manual never tells us.

Another problem with the program is the everything starts and ends with the main menu, and there is not enough memory in the Apple to hold all the *Locksmith* files in memory. Thus, the diskette is constantly being accessed any time a different utility or change must be made. This is particularly annoying when you try to copy a diskette and fail. You now have to go back to the LPL file and make some changes there. To do this, the diskette you were copying must be removed from the drive, the *Locksmith* diskette must be re-inserted, the editor loaded, the LPL file must be loaded, the changes made, the LPL file must be saved, the copy option selected, the *Locksmith* diskette removed and finally the protected diskette must be re-inserted. If another change has to be made, and that's a real strong possibility, the whole process must be repeated again. It's certainly not a shining example of ease of use.

Literature on the new Version 6.0 indicates that it supports the expanded RAM cards from Applied Engineering and Checkmate. Hopefully *Locksmith* will set up a RAM disk in these cards to speed up operation of the program.

Overall, I think *Locksmith* is a good program, although at present it is not easy to use. It is certainly not recommended for the faint of heart or those who do not want to invest the time and effort to learn how to use it properly. If you're thinking of getting *Locksmith*, don't. Wait until the new version of it is out. If it's half as good as the ads claim it is, it will be a must buy product.

Source: Alpha Logic Business Systems, 4119 North Union Rd., Woodstock, IL 60098. **Call:** (815) 568-5166.

PROTECTION TUTORIAL — Part II

In the previous article in this series, we talked about some of the early techniques that were used to make it difficult to copy diskettes. Early techniques were simple, but effective. But as Apple users became more sophisticated, more complicated ways of implementing copy protection became necessary.

Before we get into some of these more advanced techniques, it will be helpful for us to understand just how a diskette is formatted and how information is stored on it. While this is normally a subject that is generally meant for technical types, don't be concerned. We are going to assume you have no technical expertise and explain everything from scratch. So sit back and get comfortable, you're about to learn a little bit more about the *black magic* of copy protection.

Formatting a disk

If you have ever placed a new diskette into a disk drive and tried to save a program onto it, you undoubtedly heard your drive make a lot of noise and finally give up, beep and print the message **I/O ERROR**. Go ahead, try it, you won't damage anything. The reason this happens is that diskettes fresh out of the box have absolutely no information stored on them. Such a disk is not divided up into tracks or sectors and thus the Apple doesn't know where to store data, which is why it gives the I/O ERROR message.

For the Apple computer to be able to use a diskette, certain information must first be stored on it that can later be used to tell the computer exactly where the magnetic head is located at any particular point in time. This information is put on the diskette when you initialize it by using DOS's INIT command. The INIT command calls up a machine language program that turns the drive on, moves the magnetic recording head in the disk drive as far away from the center of the diskette as possible (similar to moving the arm and needle of a record player to the very first selection of a record) and finally starts recording magnetic information on the diskette. This information divides the diskette up into 35 tracks that each have 16 sectors in them. More about this later.

The magnetic head in the disk drive is mounted on an arm that moves in and out, from the outer circumference of the diskette towards its center. The mechanics of the disk drive are designed such, that this magnetic head can be moved in discrete steps that are each one half the width of a normal disk track. This is done by a special type of motor called a *stepper motor*.

When a DOS command is issued for the first time, the Apple has no idea where the disk's magnetic head is currently located, so it issues instructions to the stepper motor to move the head back to track zero. If the head were on track three it would only have to move back three tracks, while if it were on track 20, it would have to move back 20 tracks. Since we said the Apple doesn't know where the head is, it assumes the head is on track 80 (which doesn't exist on standard Apple disk drives) and tells the stepper motor to move the head back 80 tracks towards the outer circumference of the diskette. Since most Apple drives only work with 35 tracks, the head reaches track zero long before it moves back 80 tracks. When this happens, the arm that the head is mounted on bounces against a bumper inside the disk drive and makes that clattering noise that you hear. You can reduce the noise the disk drive makes and speed DOS up a bit by changing this number from 80 to 40. You can do this from Applesoft BASIC by typing in **POKE 48844,40**. This can be done either in the immediate mode (without a line number) or from within a program. Alternatively, if you wish to modify this number from the monitor mode, simply type **BECC:28** and then press **RETURN**. If you do this and then initialize a new diskette, the version of DOS that is put on the newly initialized diskette will have this modification on it.

Getting on the track

As I mentioned earlier, the Apple divides a diskette into 35 individual tracks that are concentric with the large hole in the center of the diskette. These tracks are not connected together in a spiral the way the grooves of a record are, but instead are more like the rings around a bullseye. Each of the 35 tracks is given a number from 0 through 34. Thus, the first track is called track 0 and the 35th (or last) track is called track 34. Track 0 is located the farthest away from the center of the diskette and track 34 is located the closest to the center.

In addition to electronically dividing a diskette into 35 tracks (remember the marks are magnetic ones and invisible to the eye) the computer also divides the diskette into sectors, which can be thought of as the equivalent of slices of a pie. DOS 3.3 divides a diskette into 16 of these wedge-shaped sections called *sectors*. Thus each track has 16 sectors. So with 35 tracks of 16 sectors each, we have a total of 560 sectors on an Apple diskette. Each sector is capable of storing 256 bytes of information, for a total storage capacity of 143,360 bytes of data. On a normal diskette, not all of this space is available to store programs because some of it is used to store DOS and one track (17) is used to hold the diskette's catalog information. Total usable space on a normal DOS 3.3 diskette then, is 126,976 bytes, or 496 sectors.

What a formatted track looks like

You will recall that earlier we said that the Apple couldn't use new diskettes fresh out of the box because they hadn't been initialized and thus didn't have certain information on them. Understanding just what that information is and how it can be changed, is the subject of this next section and is the key to understanding how and why copy-protected diskettes can be produced.

To better understand the discussion that follows, take a look at Fig. 1, which is a representation of a portion of a formatted track. From this drawing, you can see that there are many different components that make up the data storage area of a track. After a quick glance at Fig. 1, you can see that each sector of information that is stored on a diskette contains two areas known as *fields* and two areas known as *gaps*. You'll also notice that the beginning of a track also starts with a gap. We'll get back to this in a little while, but suffice it to say for now, that while Gap 1 originally starts out to be unique from the other two types of gaps, eventually, it gets converted into a Type 3 gap.

	SECTOR 0				
GAP 1	Address Field #0	Gap 2	Data Field #0	Gap 3	Address Field #1

Fig. 1 — Formatted track

If you think you're getting a little lost, just hang in there for another minute or so, and everything will start to become crystal clear. Now back to our explanation. The purpose of the gaps on the track is simply to provide for a separation between the two types of fields and also to allow the computer to have enough time to read the information off the diskette and interpret it. The only difference between the three types of gaps is their length. Some are longer than others.

Now, lets concentrate on those areas in Fig.1 that are labelled as *fields*. If you look closely, you'll see that there are only two types of fields present on a track: *address fields* and *data fields*.

What's the address?

The first field that we're going to look at is known as the *address field*, and Fig. 2 shows it in more detail. When a diskette is formatted (initialized) address fields are written onto the surface of the diskette for each and every sector. Thus, if the Apple wants to locate a particular track and sector, all it has to do is check the address fields until it finds the one it is looking for. Each address field consists of 14 bytes. The first three bytes are known as the *prologue* or starting bytes and they form a unique sequence of bytes. These specific three bytes will never be found anywhere else on a normal DOS 3.3 diskette except in the address field. This makes it possible to use them as *sign posts* to indicate where an address field starts. The three bytes that have been reserved by DOS 3.3 as address field markers are **D5 AA 96** (these are hexadecimal numbers). Every time DOS sees a **D5 AA 96** byte sequence, it knows that it has found the start of an address field.

The two bytes that immediately follow the prologue, contain information on the volume number of the diskette. Since this number is never higher than 255, it can be represented by only a single byte of data. You may therefore wonder why two bytes are used in the address field. The reason is simple. The Apple hardware cannot be used to read all 256 possible byte combinations from a diskette. It is therefore necessary to encode the data so that all 256 bytes can somehow be represented. This is done in the address field (except for the prologue and epilogue bytes) by writing out all the odd bits of a byte as one byte (XX) and all the even bits of the

ADDRESS FIELD

Prologue	Volume	Track	Sector	Checksum	Epilogue
D5 AA 96	XX YY	XX YY	XX YY	XX YY	DE AA EB

Fig. 2 – Address field format

same byte, as a second byte (YY). Splitting one 8-bit byte into two separate bytes means there will be four extra bits that have not been defined in each of these new bytes. The Apple makes sure that each of these new bytes starts with a 1 and that each bit from the original byte is separated from the next by a 1 also. Thus the XX byte would look like this:

1 B7 1 B5 1 B3 1 B1

while the YY byte would look like this:

1 B6 1 B4 1 B2 1 B0

Now, if the volume number on our disk was 1, the XX and YY bytes would be:

XX = 1 0 1 0 1 0 1 0 = AA

YY = 1 0 1 0 1 0 1 1 = AB

This method of coding bytes is called by a special name, *4 + 4 encoding*. If you're interested in figuring out what the 4 + 4 encoded values are for any particular number between 0 and 255, just run the the *4 + 4 Encoder* program listed below and enter the number of interest. It will tell you what the coded value will be.

Following the two bytes reserved for the volume number in the address field are two bytes which are reserved for the track number and another two bytes which are reserved for the sector number. As was the case with the volume number, the track and sector numbers are also stored in 4 + 4 encoded format.

There are only two more pieces of information left to talk about in the address field: the checksum and the epilogue. The checksum, which again is stored in a 4 + 4 encoded format, is used by DOS 3.3 to insure that the previous three pieces of information, the volume, track and sector numbers, are correct. DOS calculates the checksum when the diskette is formatted, by performing a mathematical operation known as an exclusive OR on these three pieces of data. It then stores the result on the diskette. This makes it possible to check for data integrity when reading the diskette by reading the first three pieces of information and calculating the checksum. This can then be compared with the checksum stored on the diskette. If they match, all is well. If not, data stored on the diskette is probably corrupted, and thus unreliable.

Just as everything must start somewhere, so too, it must end somewhere, and the three épilogue bytes mark the end of the address field for DOS. The epilogue bytes have the values **DE AA EB**. The address fields are only written once, when the diskette is initialized. Because of that, in spite of a variety of utility programs that claim to do otherwise, it is generally not possible to change the volume number of a diskette after it has been formatted. What the programs that change the volume number do is simply change the number that is displayed when the diskette is cataloged. That does not affect the true volume number of the diskette that is embedded in the address field of every sector.

Unlike the address field, which is only written once (when a diskette is formatted),

DATA FIELD

Prologue	Used Data	Checksum	Epilogue
D5 AA AD	342 BYTES DATA	XX	DE AA EB

6+2 encoded

Fig. 3 – Data field format

the data field is re-written every time information is saved out to the diskette. The data field is similar in many ways to the address field. Like the address field, it features a prologue that uniquely identifies it to DOS as a data field, a checksum to verify that the data is stored accurately and an epilogue to mark the end of the data field (see Fig. 3). In between the prologue bytes and the checksum is an area where data is stored, just as it is in the address field. The difference here, however, is that in the address field the data consisted of the volume, track and sector numbers. In this case, it consists of the user's data. This could be a program, data file, etc.

Encoding the user data

You may recall that earlier we said that since we couldn't use all of the 256 possible byte combinations to store our data on a diskette, that we had to encode it. For the volume, track and sector numbers, Apple chose to use a 4 + 4 encoding scheme. While this is useful, it is also very inefficient, because with that scheme, you'd have to write

```
               1000 ************************************
               1010 *                                  *
               1020 * HEXADECIMAL TO BINARY CONVERTER  *
               1030 *                                  *
               1040 ************************************
               1050 *
               1060 *
               1070           .OR $0300
               1080 *
FDDA-          1090 PRHEX     .EQ $FDDA
               1100 *
               1110 *
               1120 * This routine converts a hexadecimal number
               1130 * into individual binary bits that are
               1140 * temporarily stored in the 8 bytes that begin
               1150 * with the location marked TEMP.
               1160 *
0300- A2 08    1170           LDX #$8         Get length of byte
0302- 18       1180           CLC             Set carry to 0
0303- 0E 11 03 1190 LOOP      ASL BYTE        Shift high bit into Carry
0306- A9 00    1200           LDA #$0         Load the Carry
0308- 69 00    1210           ADC #$0         byte into the accumulator
030A- 9D 11 03 1220           STA BYTE,X      and store it
030D- CA       1230           DEX             Update bit counter
030E- D0 F3    1240           BNE LOOP        If not end get next bit
0310- 60       1250           RTS             End, return to caller
0311- 00       1260 BYTE      BRK             Number to be converted
0312- FF FF FF
0315- FF       1270 TEMP      .HS FFFFFFFF    Temporary storage for
0316- FF FF FF
0319- FF       1280           .HS FFFFFFFF    individual bits
               1290 *
               1300 *
               1310 * This routine takes the byte that is stored in
               1320 * location NUMBER and prints it out as a
               1330 * hexadecimal number.
               1340 *
031A- 00       1350 NUMBER    BRK
031B- AD 1A 03 1360 PBYTE     LDA NUMBER
031E- 4C DA FD 1370           JMP PRHEX
```

Table 1
Legal DOS Bytes (Hex)

96	AC	BA	D5	E6	F4
97	AD	BB	D6	E7	F5
9A	AE	BC	D7	E9	F6
9B	AF	BD	D9	EA	F7
9D	B2	BE	DA	EB	F9
9E	B3	BF	DB	EC	FA
9F	B4	CB	DC	ED	FB
A6	B5	CD	DD	EE	FC
A7	B6	CE	DE	EF	FD
AA	B7	CF	DF	F2	FE
AB	B9	D3	E5	F3	FF

out 512 bytes to a diskette in order to save just 256 bytes of data. That would allow for a total diskette storage capacity of only 88K, certainly not very attractive.

The software wizards at Apple however, devised a different encoding scheme that increased the storage capacity by over 50%. Instead of having four data bits per byte as in the 4 + 4 scheme, they decided to use 6 data bits per byte. The remaining 2 bits are split up among other bytes and the whole encoding process is somewhat complex, so we won't go into it here. Suffice it to say, that the new scheme is called 6 + 2 encoding and it converts 256 data bytes into 342 bytes that are written to the diskette, and results in the previously mentioned diskette storage capacity of 143K.

What is important for us to know from this whole discussion is that only certain bytes are used to store data on a diskette and that by changing the way they are used, we can produce copy-protected diskettes. The 6 data bits of the DOS 3.3 encoding scheme can be used to represent 64 different bytes. In addition, two bytes, D5 and AA, are reserved for use in the address and data field prologues only. Thus, only 66 unique bytes are required to store anything on a diskette. A list of the valid bytes that can be used is shown in Table 1.

Making your own protected DOS

Now that we have an idea of how information is stored on a diskette by the Apple, we can go ahead and produce our own protected DOS by making minor changes to DOS 3.3.

To prevent any standard copy program from duplicating diskettes it is only necessary to change any one or more of the prologue, epilogue or checksum bytes. The only thing to be wary of here is changing the last byte of the epilogue on either the address or data fields. A change to this byte will have no affect because, while it is always written to the diskette, its value is never checked.

In another approach to copy protection, the track or sector numbers can be modified. This is what Muse Software did with their products. They modified a version of DOS 3.2 so that it would increment the track number by two instead of one. Thus, while there were physically 35 tracks on a diskette, they were numbered 0 through 70 in increments of 2.

If you're going to change the prologue bytes, you must be careful. You may recall that earlier we said that two of the bytes in the address field (D5 and AA) were reserved bytes that don't appear anywhere else on the diskette. That is essential to insure that DOS knows how to locate the address and data fields. If you're going to change these bytes, you must make sure that whatever pattern you do decide on is unique.

One common technique that was used in earlier protection schemes was to simply reverse the first two bytes of the prologue. Alternatively, you could substitute a new value for bytes 2 or 3 of the prologue. Just make sure you use one of the bytes that are listed in Table 1.

In order to substitute new values for the standard ones, you have to know where to put them. That's the job of Tables 2 and 3. They list the locations in DOS 3.3 that have critical bytes that can be easily changed to produce a custom, protected DOS. One thing to pay attention to, is that for every parameter that you change, two separate locations must be modified: one for the routine that deals with reading data, and the other for the routine that deals with writing

Table 2
Address Field DOS Locations

Location	Byte	Address Hex	Address Decimal
Prologue Read	D5	B955	47445
	AA	B95F	47455
	96	B96A	47466
Prologue Write	D5	BC7A	48250
	AA	BC7F	48255
	96	BC84	48260
Epilogue Read	DE	B991	47505
	AA	B99B	47515
Epilogue Write	DE	BCAE	48302
	AA	BCB3	48307

data. If you do one and not the other, you're going to wind up with problems.

To put our new-found knowledge to work, let's produce a protected DOS by swapping the first two bytes of the address field prologue. To do this you can get into the monitor mode by typing **CALL -151** and type in

continued on page 8

```
10   TEXT : HOME
20   A$ = "4 + 4 BYTE ENCODER": GOSUB 420
30   PRINT :A$ = "COPYRIGHT (C) 1986 BY": GOSUB 420
40   A$ = "JULES H. GILDER": GOSUB 420
50   A$ = "ALL RIGHTS RESERVED": GOSUB 420
60   PBYTE = 795
70   FOR X = 1 TO 33
80     READ NUM
90     POKE 767 + X,NUM
100  NEXT X
110  PRINT : PRINT : PRINT : INPUT "ENTER NUMBER TO BE CONVERTED: ";
     NUM
120  IF NUM > 255 THEN  PRINT : PRINT CHR$ (7);"NO NUMBER LARGER
     THAN 255 MAY BE ENTERED": GOTO 340
130  POKE 785,NUM
140  CALL 768
150  FOR I = 8 TO 2 STEP  - 2
160    X(I) = 1
170    X(I - 1) =  PEEK (785 + I)
180    Y(I) = 1
190    Y(I - 1) =  PEEK (784 + I)
200  NEXT I
210  X = 0
220  Y = 0
230  FOR I = 1 TO 8
240    X = X + 2 ^ (I - 1) * X(I)
250    Y = Y + 2 ^ (I - 1) * Y(I)
260  NEXT I
270  PRINT : PRINT : PRINT "THE 4 + 4 ENCODED VERSION OF ";NUM
280  PRINT : PRINT "IS: ";
290  POKE 794,X
300  CALL PBYTE
310  PRINT "+";
320  POKE 794,Y
330  CALL PBYTE
340  PRINT : PRINT : PRINT : INPUT "CONVERT ANOTHER NUMBER? ";A$
350  IF  LEFT$ (A$,1) = "Y" OR  LEFT$ (A$,1) = "y" THEN 110
360  PRINT : PRINT : PRINT
370  DATA 162,8,24,14,17,3,169,0
380  DATA 105,0,157,17,3,202,208,243
390  DATA 96,10,255,255,255,255,255,255
400  DATA 255,255,0,173,26,3,76,218,253
410  END
420  L =  LEN (A$)
430  PRINT  TAB( (40 - L) / 2);A$
440  RETURN
```

SOFTWARE PROTECTION TECHNIQUES EXPOSED!

Now, for the first time, owners of Apple // series computers can learn all about the tricks and techniques used to protect Apple software. Apple Software Protection Digest, a new monthly publication, will show you how to protect, unprotect and backup your software.

- Prevent others from accessing your programs
- Make your programs difficult to copy
- Overcome protection schemes on commercial software
- Build a library of protection-oriented utility programs
- Get help with your specific problems
- Learn about the latest advances in protection hardware and software

All this and more can be yours by subscribing to the Apple Software Protection Digest. A one-year subscription is $24, two years is $42.

SUBSCRIBE TODAY!

REDLIG SYSTEMS, INC., Dept. A1357
2068 - 79th St., Brooklyn, NY 11214

Please enter my _____ year subscription to Apple Software Protection Digest.

☐ Enclosed is my check for _____

☐ Please charge my credit card: ☐ VISA ☐ MasterCard ☐ American Express

Card Number _____ Exp. Date _____ Signature _____

Name _____
Address _____
City _____ State _____ Zip _____

ASPD PROGRAM DISKETTE AVAILABLE FOR ONLY $15

Starting with this issue, we will make a DOS 3.3 diskette available every month that contains all of the programs from the current issue of the *Apple Software Protection Digest*.

To order send a check, money order or your charge card number and expiration date to:

REDLIG SYSTEMS, INC.
2068 79th Street
Brooklyn, New York 11214

REDLIG SYSTEMS, INC.
2068 79th Street
Brooklyn, New York 11214

BULK RATE
U.S. POSTAGE
PAID
BROOKLYN, N.Y.
Permit No. 631

APPLE SOFTWARE PROTECTION DIGEST

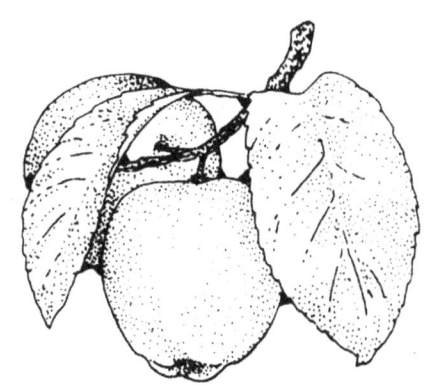

$3.00

Vol. 1 No. 3   1986

Contents

Editorial	1
Cracks Wanted	2
Crack Index	2
Letters	2
How to Crack a Program	3
Parameter Files for COPYP	6
Add Undeletable Lines to Your Program	7
Moving the Catalog to Another Track	9
REVIEW: The quickLoader ROM Card	10

Apple Software Protection Digest Publisher & Editor, Jules H. Gilder; Contributing Editor, J. Scott Barrus. Copyright © 1986 by Redlig Systems, Inc., 2068-79th Street, Brooklyn, NY 11214. All rights reserved. No part of this publication may be reproduced, or electronically transmitted or stored without the publisher's written permission. Published monthly at $24 per year by Redlig Systems, Inc. (718) 232-8429. Reprints of prior issues available at $3 each. Printed in the U.S.A.

Apple is a resitered trademark of Apple Computer, Inc.

SOME PUBLISHERS DROPPING PROTECTION

During the past few months we have seen an interesting trend starting to develop among software publishers. Many of them, under increasing pressure from corporate users, are starting to drop software copy protection from their products. The latest publisher to join the pack is Software Publishing Corp., which produces the PFS line of programs.

According to Software Publishing, they've finally realized that copy protection is a big inconvenience for the customer and they don't have to worry about protecting themselves so much any more because their business customers are protecting them and preventing employees from making copies.

I'm glad to see a movement away from copy protection. In fact, I think the whole issue of how much money is lost due to the production of illegal copies has been blown way out of proportion. There really hasn't been any hard research to determine just how much money is lost due to piracy. There also hasn't been any research done to determine how much money is lost due to the problems and inconvenience caused by copy protection, and I think that would be a real eye-opener.

Be that as it may, don't run out to buy PFS software yet. According to a Software Publishing spokesman, the protection is not going to be removed from existing products, but rather as new versions of the various programs become available.

In spite of the reasons given by Software Publishing for this move I tend to think the facts are a little different. I suspect that enough people have gotten fed up with copy protected software that they've just decided not to buy any. This is where we, the people who keep these companies afloat, can really show our strength. There is plenty of good software available that is not copy protected.

Support unprotected shareware

Much of the unprotected software that is available is being put out on a "shareware" basis. What this means is the developer makes the diskette available to anyone who wants it for a nominal fee, ususally between $10 and $20. He tells the purchaser that he is free to make copies of the diskette and distribute it to anyone he choses provided he doesn't charge more than the developer does, doesn't modify the diskette in any way and if he's purchased documentation separately he must agree not to duplicate it and give it away or sell it.

These shareware programs generally come with a sufficient amount of documentation on the diskette so that the user can learn to run the program. The shareware developer's hope is that the user will like the program so much, he'll support the developer by paying an additional fee to register his copy, get more complete printed documentation and usually one or two future updates for free. Sometimes even the source code is made available.

If you think these developers are foolish for taking this approach, think again. Several shareware developers have made over $1 million so far and their programs are as good as, or better than many commercial products costing hundreds of dollars more.

Cracks Wanted

Listed below are programs that our readers would like to unprotect. Anyone who comes up with a method of removing the protection from any of these programs will get a free three-month subscription, or extension to **ASPD**, so get those solutions in.

If you have a program that you'd like to see unprotected, please let us know, and we'll add it to our list so that some of our readers can try their hands at it.

1. Sensible Speller — DOS Version
2. Sensible Speller — ProDOS Version
3. Crush, Crumple & Chomp
4. Wizardry
5. Educational Software from Compress
6. Dazzle Draw
7. Newsroom
8. Word Handler
9. Disk-O-Check

Crack Index

In order to make life just a little more convenient for you, each issue of **Apple Software Protection Digest** will contain a list of all of the programs cracked so far and what issues these cracks appeared in. This will save you from going through all past issues of the digest in order to find a particular crack you are looking for a crack to a particular program.

Bookends — Vol. 1, No. 1, p. 7
Homeword — Vol. 1, No. 2, p. 9
Homeword Speller — Vol. 1, No. 2, p. 9
PFS Series — Vol. 1, No. 2, p. 7
Print Shop — Vol. 1, No. 1, p. 10
Print Shop Companion — Vol. 1, No. 2, p. 6
Sensible Grammar — Vol. 1, No. 2, p. 7
Time Is Money — Vol. 1, No. 2, p. 9

Don't miss a single issue SUBSCRIBE TODAY!

Letters

Dear Editor:

I liked your courtesy copy of **ASPD** and I'm going to try it for a year. I'm also ordering your diskette. I do have a problem however.

I am a writer and like *Applewriter][*, but it has two limitations which center around its copy protection. Oh, it's easy enough to make a backup copy of it (I use Locksmith 4.1). The nature of its copy protection however, makes it impossible to either put it onto a hard disk, or use it with one. I can't get the computer to recognize the slot after I've booted AW][.

My problem can be solved in one of two ways, as I see it. I need a way to modify a copy program, like Locksmith 4.1 or a way to copy Apple Writer][that leaves it unprotected. Then I could put it onto my hard disk easily. Can you tell me how to do this?

I know this much, after my experiences over the last few months, I won't buy a copy-protected program again. They are just too inconvenient to use.

Lee Baldwin
Concord, CA

The quick answer to your first question is yes, we can help you. This issue contains a full-length article devoted to unprotecting Apple Writer. If you don't want to read the whole thing, but just want the parameters for the COPYP program, they can be found in the COPYP Parameter List. The reason Applewriter doesn't recognize your hard disk is that the modified DOS that is needed to recognize your hard disk is replaced by the protected DOS of Apple Writer. If your hard disk is a Sider and you have a way of breaking out of the program into the monitor mode, you may be able to patch DOS so that it can use your hard drive. The patching information can be found in the Sider User's Guide on page 133.

Dear Editor:

I just read about your Apple Software Protection Digest. If it is as excellent as it has been reported to be, I will gladly pay the annual subscription fee. Please send me a sample issue.

By the way, I bought a game called *Crush, Crumble and Chomp* and haven't been able to make a backup copy. If you know of any way of doing so, please give me full details.

Michael Jacobs
Wolcothville, IN

Here's your sample copy Mike. I hope we've lived up to our advance billing. I'm adding your request to our Cracks Wanted list. If any of our readers can tell Mike how to back up Crush, Crumble and Chomp, let's here from you.

Dear Editor:

I was happy to see that my programs (Two Solutions to the Hide-A-Line Problem) had won your contest and were published in **ASPD #2**. I must confess though, that I have encountered a problem with the concept of hiding a line by resetting the link bytes.

The problem stems from the fact that any line hidden in this manner will cause an UNDEF'D STATEMENT error if the program does a GOTO or GOSUB to it. Has anyone else run into this dilemma?

Because of this apparent glitch, I much prefer the method of adding five colons at the start of the program line. The GOTO/GOSUB problem does not occur when using this technique. I've had lots of fun using this technique and baffling "unaware" people with it.

Thanks for the extra six months, I look forward to future issues of **ASPD**. You present ideas and concepts that many of us can experiment with and learn from, something that is missing from many Apple periodicals nowadays.

Mark Landwehr

Thanks for your letter Mark. The problem you encountered with the GOTOs and GOSUBs in the first line hiding technique is to be expected. When Applesoft encounters a GOTO or GOSUB, the 6502 starts scanning the BASIC program from the beginning (via the next line pointers) and looks at the two bytes that follow each next line pointer to see if the line that is desired has been found. Since we've changed these pointers so that they bypass the line when the program is listed, the line will also be bypassed when GOTOs and GOSUBs are encountered.

HOW TO CRACK A PROGRAM

Many people have written to me and told me that they appreciate being given step-by-step instructions on how to backup or crack a particular program. They also indicated however, that they would like to know how one goes about starting to crack a program and develop their own technique for backing it up. That's really a tough question to answer because there are almost an unlimited number of ways to go about cracking a program. To get you started however, I'll take you step-by-step through the thought processes involved in cracking Applewriter //e (DOS version). The reason this program was chosen was because one of our readers sent in a letter asking how he could remove the protection from Applewriter so that he could use it with his hard disk.

If you're not interested in knowing how Applewriter //e is unprotected, but just interested in unprotecting it, you can skip the rest of this article and simple use the COPYP parameter file that is listed elsewhere in this issue to automatically make an unprotected back up.

Know it well before you start

Before you attempt to crack any program, it is essential that you use it and become thoroughly familiar with it. If you know how the program will act in various situations, you will have an enormous advantage working for you when you try to figure out how the program is protected.

If you had become familiar with Applewriter //e before you attempted to crack it, you would have discovered that the Applewriter disk uses a fairly normal form of DOS. In fact, the diskette can be CATALOGed like a normal DOS diskette and you can use COPYA to make a copy of the diskette. While no error is generated when the copy is made, don't rejoice too quickly, because the copy will not work. Nevertheless, since the modification to standard DOS seems to be small, chances are pretty good that it won't be too difficult to crack the protection. This is generally true for most protected programs. The closer they are to standard DOS, the easier they are to crack.

Since we know that DOS 3.3 is more or less intact, we can find out what the boot program is. It's important to understand how a program boots up in order to crack its protection. By using a sector editor, such as the one available on the Copy][Plus diskette, we can look at track $1, sector $9, byte $75 (remember the $ indicates the number is a hexadecimal number), which is where we'll find the name of the program that is automatically run when the diskette is booted. In the case of Applewriter //e, the file is called OBJ.BOOT. It is a binary file and it is automatically BRUN when the diskette is booted.

The job of OBJ.BOOT is simple. It tests to see if the computer that is being used is a Apple //e. If it's a // Plus, it will run the program OBJ.APWRT][D which simply prints a message to the user telling him that an Apple //e is required to run the program. If the computer being used is a //e, OBJ.BOOT then checks to see how much memory is available. If only 64K is available, then the file OBJ.APWRT][E is run. On the otherhand, if 128K or more of RAM is available, OBJ.APWRT][F will be run.

Prepare all your tools

Before you attempt to crack a program, it is essential that you have some basic tools. To begin with, you need a sector editor that will let you read, modify and write diskette sectors. The second thing you'll need is a diskette searching program. This is a program that will let you enter a string of characters or hex values to be searched for on a diskette. Both of these capabilities are available in the Copy][Plus program (which normally retails for $39.95 but costs only $30 when you buy it through us). Next, you should have a short, in-memory search program that can be used to locate a sequence of bytes in RAM. For our Applewriter //e crack, we'll use a short machine language search routine that Bob Sander-Cederlof gives away with his S-C Macro Assembler. It's only 53 bytes long and can easily be keyed in when needed. The last thing you're going to need is a way of breaking out of the program once it's running. I have found that the Wildcard 2 board is excellent for this purpose. It allows you to press a button at any time and then gives you a menu that let's you do several things, including jumping to the monitor. It plugs into any slot in the computer and will work on any Apple or compatible except the Apple //c (which has no slots).

STEP 1: Copy it if you can

When trying to crack a protected program, always try to copy it first with COPYA. If you can't get anywhere at all, another approach will have to be taken. But if you can copy it, as is the case with Applewriter //e, you've gone a long way towards your ultimate goal. Once you've made a copy of the diskette, try to boot it up. Pay close attention to what happens during the boot process and compare it to what happens during a normal boot of the original diskette.

In the case of Applewriter //e, when the copy is booted, OBJ.BOOT is run and if an Apple //e is being used, depending on how much RAM is available, either OBJ.APWRT][E or OBJ.APWRT][F is run after it. Whichever file is activated, if the diskette is a copy, the program will detect this, zero out all of memory and then jump to Applesoft BASIC, most likely via the 'cold start' entry point at $E000. It is this jump to BASIC that turns out to be the Achilles Heel of Applewriter //e.

STEP 2: Boot the program

After you've made a backup copy of Applewriter //e, put it aside and boot the original diskette. Once the program is loaded and you get to the opening title screen, get into the monitor. I do this by pressing the button on my Wildcard 2 and selecting the jump to monitor option from the menu that is presented.

Once you're in the monitor, the whole world of Applewriter is open to you. You can examine the program code to your heart's content, but you won't be able to modify it and save it out to the diskette because you don't have access to a normal DOS. Nevertheless, there's a lot you can do to unprotect the program from this mode.

STEP 3: Search the program

Once you're in the monitor, you can search for Applewriter's Achilles Heel, the jump to BASIC which occurs when the program determines that an original diskette is not being used. You can of course search the computer's memory manually and examine every location yourself. A much easier way to do it however, is to let the computer do the hard work. If you examine page 3 of memory (addresses starting at $300) you'll find that most of it has been zeroed out. Thus, it is a handy spot for us to put in a short machine language program that will do the searching for us.

Since we don't have access to the disk drives from the monitor mode, we can't load the program in from the disk. The only other choice is to load it in from tape, for those people who still have this capability in their computers (I think it was eliminated with the enhanced Apple //e ROMs) or key it in directly. Since the program I use is short (only 53 bytes long) I key it in whenever I need it. Eventually, I'll probably put it in an EPROM that can be switched in whenever the program is needed, but that's another project.

As I mentioned earlier, this search program is one of several sample programs that come on the S-C Macro Assembler diskette from S-C Software. The program itself is easy to use and it allows you to specify the starting and ending locations of the range to be searched, the byte sequence to be searched for and it allows you to designate any particular character as a wildcard character. You can examine the full assembly language source code listing to see how it operates, or simply key in the seven lines listed below.

```
300:A9 03 8D FA 03 A9 10 8D
308:F9 03 A9 4C 8D F8 03 60
310:A2 00 A0 00 B5 02 C5 01
318:F0 04 D1 3C D0 11 C8 E8
320:E4 00 D0 F0 A5 3C 85 3A
328:A5 3D 85 3B 20 D0 F8 20
330:BA FC 90 DC 60
```

Once the search program has been keyed in, it must be initialized by typing **300G** from the monitor mode. Now you're ready to do your searching. Since we know that the jump to BASIC is associated with the protection scheme, if we find that, we can probably work our way back towards the beginning of the protection scheme code. Thus, it's important for us to locate this jump to BASIC. The machine code required to jump to BASIC should contain a three-byte sequence that looks like this:

4C 00 E0

so we'll search through memory for this sequence of bytes. We do this by placing a 3 in memory location 0 on the zero page of memory to indicate how many bytes are in the sequence of characters we're looking for. Next, we place the value of the wildcard character in location 1. Since we have no need of a wildcard character in this particular search, I just place an FF in this location. Finally, we have to enter the sequence of bytes that are being searched for starting with location 2 on zero page. In summary, the following line must be entered (from the monitor mode) to set up the search parameters:

0:03 FF 4C 00 E0

All that's left to do now is specify the range of memory locations to be searched and activate the program. Both of these tasks are done together by typing in the starting and ending addresses, separated by a period, entering a Control-Y and then pressing the RETURN key. Since RAM ends at $BFFF I decided to search all of memory from $800 to $BFFF. To do this the following line was entered while in the monitor mode:

800.BFFF <Control-Y>

Notice that I've placed spaces after the BFFF and the Control-Y. This is for ease of reading only and these spaces should not be used when you enter this line.

STEP 4: Find where it begins

When you search memory for this string of characters, you see that it appears only once, at location $2D0C. This is indicated by the search program which prints out the following line in response to your search:

2D0C- 4C 00 E0 JMP $E000

Since that's the only place in the program where the jump to BASIC occurs, chances are pretty good that starting at this location and working our way backwards, we should be able to find the protection code. As you work your way back, look for another JMP instruction or an RTS instruction. The first one you encounter on your journey back in memory will usually mark the end of some previous routine and the beginning of the routine your examining. In the case of Applewriter //e, I encountered a JMP $0200 at $2CCD. At the time I didn't pay much attention to it, although I should have because it is very unusual to jump to a subroutine that is located in the input buffer, unless of course you're trying to hide something. My failure to pay attention to this caused one false start, but that was quickly corrected. I'll get back to that in a little while.

Since the JMP instruction takes up three bytes, that means that the subroutine I was examining probably started at $2CD0. The listing of the code that resides between $2CD0 and $2D0C, where control is passed to BASIC is shown below. This listing was made by using the Apple's built-in disassembler and I have added line numbers to this listing so that it will be easy to reference a particular line.

```
100  2CD0- AD 83 C0    LDA  $C083
110  2CD3- AD 83 C0    LDA  $C083
120  2CD6- A9 03       LDA  #$03
130  2CD8- 85 01       STA  $01
140  2CDA- A0 00       LDY  #$00
150  2CDC- 84 00       STY  $00
160  2CDE- 98          TYA
170  2CDF- 91 00       STA  ($00),Y
180  2CE1- C8          INY
190  2CE2- D0 FB       BNE  $2CDF
200  2CE4- E6 01       INC  $01
210  2CE6- F0 0C       BEQ  $2CF4
220  2CE8- A6 01       LDX  $01
230  2CEA- E0 C0       CPX  #$C0
240  2CEC- D0 F1       BNE  $2CDF
250  2CEE- A2 D0       LDX  #$D0
260  2CF0- 86 01       STX  $01
270  2CF2- D0 EB       BNE  $2CDF
280  2CF4- AD 82 C0    LDA  $C082
290  2CF7- AD 82 C0    LDA  $C082
300  2CFA- 8D 0C C0    STA  $C00C
310  2CFD- 20 84 FE    JSR  $FE84
320  2D00- 20 2F FB    JSR  $FB2F
330  2D03- 20 93 FE    JSR  $FE93
340  2D06- 20 89 FE    JSR  $FE89
350  2D09- 20 58 FC    JSR  $FC58
360  2D0C- 4C 00 E0    JMP  $E000
```

STEP 5: Examine the code

Now that we know where at least some of the protection code lives, let's take a close look at it to see what it does. Because Applewriter //e wipes out all of memory before jumping to BASIC when a copied diskette is encountered, we would expect this routine to perform that task, and it does. Here is a detailed explanation of exactly what goes on when this routine is called.

In lines 100 and 110, the RAM card in the computer is write enabled, so that data can be stored in it. Lines 120 to 150 set up a pointer on page zero that will be used to indicate which memory locations are to be zeroed out. Here the program starts with location $300. Line 160 loads a zero into the accumulator and line 170 is the line that actually zeroes out the current memory location that is being pointed to. The Y-register was initially zero and is incremented in line 180. This allows the instruction in line 170 to point to every location on a particular page of memory. As long as the Y-register has not returned to zero (been incremented 256 times) the program loops back to line 170 and keeps storing zeroes in successive memory locations.

Once the Y-register does become zero again, line 200 increments the page pointer so that the next page of memory is set up to be zeroed out. As long as location $01 does not contain a zero (and it won't until the very last byte of available memory has been addressed) control passes from line 200 to line 220 where the contents of location $01 are loaded into the X-register. Line 230 checks this value to see if it is equal to $C0. If it isn't, control is passed once again to line 170. In this manner, all of memory from $300 to $BFFF (which is one less than $C000 which was just checked for) is zeroed out.

Because Applewriter //e also uses the RAM card, the program then goes on to wipe out all memory locations there as well, which is why the RAM card was write-enabled earlier. The RAM card's memory starts at $D000 and so line 250 loads a $D0 into the page counter at location $01 on page zero. Control is once again passed to line 170 and the program loops once more to zero out all successive memory locations. This time however, after a zero is stored in location $FFFF on the RAM card, the page counter is incremented again and thus returns to zero. This triggers the instruction in line 210, which causes the computer to jump to line 280 where the RAM card is turned off.

Since Applewriter //e uses the 80 column mode when it is active, the next instruction (line 300) turns off the 80 column card and activates the 40 column mode. Line 310 makes sure the Apple is set up for normal (not inverse or flashing) video while line 320 makes sure the text screen and not either of the graphic screens, is activated. Line 330 does a PR#0 to make sure the output hooks at $36 and $37 are returned to their normal condition. Similarly, line 340 does and IN#0 to restore the input hooks ($38 and $39). Finally, line 350 clears the screen and line 360 jumps to BASIC.

STEP 6: Find it on the disk

Now that we've located the protection routine and understand how it operates, we have to find out where its located on the diskette, so that it can be modified. To do this, we're going to have to use a disk scanning program which, like the short machine language program we entered earlier, will let us search for a particular byte sequence. Several such programs are available commercially. I use the one that is on the Copy][Plus diskette. You get to it by selecting the Sector Editor option and then pressing the S key. The program will then ask you if you want to enter your search string as hex codes or text. Typing an H selects the hex code mode.

Since we know from the disassembly listing that starts at $2CD0 what we're looking for the job is not to difficult. I decided to search for the first eight bytes of the routine that starts at $2CD0 — AD 83 C0 AD 83 C0 A9 03. It seemed to me that this sequence of bytes would be fairly unique, and would probably only be encountered in the protection code. After entering this data, I found that the code was stored on track 3, sector 9 and started at byte 1 (which is the second byte in the sector because we start with 0). I continued searching the diskette to see if the code would crop up somewhere else, and sure enough it did, at track 6, sector B, byte D4. The fact that the code was found in two places on the diskette suggested that the code was located in the OBJ.APWRT][E and OBJ.APWRT][F files.

STEP 7: Disable the protection

Once you find where the offending code is located on the diskette, all you have to do is disable the protection. In this case, that can easily be done by storing a $60 (the RTS code) at the very beginning of the protection scheme code. To do this you'll need a sector editor that will let you read, modify and then write a diskette sector. Always remember, NEVER WRITE ON THE ORIGINAL. Do all of your work on a copy only. Once again, I have found that Copy][Plus is the tool to handle the job. Using the copy that I made, but wouldn't boot, I stored a $60 at track 3, sector 9, byte 1 and track 6, sector B, byte D4.

STEP 8: Test it out

With patches applied to the non-working copy, it is now time to test it out. Booting up this diskette, I was delighted to see that the boot proceeded as normal and was rewarded with the normal Applewriter opening screen. But my joy was to be short-lived. After going through a short sample session, I attempted to quit Applewriter and lo and behold, I couldn't get out of it. It seems, that as part of the procedure for quitting the program, the memory wipeout routine that I just disabled, gets called into action. Back to the drawing board.

STEP 9: Find why it failed

With a lot of luck, you'll be able to skip this step. but such was not to be the case with Applewriter. At this point, I remembered the strange JMP $0200 instruction that I saw immediately before the memory wipeout routine and proceeded to examine it and the code before it more carefully. I discovered that immediately preceding the protection routine was another routine that transferred the original wipeout code into the input buffer where it was then executed by the JMP $0200 instruction. The short routine that does the moving starts at $2CBF. This apparently was the real protection routine.

Once again, I typed in the memory search program and looked for the place where this code was called from using the byte sequence: 4C BF 2C. It turns out that this sequence of bytes is located at $3B04 (when OBJ.APWRT][F is loaded). Examining the code that precedes this JMP instruction reveals the routine that is used to check and see if the disk that is in the drive is an original. This code starts at $3AF1 when OBJ.APWRT][F is loaded and is listed below.

Without going into a lot of detail, this routine calls another one that immediately follows it (at $3B08) and reads the disk. This routine checks for the correct prologue bytes in the address field of the sectors (for more information see Protection Tutorial - Part II, **ASPD** Vol. 1, No. 2, p. 20). It then checks for special information that is only present on the original Applewriter //e diskette. If it doesn't find that information, it jumps to the memory wipeout routine at $2CBF.

By the way, it's important to note that any protection scheme that accesses special information on a diskette, be it special sync bytes, extra data or a nibble counting routine, must access the diskette with an instruction such as LDA $C08C,X where X contains the slot number that the disk drive is connected

```
3AF1-  20 08 3B     JSR  $3B08
3AF4-  85 82        STA  $82
3AF6-  20 08 3B     JSR  $3B08
3AF9-  C5 82        CMP  $82
3AFB-  D0 0A        BNE  $3B07
3AFD-  20 08 3B     JSR  $3B08
3B00-  C5 82        CMP  $82
3B02-  D0 03        BNE  $3B07
3B04-  4C BF 2C     JMP  $2CBF
3B07-  60           RTS
3B08-  AE E1 02     LDX  $02E1
3B0B-  BD 8C C0     LDA  $C08C,X
3B0E-  10 FB        BPL  $3B0B
3B10-  C9 D5        CMP  #$D5
3B12-  D0 F4        BNE  $3B08
3B14-  EA           NOP
3B15-  BD 8C C0     LDA  $C08C,X
3B18-  10 FB        BPL  $3B15
3B1A-  C9 AA        CMP  #$AA
3B1C-  D0 F2        BNE  $3B10
3B1E-  EA           NOP
3B1F-  BD 8C C0     LDA  $C08C,X
3B22-  10 FB        BPL  $3B1F
3B24-  C9 96        CMP  #$96
3B26-  D0 E8        BNE  $3B10
3B28-  EA           NOP
3B29-  EA           NOP
3B2A-  BD 8C C0     LDA  $C08C,X
3B2D-  10 FB        BPL  $3B2A
3B2F-  2A           ROL
3B30-  85 80        STA  $80
3B32-  BD 8C C0     LDA  $C08C,X
3B35-  10 FB        BPL  $3B32
3B37-  25 80        AND  $80
3B39-  60           RTS
```

to. Searching a diskette for the bytes that represent this instruction — BD 8C C0 — will usually get you to the protection code, eventually. The problem is that any other routine that has a legitimate need to access the disk drive will also use similar code, so you'll have to examine a lot of code before you get to what you want. Therefore, always try to get close to your protection routine by other means first, just as we did here.

Now that we know what the true protection scheme looks like, let's use our disk scanner again and try and locate on the diskette. Remember, we're working with the copy of the original that we made only! Using the search pattern C5 82 D0 03 4C, I located three possible candidates. Finding three patterns disturbed me a bit because I had expected only two, as in the previous case. The three patterns were located on track 4, sector C, byte B1; track 7, sector C, byte 8 and track 7, sector E, byte 1. Since I had one more bit pattern than I anticipated I examined each carefully and found that while the last pattern started out the same as the other two, it was significantly different after the first several bytes and most important, it did not have the disk access instructions. This routine was therefore discarded and only the first two were used.

To eliminate the protection, once again the first byte of these two routines was replaced with a $60, the machine language code for the RTS instruction (**Re**Turn from **S**ubroutine). Thus, a $60 was placed on track 4, sector C, byte B1 and track 7, sector C, byte 8. After testing the diskette this time, the program worked perfectly. The interesting thing about this whole thing is that all it took was a two byte change on the copy of the Applewriter //e diskette to make it a working copy. The only reason it was necessary to change two bytes was because there were two different versions of the program on the diskette. Otherwise, only a single byte change would have been necessary. Isn't the power of information astounding?

If you don't have all of the tools that I used to crack this program, I suggest you get them right away, if you anticipate cracking more software. In the meantime, if you just want to make an unprotected copy of Applewriter //e, you can use the COPYP program that appeared in the last issue and the Applewriter //e parameters that are listed in the COPYP Parameters section of the digest.

I've spent a lot of time explaining the step-by-step process that I went through to crack this program so that you could understand the thought process that went on. This will help you to crack other programs, but don't expect any miracles. There are many different ways in which programs can be protected and this has only been one of them. Hopefully, however, you've gained some insight that can be applied to other programs. If you do crack any other programs, let us know how you did it so that we can share the procedure with the rest of our readers. We'll reward you with an extension of your subscription. Let's hear from you soon.

PARAMETER FILES FOR COPYP

Listed below are several parameter files for use with the COPYP program that was presented in **ASPD** Vol. 1, No. 2. You can key these lines in directly or you can do what I do and create text files that contain these lines. Then you can load in COPYP and EXEC in the appropriate file for the program you want to copy. You can keep these text files on a diskette and re-use them again whenever you want to make another copy.

Some of these files have been tested by me and some haven't. It gets to be an expensive proposition to buy each of these programs in order to test out each file. Therefore, if you submit files to us, please make sure you test them thoroughly. Also, please give us the version number of the program you're cracking. Nothing is more discouraging than trying to use a routine that is supposed to work, only to find out that it doesn't. Your reward for doing this will be a one-month addition to your subscription.

Applewriter //e

A complete explanation of how *Applewriter //e* is unprotected is included in a separate article in this issue. For those of you who are merely interested in making an unprotected copy of it and not interested in the how and the why, just add the following lines to your COPYP program and make as many unprotected copies as you want.

1000 DATA 4,12,177,76,96
1010 DATA 7,12,8,76,96

Financial Cookbook

Financial Cookbook from Electronic Arts is a program that can be easily unprotected by changing just a single byte in the program. The reader who supplied the information for unprotecting this program and the next couple of programs neglected to tell us what the value of the original byte that is being changed was.

Since we have been unable to contact him so far, we decided to add a slight modification to COPYP that would enable you to unprotect a program without having to know what the original value of the byte that's being changed is. This of course bypasses the built-in safeguard that doesn't let you modify a different version of the program (which is determined by checking to see that the original value of the byte is what it should be) but it can come in handy sometimes.

continued on page 11

ADD UNDELETABLE LINES TO YOUR PROGRAM

For those of you who write programs in Applesoft BASIC this next program will be of some interest to you. Did you ever see some commercial programs that had a copyright notice and author credit listed at the bottom of the program using line numbers that somehow could not be deleted? Have you ever wondered how you could do the same thing? It's easy and this program will help you to do it.

Most Applesoft BASIC programmers eventually discover that the highest line number that can be entered in an Applesoft program, from the keyboard, is 63999. That next to the last phrase "...from the keyboard..." is the key here however. The designers of Applesoft, for some reason, decided to make it illegal to have line numbers that were greater than 63999. Therefore, everytime that a line is entered from the keyboard, the computer checks to see if the line number is greater than 63999. If it is, the computer gives you a SYNTAX ERROR message. Since the checking is done as the line is entered, if we can find someway to bypass the input routine, we can have larger line numbers in our program and everything will work fine. As an added bonus, once we have this larger numbered line in our program, there will be no convenient way to delete it.

To make life easy, what I generally do is write out the lines that are to become permanent additions to my program as a separate file and then I run this short program, while that file is in memory. I then save the resulting program, which is usually just REMs with my name and a copyright notice in them, out to disk. When I finish developing an Applesoft program, I then merge the newly developed program with my short credit file program and I now have a program that contains the proper credit to me in lines that are difficult (but not impossible) to delete.

This program, *All Line Numbers to 65535* does just what its name implies, it changes all line numbers in any particular program to 65535. For those of you who may be wondering just how its possible to have a program with more than one identical line number, I'll explain in a minute. Suffice it to say that you can't have it if the lines are being entered from the keyboard, because the moment you enter a second line with a number that is identical to an already existing line, the old line with the same

```
              1000 ****************************************
              1010 ***                                   ***
              1020 ***     ALL LINE NUMBERS TO 65535     ***
              1030 ***                                   ***
              1040 ***       Copyright (C) 1986 by       ***
              1050 ***           Jules H. Gilder         ***
              1060 ***         All Rights Reserved       ***
              1070 ***                                   ***
              1080 ****************************************
              1090 *
              1100 *
              1110 * Equates
              1120 *
0006-         1130 TXTPTR            .EQ $06
0008-         1140 POINTER           .EQ $08
0067-         1150 TXTTAB            .EQ $67
00AF-         1160 PRGEND            .EQ $AF
FC58-         1170 HOME              .EQ $FC58
FDED-         1180 COUT              .EQ $FDED
              1190 *
              1200                   .OR $300
              1210 *
0300- 20 58 FC 1220        JSR HOME           Clear the screen.
0303- A9 49    1230        LDA #TEXT          Point to the text
0305- A0 03    1240        LDY /TEXT          that is to be printed.
0307- 20 38 03 1250        JSR MSGPRT         Print it.
030A- A5 67    1260        LDA TXTTAB         Get the start of
030C- A4 68    1270        LDY TXTTAB+1       program pointer
030E- C5 AF    1280 ENDCHK CMP PRGEND         Compare with the
0310- 90 05    1290        BCC NEXT           end of program
0312- C4 B0    1300        CPY PRGEND+1       pointer to see if
0314- 90 01    1310        BCC NEXT           we're done yet.
0316- 60       1320        RTS                Yes, we're done.
              1330 *
              1340 * This section of the program saves the
              1350 * pointer to the current line and then
              1360 * replaces the line number in that line
              1370 * with the number stored in LINNBR, in
              1380 * this case #$FFFF which is 65535. Next,
              1390 * the pointer is updated to point to the
              1400 * next line.  The program then jumps to
              1410 * a routine that checks to see if we've
              1420 * reached the end of the program.
              1430 *
0317- 85 08    1440 NEXT   STA POINTER        Save the line
0319- 84 09    1450        STY POINTER+1      pointer.
031B- A2 00    1460        LDX #$0            Initialize the
031D- A0 02    1470        LDY #$2            offset counters.
031F- BD A2 03 1480        LDA LINNBR,X       Get the low byte
0322- 91 08    1490        STA (POINTER),Y    of the new number
0324- E8       1500        INX                and replace the
0325- C8       1510        INY                old one.
0326- BD A2 03 1520        LDA LINNBR,X       Get the new high
0329- 91 08    1530        STA (POINTER),Y    and replace old.
032B- A0 00    1540        LDY #$0
032D- B1 08    1550        LDA (POINTER),Y    Update POINTER to
032F- 48       1560        PHA                point to the next
0330- C8       1570        INY                line.
0331- B1 08    1580        LDA (POINTER),Y
0333- A8       1590        TAY
0334- 68       1600        PLA
0335- 4C 0E 03 1610        JMP ENDCHK
              1620 *
              1630 * This is the message printing routine.
              1640 *
0338- 85 06    1650 MSGPRT STA TXTPTR         Store the pointer
033A- 84 07    1660        STY TXTPTR+1       to the message.
033C- A0 00    1670        LDY #$0            Initialize offset.
033E- B1 06    1680 LOOP   LDA (TXTPTR),Y     Get next character.
0340- F0 06    1690        BEQ ENDPRT         Done yet?
0342- 20 ED FD 1700        JSR COUT           No, print it.
0345- C8       1710        INY                Point to next character.
0346- D0 F6    1720        BNE LOOP           Go get it.
0348- 60       1730 ENDPRT RTS                Return to caller.
              1740 *
0349- C1 CC CC
034C- A0 CC C9
034F- CE C5 A0
0352- CE D5 CD
0355- C2 C5 D2
0358- D3 A0 D4
035B- CF A0 B6
035E- B5 B5 B3
0361- B5          1750 TEXT    .AS -"ALL LINE NUMBERS TO 65535"
0362- 8D 8D       1760         .HS 8D8D
0364- C2 D9 A0
```

number gets erased and is replaced by the new one.

Multiple lines with the same number are possible however. To accomplish this bit of micro magic, we must first type in lines with ordinary line numbers. Since we know what the structure of a BASIC line is as it is stored in memory (see **ASPD**, Vol. 1, No. 1, p. 2) we can go into the monitor mode and change the line number bytes manually so that they contain any line numbers that we wish.

To simplify and automate the process, all you have to do is enter this short program and it will do the job in a fraction of a second.

Make it hard to modify

While my primary use for this program is to produce undeletable credit lines for Applesoft programs that I write, it is also possible to use this program to make it difficult for someone else to modify your programs. If you give all your lines in a program the same high number, it will be hard to change any line in the program. A word of caution is needed here however. If entire programs are going to have identical line numbers in them, then you won't be able to use GOTOs, GOSUBs and THENs followed by a line number, because there will be no way of telling the computer to go to a specific line.

How it works

Operation of the program is fairly straight-forward. After clearing the screen and printing out the title page (lines 1220-1250) the program gets the start of program pointer (lines 1260-1270) so it knows where to begin and then falls into a routine to check if the end of the program has been reached yet (lines 1280-1320). The check is made by comparing the current location in memory, which is stored in the accumulator and the Y-register with the end of program pointer located on Zero page at AF and B0.

If the end of the Applesoft program has not been reached, the machine-language program branches to line 1440 where the current memory pointers are saved. In lines 1460 and 1470 the X and Y registers, which are used as offset counters, are setup so that they can be used to retrieve the two bytes of the new line number and store it in place of the old line number. This actual replacement in done in lines 1480 to 1530 and the pointer that tells the program where the next line to be worked on is located is updated in lines 1540 to 1600. Lines 1650 to 1730 comprise the routine that is used to print text out to the screen and lines 1770 to 1840 contain the text itself. Finally, line 1880 contains the line number that is going to be used to replace all of the existing ones. It is stored low byte first and in this case is $FFFF, which represents the number 65535.

```
0367- CA D5 CC
036A- C5 D3 A0
036D- C8 AE A0
0370- C7 C9 CC
0373- C4 C5 D2    1770          .AS -"by Jules H. Gilder"
0376- 8D          1780          .HS 8D
0377- C3 CF D0
037A- D9 D2 C9
037D- C7 C8 D4
0380- A0 A8 C3
0383- A9 A0 B1
0386- B9 B8 B6    1810          .AS -"COPYRIGHT (C) 1986"
0389- 8D          1820          .HS 8D
038A- C1 CC CC
038D- A0 D2 C9
0390- C7 C8 D4
0393- D3 A0 D2
0396- C5 D3 C5
0399- D2 D6 C5
039C- C4          1830          .AS -"ALL RIGHTS RESERVED"
039D- 8D 8D 8D
03A0- 8D 00       1840          .HS 8D8D8D8D00
                  1850 *
                  1860 * Number to which all lines are changed.
                  1870 *
03A2- FF FF       1880 LINNBR   .HS FFFF
```

```
  1  REM BASIC PROGRAM TO INSTALL ALL LINES TO 65535
  2  REM
 10  TEXT : HOME
 20  PRINT : PRINT : PRINT : PRINT
 30  PRINT "INSTALLING 'ALL LINES TO 65535'..."
 40  FOR X = 768 TO 931
 50      READ Y
 60      POKE X,Y
 70  NEXT X
 80  PRINT : PRINT : PRINT : PRINT "INSTALLATION COMPLETE."
 90  PRINT : PRINT "TYPE 'CALL 768' TO RUN PROGRAM."
100  DATA 32,88,252,169,73,160,3,32
110  DATA 56,3,165,103,164,104,197,175
120  DATA 144,5,196,176,144,1,96,133
130  DATA 8,132,9,162,0,160,2,189
140  DATA 162,3,145,8,232,200,189,162
150  DATA 3,145,8,160,0,177,8,72
160  DATA 200,177,8,168,104,76,14,3
170  DATA 133,6,132,7,160,0,177,6
180  DATA 240,6,32,237,253,200,208,246
190  DATA 96,193,204,204,160,204,201,206
200  DATA 197,160,206,213,205,194,197,210
210  DATA 211,160,212,207,160,182,181,181
220  DATA 179,181,141,141,194,217,160,202
230  DATA 213,204,197,211,160,200,174,160
240  DATA 199,201,204,196,197,210,141,195
250  DATA 207,208,217,210,201,199,200,212
260  DATA 160,168,195,169,160,177,185,184
270  DATA 182,141,193,204,204,160,210,201
280  DATA 199,200,212,211,160,210,197,211
290  DATA 197,210,214,197,196,141,141,141
300  DATA 141,0,255,255
```

To make entering the program easy, I have included a short Applesoft BASIC program that will automatically load the machine language program for you. After the program is entered, you can execute it by typing **CALL 768**. If you do that while the BASIC loading program is in memory, all its line numbers will be changed to 65535. If you then try re-running the program, you see that it executes without a problem because it contains no GOTOs or GOSUBs.

MOVING THE CATALOG TO ANOTHER TRACK

One very effective way to protect programs from being copied is to change the track that the catalog is stored on. Normally it's stored on track 17 ($11) from sectors 15 ($F) to 1. While changing the catalog track will stop the standard copy programs (COPYA, FID, MUFFIN) it, of course, will not stop the bit copier programs from duplicating a diskette that uses this technique. However, if you combine this technique with some of the other copy protection schemes we've discussed so far, or if you move the catalog to track 37 or higher, even the popular nibble copier programs won't be able to duplicate your diskette.

While most of track 17 is devoted to the catalog, sector 0 of this track has a special job. It contains what is known as the **VTOC** (for **V**olume **T**able **O**f **C**ontents) and it keeps track of which sectors have been used and which are available for future storage. In addition to keeping track of which sectors are available, the presence of this special sector makes it possible for you to lock out any track and/or sector on the diskette and make sure that it won't be written to. This is helpful if you want to "bury" a serial number on the diskette somewhere. We'll get back to a more detailed discussion of the VTOC later.

Moving the VTOC

There are several different approaches that can be used to move the contents of track 17. You can choose to move just the VTOC, just the catalog data or both. If you move just the VTOC, you'll still be able to run programs under normal DOS, you just won't be able to save anything out to the diskette without the risk of damaging it. Nevertheless let's start by moving the VTOC. Moving the VTOC is perhaps a misconception because we're not going to take an initialized diskette and then move it's VTOC, although it is possible. Instead, we're going to modify DOS and then use this modified DOS to initialize a new diskette. The modification that we make to DOS will cause the new diskette to be initialized with the VTOC on another track. The modification that we have to make to DOS to move the VTOC is a simple one and consists of changing only a single byte of memory. That byte is located at **44033 ($AC01)**, and it is the location that contains the number of the track on which the VTOC is located.

This location is used both by the routine that initializes a diskette and by the routines that load or save programs to a diskette. Under normal circumstances the number stored in 44033 is 17 ($11).

We can change the VTOC track by simply POKEing a new number into location 44033. For example, from BASIC we can type in the following line in the immediate mode (no line number) and cause the VTOC to be saved out to track 37 where it cannot be copied by standard copy programs.

POKE 44033,37

As you will recall, we discussed how to add up to 5 tracks to your diskettes in the first issue of **ASPD** (Vol. 1, No. 1, p. 8). Since none of the commercial bit copier programs copies more than 36 tracks, storing the VTOC and catalog onto one of these extra tracks is an effective copy protection scheme.

You can move the catalog too

To make your files inaccessible to normal DOS, you can move the catalog sectors to track 37 as well. This would make it almost impossible to access the programs on a copied version of the diskette, especially if the space on track 17 is released and used to store programs on. To change the number of the track that DOS goes to, to look for the catalog information, it is only necessary to change two locations in DOS. They are **46012 ($B3BC)** and **44764 ($AEDC)**. The first location is used to tell DOS which track to write the directory onto, and the second location tells DOS which track to format as a directory track. Both of these locations must contain the same track number, which is normally 17. Once again, by changing the number in these two locations, you can produce a diskette that has its catalog information on track 37, which cannot be copied by most copy programs that are available. The following BASIC line executed in the immediate mode will make the changes for you:

POKE 46012,37 : POKE 44764,37

There is a big advantage to doing this. By putting the catalog and VTOC on a track that cannot be copied, you can tell users of your protected diskette that they can make backup copies of the diskette with COPYA, which will not run, and save them in case the original becomes damaged. Since odds are small that the damage will occur on the 37th track, most of the time, users will be able to restore their damaged original by recopying their backup copy onto the original. Of course, if the damage does occur on the 37th track, the diskette will have to be replaced.

Tell the VTOC about the changes

Once you've modified DOS so that it will produce a 37-track diskette and moved your VTOC and catalog onto it, you must also tell the VTOC that track 37 is used and that track 17 is available. You do this by changing two locations in DOS which contain information that tells DOS where the catalog track is located. These locations are **44741 ($AEC5)** and **44745 ($AEC9)**. The first location (44741) contains the number of the track on which the directory is located, multiplied by four, while the second location (44745) contains four times the directory track number plus four. Thus, for standard DOS, 44741 contains 68 ($44) while 44745 contains 72 ($48). Interestingly enough, if we use 68 as an offset into track 17, sector 0 (the VTOC sector) we get exactly to the point where we have four bytes that are used to mark the availability of track 17. This is not just a coincidence, because these two locations are used by DOS to create the VTOC bit map.

Thus, after we make the necessary changes to move our directory (or catalog) onto track 37, we have to make these changes too. They can easily be implemented by typing in the following line in the immediate mode:

POKE 44741,68 : POKE 44745,72

Now you have completed the modifications necessary to move the VTOC and the catalog to a different track. All that's left for you to do is initialize your new diskette. Don't forget, if you're using more than 35 tracks on your diskette, you'll have to modify DOS as described in **ASPD** Vol. 1, No. 1. While I've concentrated on showing you how to move the catalog and VTOC to an extra, nonstandard track, there is obviously no reason why it cannot be moved to any other track on the diskette. The reason I've concentrated on these extra tracks is, as I mentioned earlier, they cannot be easily copied with the current crop of copy programs.

To make the whole task of producing

custom diskettes easier, I have included a short BASIC program that will take care of all the nitty gritty details for you. All you have to do is answer the questions it asks about the number of tracks you want on the diskette and where you want the catalog track located. The program does the rest.

A challenge and a gift

For those of you who have the time and the inclination, here's a small challenge for you. Use the information I have just presented to you to come up with a program that will produce a diskette that has two catalog tracks on it. You should provide a means of switching back and forth between the standard catalog and the hidden one so that programs can be saved on one or the other. Provision should also be made to update both VTOCs whenever either one is modified so that nothing will be accidentally overwritten.

The simplest way to update the VTOCs is to first make sure that the track with the hidden catalog on it is locked out as an in-use track on that normal VTOC. You can do this by storing zeroes in the appropriate bit map locations on track 17, sector 0 (remember the offset to the starting location of the bit map can be calculated by multiplying the track number by four. Thus the bit map for track 37 would start at byte 148 ($94) in the VTOC sector. To lock out an entire track, four successive bytes must be set to zero. After the standard VTOC has been modified to protect the hidden VTOC, just read the standard VTOC sector into memory, modify byte number 1 (the second byte in the sector) so that it is equal to the track that the hidden catalog is stored on and write it out again to the VTOC sector of the hidden catalog track. Now, if you always copy the the VTOC sector of the catalog that has just been modified (the currently active one) to the VTOC sector that was not modified (the inactive one), remembering to adjust that second byte to the correct track number, you'll always have both VTOCs properly updated and not have to worry about accidentally overwriting something on your diskette.

For your efforts in developing this program, the winner will get fame and recognition by having it published in **ASPD**, the satisfaction of having developed your own protection scheme and a *free 6-month extension to your subscription*. The second best entry will get a *free 3-month extension*. You may use any programs that have already appeared in **ASPD** as a starting point if you think they'll be helpful, so let's see you get those entries in.

If you need more information on just how the catalog track is formatted you can look in Apple's DOS manual or in one of the handiest books I've found on the subject, *Beneath Apple DOS*. If you have difficulty find this book, which is published by Quality Software, you can order it through us at a 10% discount, for only $17.95.

REVIEW: The quikLoader ROM Card

One of the most useful accessories that you can purchase to help you crack programs is the quikLoader ROM Card from the Southern California Research Group (SCRG). Designed to be used in an Apple][, Apple][Plus or Apple //e, the quikLoader card can hold up to 256 programs in ROM with a total memory capacity of almost half a megabyte. Programs can be written in machine language or either Integer or Applesoft BASIC.

The main reason the quikLoader card is such a helpful tool in cracking programs is that it can be used to interrupt a running program and let's you select from a menu, any other program you'd like to have run. When the card is enabled, one of the eight possible ROM chips that are installed on it, is selected for response to addresses in the $C100 to $FFFF memory range. At the same time, motherboard response in this range is inhibited. This is great for the cracker because he can now reset directly into the monitor or run any other program without having to worry about overcoming protection schemes in programs that make it impossible to break out of the program by pressing RESET. When you have a quikLoader in your computer, anytime the RESET or Control-RESET key is pressed, the card is enabled and ROM chip 0 is selected. The result is that when RESET is pressed, a program in chip 0 is run. This program is called QLOS (for quikLoader Operating System).

The action that QLOS takes when a reset is encountered depends on which key was pressed just before or, at the same time as the RESET key and the status of the power-up byte at $3F4. By pressing the appropriate key concurrently with Control-RESET, you can choose from a variety of resets. Included in this list are a normal reset, forced power-up reset, forced disk boot, a catalog of the quikLoader ROM(s), execution of specific programs from the ROM(s). Below is a list of the actions allowed when a reset is encountered, and the keys that must be pressed to implement them.

Z - Move Integer BASIC, the monitor ROM and DOS into RAM, initialize DOS and and enter Applesoft BASIC.
n - (number 0-7) Run a program on chip n.
Q - quikLoader catalog (referred to as katalog to differentiate from a disk catalog).
H - Do a Z-Reset and then run the HELLO program.
B - Boot DOS by moving DOS to RAM, initializing it and entering Applesoft.
D - Disk boot.
C - Catalog a diskette.
M - Enter the monitor mode.
S - Soft reset (slot 0, 16K RAM card reset).
X - Go to the mini assembler.

In addition to these reset options, there is an additional one call A-reset. This is encountered when an undefined key is pressed. In an A-reset, the computer jumps to the address contained in $FFFC and $FFFD on the motherboard (the main Apple circuit board) if the power-up byte is good. If the power-up byte is not good, the computer jumps to the power-up routine on chip six of the quikLoader.

If you replace the power-up routine that is stored in the chip 0 ROM with one of your own programs, you can have the quikLoader card do anything you want when the RESET (or Control-RESET) key is pressed.

Uses very little RAM

The design philosophy behind the quikLoader is to transfer programs that are stored on EPROMs into RAM for execution. However, programs can be run while they reside in the ROM card (that's how QLOS is run). When this is done, very little user RAM is needed. The memory that it does need is primarily used for pointers, counters and temporary storage. Zero page locations are used for most temporary storage and certain routines that must run in RAM are loaded either into the input buffer at $200 or the bottom of the 6502 stack at $100. These locations were chosen by the board's designer Jim Sather (author of *Understanding Your Apple*) so as to minimize any likely interference with user programs. And his goal was achieved.

Using the board's B-RESET feature, you can load DOS into the Apple and very few memory locations will be changed. There's no multi-stage boot process involved that wipes out large chunks of memory. DOS is loaded directly from the card into the final location in memory where it will be run. Thus, it is a simple matter to boot up a protected diskette, load the program into memory, boot normal DOS from the quikLoader card, and then save the program out to an unprotected diskette.

It comes with software

The quikLoader card has eight sockets on it for EPROMs. When you buy the card, you'll get it with some EPROMs already in it. These will contain DOS 3.3, Integer BASIC, FID and COPYA. These programs are licensed from Apple Computer. SCRG also has other programs available in ROM for use with this board. These include the Beagle Bros. Double-Take utility and Central Point's Copy][Plus. And, if you send them your configured version of AppleWorks on a diskette, they'll burn it into ROM for you so that you can be up and running with it in less than 2 seconds.

The board is extremely versatile and can accomodate any combination of EPROMs from the 2K 2716s to the 64K 27512s. If completely populated with 64K EPROMs, the quikLoader can store almost a half megabyte of data. Since the card can be plugged into any slot except slot 0 (but including slot 3 in the Apple //e) it is possible to store over 3 MB of data in EPROMs and have any of it instantly available.

Support is superb

For those of you who may not have heard of SCRG, it's a small company that sells a number of hardware accessories for the Apple. But don't hold its size against it, because you'll be hard pressed to find another company, even a Fortune 500 one, that supports its products as well as SCRG does. While my quikLoader card has always worked well and I've never encountered any problems, the company sent around a notice that a change had been made to the card and the ROMs to enable it to work with the 27512 EPROMs (I bought mine before these chips were available). And though SCRG was not obligated to, it offered to update my card for free if I sent it back to them. I did, and they turned it around very quickly. In the years that I have owned this card, I have had several ocassions to call the company and ask technical questions about how or why something was done, or if the card could be used for specific applications. I always found someone technically knowledgeable to talk to, usually Phil Wershba himself (he's the president). In those rare circumstances when he couldn't answer my questions, the designer, Jim Sather could.

SCRG offers a 6 month warranty on everything it sells, but I have found that if you encounter a problem even after the warranty expires, that the company will take care of it for you anyway (if possible), at no charge. Another nice practice of this company is its 10-day free trial period. You can order any of their products and try them for 10 days. If for some reason you're not happy with a product, all you have to do is return it for a prompt refund. If you're going to be doing a lot of program cracking, or if you just want the added convenience of having your most frequently used programs in ROM ready for instant access, then this card is a must for you. **Price:** $179. **Source:** Southern California Research Group, P.O. Box 593, Moorpark, CA 93020.

COPYP Files *continued from page 6*

The checking routine is bypassed by adding line 485, which is listed below and setting the old value of the byte to 0.5. Actually, any value between 0 and 1 will do, but 0.5 is easy to remember. Thus the parameter file for *Financial Cookbook* becomes:

485 IF OV > 0 AND OV < 1 THEN 500
1000 DATA 1,6,8,0.5,98

COPYP will now make a backup copy of the program and, without checking to make sure this is the correct version of the program, modify the diskette so that it will work.

Hayes Terminal Program

Like the previous program, this one was submitted without the value of the byte that is to be changed, Since we do not have a copy of this program, we can't check it and find the value of the original byte.

485 IF OV > 0 AND OV < 1 THEN 500
1000 DATA 16,3,157,0.5,37

Microwave

Although this program is a few years old, it has proven to be a very popular one and for that reason, cracking information is included here.

485 IF OV > 0 AND OV < 1 THEN 500
1000 DATA 2,1,218,0.5,173
1010 DATA 2,1,219,0,5,3
1020 DATA 2,1,220,0.5,129
1030 DATA 2,1,221,0.5,96

That's all it takes to unprotect Microwave.

Give us a hand

In order for this publication to be really useful to you, you have to get involved. Tell us what you'd like to see and also contribute your favorite cracks to us. If you took the time out to unprotect a program, chances are that someone else is interested in it too. Remember, you get a one-month subscription extension for every program crack you submit and we use. So let's see those helpful hints.

ASPD PROGRAM DISKETTE AVAILABLE FOR ONLY $15

Starting with this issue, we will make a DOS 3.3 diskette available every month that contains all of the programs from the current issue of the *Apple Software Protection Digest*.

To order send a check, money order or your charge card number and expiration date to:

REDLIG SYSTEMS, INC.
2068 79th Street
Brooklyn, New York 11214

REDLIG SYSTEMS, INC.
2068 79th Street
Brooklyn, New York 11214

BULK RATE
U.S. POSTAGE
PAID
BROOKLYN, N.Y.
Permit No. 631

APPLE SOFTWARE PROTECTION DIGEST

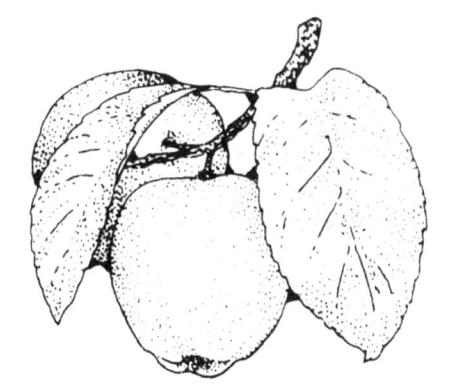

$3.00

Vol. 1 No. 4   1986

Contents

Editorial 1
Crack Index 2
Letters 2
Bugs 2
Protect and Unprotect Programs
with Muffin Plus and Demuffin .. 3
Protection Tutorial - Part III
    All About Synch Bytes 7
Cracks Wanted 8
How To Restore Lost Applesoft
Programs 9

Apple Software Protection Digest

Publisher & Editor, Jules H. Gilder; Contributing Editor, J. Scott Barrus. Copyright © 1986 by Redlig Systems, Inc., 2068 - 79th Street, Brooklyn, New York 11214. All rights reserved. No part of this publication may be reproduced, or electronically transmitted or stored without the publisher's written permission. Published monthly at $24 per year by Redlig Systems, Inc. (718) 232-8429. Reprints of prior issues available at $3 each. Printed in the U.S.A.

Apple is a registered trademark of Apple Computer Inc.

HELP SPREAD THE WORD

As you can see we've gotten issue #4 of the digest out and cut down on the delay between issues. Things are starting to finally run a little smoother now and we've just started doing the typesetting for the newsletter in-house. This should significantly cut down on our costs and more importantly, make it easier for us to get the newsletter ready for publication. By going in-house we've eliminated a lot of delays that were caused by the fact that we had to travel some distance to get to the typesetter. It also precluded the possibility of turning articles into typeset material the same day. All that has now changed.

Now that we're back on track, we'd like to move ahead somewhat and try to build the subscription list, and we're asking you to help. Show the digest to your friends who have Apple // computers (or clones like the Laser 128). I think that once they see it, they'll like it and want to order it for themselves.

Get a free digital watch pen

We think you'll tell your friends about us because you like our publication and they will too. But, as a little extra incentive to you, we'll send you a beautiful, free digital watch pen for every new subscriber who subscribes to the digest and mentions your name. Obviously, a new subscriber can only mention the name of one already existing subscriber, but there's no limit on the number of new subscribers who can mention your name. Thus, if ten people subscribe because they heard about us from you, you'll get ten digital watch pens. This is a limited offer and will only be good for one month, so hurry up and get those subscriptions in quickly.

Special group discounts

In order to encourage group purchases of the digest, we have established a special discount of 16.7% whenever ten or more subscriptions are ordered at the same time. This means that the normal $24 subscription will cost only $20 a year. In order to qualify for this special rate, at least ten subscriptions must be ordered at once and they must be paid for with one group check (or charge). The free pen and discount offer cannot be combined.

Let's hear from you

One of the most useful features of any publication is the section that provides feedback from the readers. This is the **Letters** section. This is the place where you can air your opinions (even if we don't agree with them) and ask for help. It's also the place where we find out how we're doing. Certain things we know, like we're late and should try to improve our schedule. Other things we don't, like how do you find the material presented? Is it too simple or too complicated? Is there something you don't like? Is there something you'd like included? Let us know, we'll try to accomodate you.

Jules H. Gilder
Publisher & Editor

Crack Index

In order to make life just a little more convenient for you, each issue of **Apple Software Protection Digest** will contain a list of all the programs cracked so far, and what issues those cracks appeared in. This will save you from going through all past issues of the digest in order to find a particular program.

Applewriter //e - Vol. 1, No. 3, p. 3
Bookends - Vol. 1, No. 1, p. 7
Financial Cookbook - Vol. 1, No. 3, p. 6
Hayes Terminal Program - Vol. 1, No. 3, p. 11
Homeword - Vol. 1, No. 2, p. 9
Homeword Speller - Vol. 1, No. 2, p. 9
Microwave - Vol. 1, No. 3, p. 11
PFS Series - Vol. 1, No. 2, p. 7
Print Shop - Vol. 1, No. 1, p. 10
Print Shop Companion - Vol. 1, No. 2, p. 6
Sensible Grammar - Vol. 1, No. 2, p. 7
Time Is Money - Vol. 1, No. 2, p. 9

Don't miss a single issue SUBSCRIBE TODAY!

BUGS

Although we spend a lot of time testing and rechecking all the information we present here, every once in a while a problem will still crop up. As soon as I find out about it, I'll let you know in this column. It is my sincere hope that this column will be missing from most issues, and very short in those issues in which it is included.

Print Shop Copier

Many of you have written in and complained of problems with the Print Shop Copy program from the first issue of **ASPD**. Interestingly enough, there were almost as many solutions to the problem as there were writers about it. All of you however treated the symptom, and thus while each of these fixes worked, none got down to the real cause of the problem, which lies in line 100 of Apple's original COPYA program.

This line sets up the start of the copy buffer. Since we've added some lines to the program the space between the end of the program and the beginning of the buffer — which is needed to store program variables — has been reduced considerably and thus causes the program to crash frequently. I had actually already discovered this when I wrote COPYP in the last issue, but didn't have time to get it into the issue. The problem can be eliminated altogether by simply adding the following line to the Print Shop Copier program:

100 POKE 715, PEEK (110) + 2

I'm sorry for any inconvenience I may have caused you.

Print Shop Companion

There was an omission in the listing of the parameters to be used to back up the program. Line 72 should have read: **POKE 863,34**. Thus line 72 should look like this:

72 POKE 863,34

This will tell the program not to copy the last track and eliminate I/O Error messages.

Tutorial — Part II

On page 8 of the last issue, where the modifications are listed from making a protected DOS, the second occurence of line 1 was incorrect. It should read:

1. B955:D5 N B95F:AA N BC7A:D5 N BC7F:AA

This will now restore normal DOS.

Letters

Dear Editor:

I continue to enjoy your magazine. I don't care if the issues are late, just keep them coming! I will certainly renew my subscription when it is due. I wonder if anyone has a crack for the program, "The Game Show" by Advanced Ideas. It involves reading half tracks and the disk is a combination of DOS 3.3 and DOS 3.2 and it is beyond my skills so far.

As far as your **Cracks Wanted** list is concerned, Sensible Speller was covered in Hardcore Computing, issues 9, 10, 11, 13, 15, 16 and 23. It was also covered in the 1985 Pirate's Harbor disk. Crush, Crumble and Chomp was in Hardcore's issue 7. Wizardry was covered in the Bootlegger's disk #2 and Hardcore in issue's 8, 20, 23, 26 and 29. Dazzle Draw was covered in the 1985 Pirate's Harbor disk and Hardcore 21 and 26. I have not seen cracks for Compres Software, Word Handler or Disk-O-Check anywhere.

Brian Symonds
Powell River, B.C.

I'm glad to here that you enjoy our publication so much. I appreciate your tolerance of our lateness. We are trying to overcome it. We have just purchased a laser printer to do the typesetting in-house and cutdown on costs and time. Parts of this issue were set on the laser printer and the entire next issue will be too. I don't know if anyone has crack "The Game Show" yet, but we'll add it to our list. Thanks for all the info on where the other programs on our list have already been cracked. That should be helpful to a lot of people. Nevertheless, we'd like to see other approaches to cracking these programs.

PROTECT AND UNPROTECT PROGRAMS WITH MUFFIN PLUS AND DEMUFFIN PLUS

Whenever you're trying to protect or unprotect programs, its always important that you have the correct tools to do the job. One of the tools that I have found very useful over the years is a program called *DEMUFFIN PLUS*. If the name of this program sounds familiar to you, it should, because it is a modification of a program that Apple gives away on its DOS 3.3 System Master diskette. That program is called *MUFFIN*, and was originally designed to bridge the gap between Apple's old DOS 3.2 operating system, and the subsequent DOS 3.3 operating system. When *MUFFIN* was run, it allowed the user to take files (of all types) that were stored on a DOS 3.2 diskette and transfer them over to a DOS 3.3 diskette.

If you've ever tried using a DOS 3.2 diskette (are there still any around) on a DOS 3.3 system, you will notice that the Apple stubbornly refuses to recognize it and prints out an **I/O Error** message to the user. The reason for this is that the diskette is formatted differently than a DOS 3.3 diskette is. To get around this problem, the software wizards at Apple Computer designed a program that could use two different RWTS (Read and Write a Track and Sector) routines. One RWTS routine would be the standard one that is in DOS 3.3 and located in memory at $B800. The other one would be the 13-sector DOS 3.2 RWTS and it would be located in memory at $1900. The RWTS routine is the core of any DOS and is the routine that makes it possible for the computer to write information to, or read information from, a diskette.

Shortly after Apple came out with its DOS 3.3 and *MUFFIN* programs, some bright programmer decided that he was going to replace the resident copy of the DOS 3.2 RWTS with a copy of the DOS 3.3 RWTS. He apparently reasoned that if he could then interrupt a running protected program by pressing the RESET key (non-autostart ROMs that dropped you into the monitor when RESET was pressed were widely available) and somehow load in this modified *MUFFIN* program which was called *DEMUFFIN PLUS*, programs could then be transferred from a diskette with the protected DOS on it to a diskette with standard DOS 3.3 on it. An that's what was done. After *DEMUFFIN PLUS* was produced, it was stored out on a cassette tape and loaded in when needed.

While most people are primarily interested in transferring programs from a protected diskette to an unprotected one, if you've created your own protected DOS (see **ASPD** Vol. 1, No. 2, p. 22) you'll want some method of transferring programs the other way, from unprotected diskettes to protected ones. That's where a new program, which I call *MUFFIN PLUS*, comes in. In the rest of this article, I will show you how to make both of these programs and how to use them.

Here's what you'll need

To make the *DEMUFFIN PLUS* program, you will need a DOS 3.3 System Master with the *MUFFIN* program on it and an Apple computer that has Integer BASIC with the Programmer's Aid ROM available. If you have a 16K RAM card (or an Apple //c or //e) and you boot your system with the System Master diskette, Integer BASIC and the Programmer's Aid ROM will automatically be loaded for you into the RAM card memory. If your Apple does not have the extra 16K of memory and you don't have the Programmer's Aid ROM installed in your computer along with Integer BASIC, don't dispare, you'll still be able to make *DEMUFFIN PLUS*.

The reason we need to have the Programmer's Aid ROM available is because there is a very handy machine language program in it that let's you relocate machine language programs. By relocate, I mean move the program from its current location in memory to another one in such a manner so that it can run at the new location without any difficulty. Those of you somewhat familiar with the Apple monitor ROM might think that you can already do that by using the memory move command that is built into the F8 ROM. That will only work under special circumstances. Most of the time, Apple machine language programs are written in such a way, that they are tied to a specific location in memory. Thus if you move the program to a new memory location, it won't work because it is still going to search for some of the information it needs at the old location. However, if as you move the program, you replace the old addresses that were referenced, with the matching ones for the new location of the program, then everything will run fine. This process of moving and updating the program and its references to specific memory locations is called relocation.

As I mentioned earlier, this special relocation program is only available in those Apples that have 64K or more of memory or Integer BASIC with the extra Programmer's Aid ROM added to it. However, to accommodate those readers who do not meet either of these conditions, I have rewritten the Apple relocation program so that it does not require the Integer or Programmer's Aid ROMs. This program, called *6502 RELOCATOR*, is listed below. This version of the *6502 RELOCATOR* program has been specially modified so that it can run wherever it is loaded into memory. It is not tied to any specific memory locations. Unless you have a machine language program on page three that has to be worked on, you'll probably find it most convenient to load and run the relocator program at address $300. To make it easy to use, I have included a short BASIC program listing that will automatically enter the *6502 RELOCATOR* program for you. For those of you who do not like to type, the *6502 RELOCATOR* is available on **ASPD Diskette #3** along with all of the others programs in this issue. The diskette is available for $15.

In order to make *DEMUFFIN PLUS*, it is necessary to move the standard DOS 3.3 RWTS from its usual location of $B800 to $1900. Since the RWTS code references specific locations within itself, it is necessary to modify those specific references before we run the program, hence the need for the relocator.

Making DEMUFFIN PLUS

The first thing you have to do once you have a copy of *MUFFIN*, is to activate the relocator program. If you have an Apple with Integer BASIC in it and the Programmer's Aid ROM, activate Integer BASIC by typing INT. If you're using my modified version of the *6502 RELOCATOR*, just RUN the BASIC version, or BLOAD and CALL the program at 768. In either case, the next step is for you to BLOAD the *MUFFIN* program. *MUFFIN* loads in at location $803.

After *MUFFIN* has been loaded into memory, you must get into the monitor mode. You can do this by typing **CALL -151**. Once in the monitor, people not using my program must type **D4D5G** to activate the *6502 RELOCATOR* program. The program is designed to work with the monitor's Control-Y capabilities. To start the relocation process, type in the following:

1900<B800.BFFF Control-Y*

In the above instructions, you don't type the word "Control-Y", but rather, you hold down the **Control** key while at the same time you press the **Y** key. Then you let both of them go. Also, don't type a space after BFFF. I've put it in here so that it's a little easier to read. Don't forget to type the asterisk (*) immediately after the Control-Y. Now that you've told the relocator which block of code is being moved ($B800-$BFFF) and where it is going ($1900), you've got to tell the relocator which portions of this block contain instructions that have to be changed, and which portion contains data that must only be moved and not updated. Let's tackle the instruction segment first. Type in the following line and then press return:

1900<B800.BA10 Control-Y

Next, you want to move a section of data without modifying it. This is done by typing in the following line:

.BC57M

Don't forget the period preceding the BC57M, it's very important. Finally, you want to move another section of program and have all the internal references updated. This is done by typing:

.BFFF Control-Y

At this point, you might want to consider saving this file out to the diskette because we'll need it again later to make up the program *MUFFIN PLUS*. You can save it out by typing:

BSAVE MUFTEMP,A$803,L$1900

Now that all of the DOS 3.3 code has been properly relocated and you've saved a copy for use again later, the next thing to do is to modify the *MUFFIN* program itself so that it will display the correct title and so it will work as we

```
               1000 ****************************************
               1010 ***                                    ***
               1020 ***            6502 RELOCATOR          ***
               1030 ***                                    ***
               1040 ***            by S Wozniak            ***
               1050 ***                                    ***
               1060 ***       Modified to eliminate        ***
               1070 ***       the need for the Sweet-16    ***
               1080 ***       Interpreter and to be        ***
               1090 ***       completely relocatable by    ***
               1100 ***                                    ***
               1110 ***            JULES H. GILDER         ***
               1120 ***                                    ***
               1130 ***         Copyright  (C) 1982        ***
               1140 ***         All Rights Reserved        ***
               1150 ***                                    ***
               1160 ****************************************
               1170 *
               1180 *
               1190 * Equates
               1200 *
0000-          1210         BEGIN       .EQ $0
0002-          1220         R1L         .EQ $2
0002-          1230         FROMBEG     .EQ $2
0004-          1240         FROMEND     .EQ $4
0008-          1250         TOBEG       .EQ $8
000B-          1260         INST        .EQ $B
002F-          1270         LENGTH      .EQ $2F
0034-          1280         YSAV        .EQ $34
003C-          1290         A1L         .EQ $3C
0042-          1300         A4L         .EQ $42
0100-          1310         STACK       .EQ $100
0200-          1320         IN          .EQ $200
03F8-          1330         CNTRLY      .EQ $3F8
F88E-          1340         INSDS2      .EQ $F88E
FCB4-          1350         NXTA4       .EQ $FCB4
FF58-          1360         RETURN      .EQ $FF58
               1370 *
               1380                     .OR $300
               1390 *
               1400 * Do a subroutine jump to a known RTS
               1410 * instruction to push the address of
               1420 * beginning of the program +2 on the
               1430 * stack.  Then add 36 ($24) bytes to
               1440 * this address to get the beginning of
               1450 * the program.
               1460 *
0300- 20 58 FF 1470         JSR RETURN         Put program start
0303- BA       1480         TSX                address on the
0304- BD 00 01 1490         LDA STACK,X        stack and then
0307- 85 01    1500         STA BEGIN+1        retrieve it.
0309- CA       1510         DEX
030A- BD 00 01 1520         LDA STACK,X
030D- 18       1530         CLC
030E- 69 24    1540         ADC #$24           Adjust starting
0310- 85 00    1550         STA BEGIN          address.
0312- 90 02    1560         BCC INITY
0314- E6 01    1570         INC BEGIN+1
               1580 *
               1590 * Set up the Control-Y vector with the
               1600 * address of the start of the program.
               1610 *
0316- A9 4C    1620 INITY   LDA #$4C
0318- 8D F8 03 1630         STA CNTRLY
031B- A5 00    1640         LDA BEGIN
031D- 8D F9 03 1650         STA CNTRLY+1
0320- A5 01    1660         LDA BEGIN+1
0322- 8D FA 03 1670         STA CNTRLY+2
0325- 60       1680         RTS
               1690 *
               1700 * This is the beginning of the actual
               1710 * relocation routine.
               1720 *
0326- A4 34    1730 RELOC   LDY YSAV           Initialize Y-register
0328- B9 00 02 1740         LDA IN,Y           Get next character.
032B- C9 AA    1750         CMP #'*+$80        Is it a *?
032D- D0 0C    1760         BNE RELOC2         No, relocate code.
032F- E6 34    1770         INC YSAV           Yes, incr. pointer.
0331- A2 07    1780         LDX #$7            Get move
0333- B5 3C    1790 INIT    LDA A1L,X          parameters of
0335- 95 02    1800         STA R1L,X          block.
0337- CA       1810         DEX
0338- 10 F9    1820         BPL INIT
033A- 60       1830         RTS
```

want it to. This is done by typing in the following lines while still in the monitor mode.

```
1155: 00 1E
115B: D9 03
1197: A0 20
15A0: A0 D2 C5 D3 C9 C4 C5 CE
15A8: D4 A0 C4 AE CF AE D3 AE
15F7: A0 A0 A0 A0 C4 C5 CD D5
15FF: C6 C6 C9 CE A0 D0 CC D5
1607: D3 A0
161E: CD CF C4 D3 A0 C2 D9 A0
1626: CA D5 CC C5 D3 A0 C8 AE
162E: A0 C7 C9 CC C4 C5 D2
20A0: A9 1E 8D B9 B7 20 FD AA
20A8: 48 A9 BD 8D B9 B7 68 60
```

Once these lines have been typed in, you have completed the task of changing *MUFFIN* into *DEMUFFIN PLUS* and all that's let for you to do is to save it out to disk. You can do this by typing:

BSAVE DEMUFFIN PLUS,A$803, L$1900

You now have a useful utility that can be used to unprotect many programs.

Using DEMUFFIN PLUS

Now that you have this very handy tool, the next thing you have to learn is how and when to use it. *DEMUFFIN PLUS* cannot be used with all protected programs, only those that have a DOS that has not been too heavily modified. One good indication of such programs are those that display the Applesoft prompt ( ]) at some time during the boot-up process. If you see that prompt, even for only a short period of time, chances are pretty good that you'll be able to use *DEMUFFIN PLUS* with the program. If you don't see the prompt, there's no guarantee that *DEMUFFIN PLUS* won't work, but the likelihood of it working is considerably smaller.

Before you start to crack a diskette with *DEMUFFIN PLUS*, make sure you have all the tools you'll need. First, you'll need a blank, initialized diskette. Next, you'll need some way of breaking out of the program you want to copy once it has booted. This could be an Integer BASIC ROM card, an interrupter card such as the WildCard 2, or a modified F8 ROM that will drop you into the monitor when RESET (or Control-RESET) is pressed. If you have an Apple computer that will still let you use the cassette tape (those routines were eliminated from the new enhanced //e ROMs) *DEMUFFIN PLUS* can be saved out to tape by typing:

```
              1840 *
              1850 * Here the next three bytes are copied
              1860 * and examined and the length of the
              1870 * instruction is calculated.
              1880 *
033B- A0 02   1890 RELOC2  LDY #$2        Copy the next
033D- B1 3C   1900 GETINS  LDA (A1L),Y    3 bytes.
033F- 99 0B 00 1910        STA INST,Y
0342- 88      1920         DEY
0343- 10 F8   1930         BPL GETINS
0345- 20 8E F8 1940        JSR INSDS2     Calculate the
0348- A6 2F   1950         LDX LENGTH     length.
034A- CA      1960         DEX            0=1-byte, 1=2-byte,
034B- D0 0C   1970         BNE XLATE      2=3-byte.
034D- A5 0B   1980         LDA INST       Is it Zero
034F- 29 0D   1990         AND #$D        page mode?
0351- F0 2A   2000         BEQ STINST     No, Immediate.
0353- 29 08   2010         AND #$8        Yes, clear the
0355- D0 26   2020         BNE STINST     high byte.
0357- 85 0D   2030         STA INST+2
              2040 *
              2050 * This section of code checks to see if
              2060 * the address of the instruction is in
              2070 * the range of the block of code being
              2080 * relocated. If it is, then the
              2090 * address is adjusted.
              2100 *
0359- A0 00   2110 XLATE   LDY #$0        Compare the
035B- A6 04   2120         LDX FROMEND    instruction address
035D- E4 0C   2130         CPX INST+1     with the end
035F- A5 05   2140         LDA FROMEND+1  address of the
0361- E5 0D   2150         SBC INST+2     source block.
0363- 90 18   2160         BCC STINST     It's larger.
0365- 38      2170         SEC
0366- A5 0C   2180         LDA INST+1     Compare it with
0368- E5 02   2190         SBC FROMBEG    start address of
036A- AA      2200         TAX            source block.
036B- A5 0D   2210         LDA INST+2
036D- E5 03   2220         SBC FROMBEG+1
036F- 90 0C   2230         BCC STINST     It's smaller
0371- 48      2240         PHA            It's in the range
0372- 8A      2250         TXA            so adjust it
0373- 18      2260         CLC            for its new
0374- 65 08   2270         ADC TOBEG      location.
0376- 85 0C   2280         STA INST+1
0378- 68      2290         PLA
0379- 65 09   2300         ADC TOBEG+1
037B- 85 0D   2310         STA INST+2
037D- A2 00   2320 STINST  LDX #$0        Copy the fixed
037F- B5 0B   2330 STINS2  LDA INST,X     instruction to
0381- 91 42   2340         STA (A4L),Y    its new location.
0383- E8      2350         INX
0384- 20 B4 FC 2360        JSR NXTA4      Update pointers.
0387- C6 2F   2370         DEC LENGTH
0389- 10 F4   2380         BPL STINS2     End of instruc?
038B- 90 AE   2390         BCC RELOC2     End of block?
038D- 60      2400         RTS
```

803.2103W

and reloaded from tape again when it is needed later by typing:

803.2103R

Both of these tape commands must be typed while you're in the monitor mode — that means the prompt character is an asterisk (*). If you're not going to use the cassette tape, most of the time you should be able to work around it by loading *DEMUFFIN PLUS* into an area of memory that does not get destroyed during the boot-up process.

I usually load *DEMUFFIN PLUS* into memory starting at $6000. This is a fairly safe area. Once the protected DOS has been loaded in, you should get into the monitor using any one of the techniques I discussed earlier. Once you're in the monitor, you'll have to move the *DEMUFFIN PLUS* program back down in memory where it belongs and then start the program running. You can do both of these things at once by typing:

803<6000.7900M N 803G

The spaces before and after the N are important, so don't leave them out. The command preceding the N performs the memory move, while the command after it causes the computer to jump to location $803 and execute the program that is stored there. The N and the spaces are just used to separate multiple monitor commands on the same line.

Once the program is running, you'll be presented with an opening screen and a two-choice menu. The first choice is to convert the programs and the second is to quit. After selecting choice 1, you'll be asked for the source and destination drives and the name of the file you want transferred. Here you may answer with a name, an equals sign (=) or a partial name and equals sign, just as in FID. That's all there is to it.

How to make MUFFIN PLUS

Earlier we said that *DEMUFFIN PLUS* was a handy tool to use for transferring programs from a diskette with protected DOS to standard DOS 3.3. If you are developing your own protected programs however, you'll want a way of transferring your programs from a standard 3.3 DOS diskette to a diskette with your own protected DOS on it. To do this, we use another variation of the *MUFFIN* program which I call *MUFFIN PLUS*.

You start out making *MUFFIN PLUS* the same way you make *DEMUFFIN PLUS*. If you saved out the program MUFTEMP as suggested earlier, all you have to do is BLOAD it. Otherwise you have to load *MUFFIN* into memory and then you move and relocate the standard DOS 3.3 code done in memory to $1900, just as I told you how to do it for *DEMUFFIN PLUS*. Once this code has been relocated, or MUFTEMP has been loaded, you actually have a working copy of *MUFFIN PLUS*, however, to prevent you from confusing it with MUFFIN, you should key in the following lines, from the monitor mode, to change the title that is displayed when the program is run.

```
15F7: A0 A0 A0 A0 A0 CD D5 C6
15FF: C6 C9 CE A0 D0 CC D5 D3
1607: A0 A0
161E: CD CF C4 D3 A0 C2 D9 A0
1626: CA D5 CC C5 D3 A0 C8 AE
162E: A0 C7 C9 CC C4 C5 D2
```

This program should now be saved out to a diskette by typing:

BSAVE MUFFIN PLUS,A$803,L$1900

In operation, *MUFFIN PLUS* works the same way that *DEMUFFIN PLUS*

```
1    REM BASIC PROGRAM TO INSTALL 6502 RELOCATOR
2    REM
10   TEXT : HOME
20   PRINT : PRINT : PRINT : PRINT
30   PRINT "INSTALLING 'RELOCATOR'..."
40   FOR X = 768 TO 909
50      READ Y
60      POKE X,Y
70   NEXT X
80   PRINT : PRINT : PRINT : PRINT "INSTALLATION COMPLETE."
90   PRINT : PRINT "TYPE 'CALL 768' TO RUN PROGRAM."
100  DATA 32,88,255,186,189,0,1,133
110  DATA 1,202,189,0,1,24,105,36
120  DATA 133,0,144,2,230,1,169,76
130  DATA 141,248,3,165,0,141,249,3
140  DATA 165,1,141,250,3,96,164,52
150  DATA 185,0,2,201,170,208,12,230
160  DATA 52,162,7,181,60,149,2,202
170  DATA 16,249,96,160,2,177,60,153
180  DATA 11,0,136,16,248,32,142,248
190  DATA 166,47,202,208,12,165,11,41
200  DATA 13,240,42,41,8,208,38,133
210  DATA 13,160,0,166,4,228,12,165
220  DATA 5,229,13,144,24,56,165,12
230  DATA 229,2,170,165,13,229,3,144
240  DATA 12,72,138,24,101,8,133,12
250  DATA 104,101,9,133,13,162,0,181
260  DATA 11,145,66,232,32,180,252,198
270  DATA 47,16,244,144,174,96
```

does. The only difference is that you must have an initialized protected diskette ready before the program is run. In addition, since you are doing the protection it's an easy matter for you to first load *MUFFIN PLUS* into memory where it belongs and then modify your DOS so that it is a protected DOS. This makes it a little easier to get *MUFFIN PLUS* up and running.

If you come up with any interesting uses for either *MUFFIN PLUS* or *DEMUFFIN PLUS*, let us know and we'll pass it along to everyone else.

---

continued from page 11

```
1    REM BASIC PROGRAM TO INSTALL AMPER RESTORE
10   TEXT : HOME
20   PRINT : PRINT : PRINT : PRINT
30   PRINT "INSTALLING 'AMPER RESTORE'..."
40   FOR X = 768 TO 970
50      READ Y
60      POKE X,Y
70   NEXT X
80   PRINT : PRINT : PRINT : PRINT "INSTALLATION COMPLETE."
90   PRINT : PRINT "TYPE 'CALL 768' TO RUN PROGRAM."
100  DATA 169,76,141,245,3,169,18,141
110  DATA 246,3,169,3,141,247,3,76
120  DATA 23,3,169,174,32,192,222,160
130  DATA 0,32,88,252,185,126,3,240
140  DATA 6,32,237,253,200,208,245,165
150  DATA 103,24,105,3,133,6,165,104
160  DATA 133,7,160,1,145,103,136,200
170  DATA 177,6,208,251,152,24,105,5
180  DATA 160,0,145,103,165,103,133,6
190  DATA 165,104,133,7,169,0,133,8
200  DATA 177,6,200,208,2,230,7,201
210  DATA 0,208,241,165,8,201,2,240
220  DATA 4,230,8,208,235,200,152,208
230  DATA 2,230,7,133,105,133,107,133
240  DATA 109,133,175,165,7,133,106,133
250  DATA 108,133,110,133,176,96,166,210
260  DATA 197,211,212,207,210,197,141,141
270  DATA 194,217,160,202,213,204,197,211
280  DATA 160,200,174,160,199,201,204,196
290  DATA 197,210,141,195,207,208,217,210
300  DATA 201,199,200,212,160,168,195,169
310  DATA 160,177,185,184,178,141,193,204
320  DATA 204,160,210,201,199,200,212,211
330  DATA 160,210,197,211,197,210,214,197
340  DATA 196,141,141,141,210,197,193,196
350  DATA 217,174,141
```

PROTECTION TUTORIAL — Part III
ALL ABOUT SELF-SYNC BYTES

Last time we discussed how a track on a diskette is formatted. You may recall that we said the Address and Data fields on the diskette are separated by gaps. What we did not say was just what these gaps were composed of. They are formed by writing a series of special bytes to the diskette that are called *self-sync* bytes. Self-sync bytes get their name from the property that they have of being able to automatically bring the disk drive hardware into synchronization with the data that is stored on the diskette.

The newcomer to understanding disk drive operation might wonder why this is necessary. The explanation is simple. Data is stored on the diskette as individual bits, but must be retrieved as 8-bit bytes. The problem, however, is that when the computer starts reading information from a diskette, it has no way of knowing where a particular byte begins. When the disk drive starts to read data, it starts from whatever position the read head is located at. Since we're reading 8-bit bytes from the diskette, there's only a one-in-eight chance that it has started reading data from the beginning of a byte as we'd like it to. Without some sort of special marker bytes, the computer has no way of knowing where the start of a series of bits begins.

To clarify the situation a little, let's make believe that the following series of bits were read from the disk drive:

```
11011111   10101011   1010
   DF          AB
```

If we begin interpreting our data with the first bit, we find that the first two bytes that we've read are DF and AB. If, on the otherhand, the read head was located at a position where it would start reading data from the diskette at the second bit of the above data stream, then the data would be interpreted as:

```
10111111   01010111   010
   BF          57
```

As you can see from this very simple example, the first two bytes have now become BF and 57, a far cry from what our original data was. Thus, it becomes clear why where we begin reading our data is such a critical matter.

Self-sync bytes have 10 bits

To overcome this problem of deciding where to start reading data, the designers of Apple's disk drive decided to define a special byte called a self-sync byte. The one thing that differentiates this byte from all other bytes is that it is composed of 10 bits, with the extra two bits always being zeroes. In normal DOS, the self-sync byte is an FF with two zero bits appended to it. In the modified DOS that's used in many protection schemes, this FF byte has been changed to other values. But, while the value may change, one thing doesn't. The two extra bits are always zeroes.

At this point, if you are the least bit curious, you're probably wondering how these special bytes can bring the hardware into sync with the data coming of the diskette. It's not difficult to understand, but first we must know that the Apple hardware will not start reading a byte from the diskette unless the first bit is a 1. So, if it encounters a zero bit first, it will skip over it and wait for the next "1"-bit to appear. Knowing this, it is now possible to figure out how many self-sync bytes will be necessary to guarantee that the hardware is synchronized with the data. To do this, we should first write out the bits for about half a dozen self-sync bytes. They would look like the first line in the diagram below. As you can see, I have included spaces between each sync byte, but when they are read off the diskette, they would simply appear as a continuous stream of bits. Now, if we start to read this stream of data (e.g. the first time we start with the first bit, the second time we start with the second bit, etc.) we can find out how many sync bytes we'll have to read before we can be sure that the data we are reading is accurate.

If we look at the chart above, we find that it takes a maximum of four self-sync bytes to insure synchronization. No matter where we start reading data, by the time we've reached the fifth byte, we know we must be reading an $FF. For this reason, the gaps on a diskette track must have a minimum of five self-sync bytes.

How Self-Sync Bytes Synchronize Data and Hardware

Start Bit	Data Read From the Diskette						Syncs on Byte
	Byte 1	Byte 2	Byte 3	Byte 4	Byte 5	Byte 6	
1	1111111100	1111111100	1111111100	1111111100	1111111100	1111111100	1
2	111111100	1111111100	1111111100	1111111100	1111111100	1111111100	2
3	11111100	1111111100	1111111100	1111111100	1111111100	1111111100	2
4	11111001	111111100	1111111100	1111111100	1111111100	1111111100	3
5	11110011	1111100	1111111100	1111111100	1111111100	1111111100	3
6	11100111	11111001	111111100	1111111100	1111111100	1111111100	4
7	11001111	11110011	1111100	111111100	1111111100	1111111100	5
8	10011111	11100111	11111001	111111100	1111111100	1111111100	5
9	0011111111	0011111111	0011111111	0011111111	0011111111	0011111111	1
10	0111111110	0111111110	0111111110	0111111110	0111111110	0111111110	1

Synchronizing Data and Hardware With 8-Bit Bytes

Start Bit	Byte 1	Byte 2	Byte 3	Byte 4	Byte 5	Byte 6	Syncs on Byte
	E4	92	E4	92	E4	92	
1	11100100	10010010	11100100	10010010	11100100	10010010	1
2	11001001	0010010111	0010010010	010111001	00	10010010	6
3	10010010	010111001	0010010010	010111001	00	10010010	6
4	0010010010	010111001	00	10010010	11100100	10010010	4
5	01001001	0010111001	00	10010010	11100100	10010010	4
6	10010010	010111001	00	10010010	11100100	10010010	4
7	00	10010010	11100100	10010010	11100100	10010010	2
8	0	10010010	11100100	10010010	11100100	10010010	2
9		10010010	11100100	10010010	11100100	10010010	2
10		0010010111	0010010010	010111001	00	10010010	6
11		010010111	0010010010	010111001	00	10010010	6
12		10010111	0010010010	010111001	00	10010010	6
13		0010111001	00	10010010	11100100	10010010	4
14		0101110010	0	10010010	11100100	10010010	4
15		10111001	00	10010010	11100100	10010010	4
16		0	11100100	10010010	11100100	10010010	3

Self-sync bytes can be eliminated

While it is not generally known, it's not absolutely necessary to have the 10-bit self-sync bytes on a diskette. If you choose the right combination of bytes, and there are several, you can synchronize the disk hardware and data with ordinary 8-bit bytes. You do pay a price for this however. Generally speaking you will need at least one more 8-bit sync byte. So, instead of requiring a minimum of four 10-bit sync bytes to guarantee synchronization, you'd need a minimum of five 8-bit sync bytes. Interestingly enough, both situations result in the same number of bits (40) to insure synchronization. One bit pattern that will insure synchronization within 5 sync bytes is **E4 92**. Let's check this out as we did with the 10-bit sync bytes. As you can see from the table above, no matter which of the first 16 bits you start reading the diskette from, by the time you have reached the 6th byte, the hardware and the data are in sync.

Self-sync bytes can't be copied

Why have we spent so much time trying to understand self-sync bytes? The answer is simple, they can be used to great advantage in copy protection schemes. Many people have asked me, "Why can't you write a program that simply reads a series of bits off of one diskette and writes it out to another diskette?" That's a good question, and at first glance you would think that it would be a simple matter to do just that. There is a problem however, and that is, *self-sync bytes cannot be copied*. The hardware in the Apple computer is setup in such a way, that only 8-bit bytes can be read from the diskette and stored in memory. If a 10-bit sync byte is read, the two trailing zeroes are lost. You may be wondering why it's so important to identify self-sync bytes. It's important because with their help, it becomes possible to identify the beginning and the end of a track. This is necessary on soft-sectored systems like the one used for the Apple, because there is no physical marker on the diskette that can be used to tell the computer where a track begins. Hard sector diskettes have a hole punched at sector zero, so the disk drive hardware can be used to locate the beginning of a track.

From our discussion of the track format in the last issue (**ASPD** Vol. 1, No. 2, p. 20) we learned that there are three types of gaps on a track: one that marks the beginning of a track, one that separates the address field from the data field and one that separates the data filed from the next address field. As it turns out, the gap that marks the beginning of a track is easily identified because it turns out to be the longest gap on the track. Thus, when nibble copy programs go to copy a track, they read the track into RAM and analyze it, searching for a large group of $FFs. Once they find this group of $FFs, they assume that they have located the beginning of the track and mark its location. Next, the bit copier programs look for a second occurrence of this large group of $FFs. Once they find it, they know that they've located the spot where the track starts to repeat itself. They then backup to the spot just before these $FFs began and mark that as the end of the track. Now that the bit copier knows where the start and finish of the track is, all it has to do is write this information back out to the diskette. As it does that it makes assumptions as to which bytes are sync bytes. If the track overlaps itself when it is written back out to the diskette, the bit copier will then start removing either zeroes from sync bytes, or sync bytes themselves to shorten the length. If bytes are removed, a problem will result in those programs that contain a nibble counting scheme.

After software developers analyzed the bit copiers and realized that they were looking for large groups of $FFs, they decided to use different bytes for self-sync bytes, temporarily making the nibble copy programs ineffective. Some developers even went so far as to use many different self-sync bytes on the same diskette. The next generation of nibble copy programs learned to overcome this new protection ploy by incorporating sophisticated disk reading routines that could detect the presence of the two trailing zeroes that were tacked onto self-sync bytes. With these reading techniques, it was no longer important what the sync byte was, the nibble copiers could detect them because they could find the two zero bits that are characteristic of self-sync bytes.

Use your own sync bytes

If you want to create your own protection scheme by changing the byte that's used as a self-sync byte, it's very easy to do. All you have to do is change one location in memory — location 48224 ($BC60). This location is near the beginning of the routine that's called by DOS's formatter and writes the address headers. It's entered with a number in the Y-register that tells the routine how many self-sync bytes to write. An LDA instruction at 48223 ($BC5F) gets the byte that will be stored as the self-sync byte on the diskette. You can change this value from an $FF to any other legal value (see chart of legal diskette bytes in **ASPD** Vol. 1, No. 2, p. 22) from BASIC. For example, if we wanted to change the normal self-sync byte to $FE, we would type in the following line:

POKE 48224,254

That's all there is to it. While it's easy to change the sync byte, your software must check for its presence to make it effective as a software protection scheme. In addition, it will not prevent current copy programs from backing up your diskette. In a future issue of **ASPD** we will talk about producing a useful protection scheme using modified sync bytes, bit insertion and nibble counting.

Cracks Wanted

Listed below are programs that our readers would like to unprotected. Anyone who comes up with a method of removing the protection from any of these programs will get a free three-month subscription, or extension to ASPD, so get those solutions in.

If you have a program that you'd like to see unprotected, please let us know, and we'll add it to our list so that some of our readers can try their hands at it.

1. Sensible Speller - DOS
2. Sensible Speller - ProDOS
3. Crush, Crumble & Chomp
4. Wizardry
5. Compress Software
6. Dazzle Draw
7. Newsroom
8. Word Handler
9. Disk-O-Check
10. The Game Show
11. Batter Up!
12. Certificate Maker

HOW TO RESTORE LOST APPLESOFT PROGRAMS

Many programs that are written in Applesoft appear to wipe themselves out when they're finished or when the program detects an attempt by the user to break out of the program by pressing Control-C or Control-RESET. Other programs contain special REM statements, which I call Wipeout REMs, that will automatically erase the program when you try to list it. The RAM disk formatter that was used with the Synetix 294K RAM card contained many statements of this type. These REM statements are easy to produce (I'll show you how to produce them in the next issue of **ASPD**) and provide protection from novice or casual users who want to examine, copy or otherwise manipulate your program code. They can be overcome however in many ways, and a program that can restore programs that are erased by the NEW or FP commands can be a powerful tool.

Another use for such a restoring capability comes up when you're trying to transfer Applesoft files from a protected disk to an unprotected one. This can be done by loading the program in from the protected disk. Once you get the Applesoft prompt back, you get into the monitor by typing **CALL -151**. Then type **AF.B0**. This command will print out two hexadecimal numbers for you which represent the low byte and the high byte of the end of the current BASIC program. Usually we know where an Applesoft program begins, at $801. However, if you don't want to take any chances, you can examine the start of program pointers which are located on page zero at locations $67 and $68.

Now that you know where the program starts and ends, you can move it up, out of the way of DOS's bootup process. I usually move the BASIC program up to $6000 and then boot a normal DOS 3.3 slave diskette. A slave diskette is one that is created by just using the INIT command and not using MASTER CREATE. Once DOS 3.3 has been loaded into the computer, **BLOAD &RESTORE**. Then move the BASIC program down from the $6000 memory range and restore the BASIC program by typing **CALL 768**. Once **&RESTORE** has been run, it can subsequently be invoked by typing **CALL 768** again or by typing **&RESTORE**.

To clarify the situation, let's take a fictional BASIC program that is on a

```
              1000 ******************************************
              1010 ***                                     ***
              1020 ***              &RESTORE               ***
              1030 ***                                     ***
              1040 ***         COPYRIGHT (C) 1982 BY       ***
              1050 ***            JULES H. GILDER          ***
              1060 ***          ALL RIGHTS RESERVED        ***
              1070 ***                                     ***
              1080 ******************************************
              1090 *
              1100 *
              1110 *
              1120          .OR $300
              1130 *
              1140 *
              1150 * CONSTANTS
              1160 *
004C-         1170 JUMP    .EQ $4C         JMP op code
00AE-         1180 RESTORE .EQ $AE         RESTORE token
              1190 *
              1200 *
              1210 * EQUATES
              1220 *
0006-         1230 POINTER .EQ $6
0008-         1240 TESTBYT .EQ $8
0067-         1250 TXTTAB  .EQ $67
0069-         1260 VARTAB  .EQ $69
006B-         1270 ARYTAB  .EQ $6B
006D-         1280 STREND  .EQ $6D
00AF-         1290 PRGEND  .EQ $AF
03F5-         1300 AMPERSD .EQ $3F5
DEC0-         1310 SYNCHR  .EQ $DEC0
FC58-         1320 HOME    .EQ $FC58
FDED-         1330 COUT    .EQ $FDED
              1340 *
              1350 *
              1360 * This is where the ampersand jump
              1370 * vector is set up. After set-up,
              1380 * a relative jump is made to the
              1390 * second entry point of the program.
              1400 *
0300- A9 4C   1410         LDA #JUMP       Get the JMP
0302- 8D F5 03 1420        STA AMPERSD     op-code & store
0305- A9 12   1430         LDA #START      it and the
0307- 8D F6 03 1440        STA AMPERSD+1   address of the
030A- A9 03   1450         LDA /START      start of this
030C- 8D F7 03 1460        STA AMPERSD+2   program.
030F- 4C 17 03 1470        JMP START2      Go to START2.
              1480 *
              1490 *
              1500 * There are two entry points to this
              1510 * program. One is via the &RESTORE
              1520 * command (START) and one by a CALL 768
              1530 * (START2). At START, the program
              1540 * looks at the information that follows
              1550 * the & to see if it is the RESTORE
              1560 * token. This is done by SYNCHR. If
              1570 * not RESTORE a syntax error is
              1580 * generated. Once syntax has been
              1590 * checked, the program title is
              1600 * printed out.
              1610 *
0312- A9 AE   1620 START   LDA #RESTORE    Does the RESTORE
0314- 20 C0 DE 1630        JSR SYNCHR      token follow the &?
0317- A0 00   1640 START2  LDY #$0         Yes, zero character pointer.
0319- 20 58 FC 1650        JSR HOME        Clear the screen.
031C- B9 7E 03 1660 LOOP1  LDA TEXT,Y      Get a character.
031F- F0 06   1670         BEQ NEXT        If done go to NEXT.
0321- 20 ED FD 1680        JSR COUT        Print a character.
0324- C8      1690         INY             Increment the pointer.
0325- D0 F5   1700         BNE LOOP1       Get more characters.
              1710 *
              1720 *
              1730 * This section of program resets the
              1740 * start of program pointers that are
              1750 * wiped out when a NEW or Control-B
              1760 * are entered.
              1770 *
0327- A5 67   1780 NEXT    LDA TXTTAB      Get program start
0329- 18      1790         CLC             low byte. Calculate
032A- 69 03   1800         ADC #$3         and save the starting
032C- 85 06   1810         STA POINTER     line's low byte.
032E- A5 68   1820         LDA TXTTAB+1    Get program start
```

protected diskette. After booting the protected diskette, we reset into the monitor and find the beginning and end of the program by typing:

67.68 N AF.B0

For our fictitious program, the computer responds by printing:

0067- 01
0068- 08
00AF- 97
00B0- 21
*

Next, we move the program up in memory, out of harms way by typing:

6001<801.2197M

With the the program safe from destruction, we boot a DOS 3.3 diskette and **BLOAD &RESTORE**. Then we move our BASIC program back down where it belongs getting into the monitor mode with **CALL -151** and then typing:

801<6001.7997M

Finally, we restore the program by typing **CALL 768**.

What makes it possible for a program like *&RESTORE* to resurrect a dead Applesoft program is the fact that the designers of the Applesoft language wanted to have an efficient language and decided that it was not necessary to actually erase the contents of memory every time a NEW or FP command was issued. Instead, they just changed the information stored in the end of program pointer and erased only two bytes of data from the program. Thus, the program is still in memory, it's just that Applesoft doesn't know where to look for it. By restoring the two bytes that were erased (the pointer to the second line of the Applesoft program), and searching through memory until the end of the program is found and restoring the PRGEND pointer, the program can be brought back to life, as if it were always there.

While *&RESTORE* will bring back programs that were NEWed or FPed, it will not help a bit if the program has been wiped out by zeroing out all of memory with a program such as *Wipeout 1* or *Wipeout 2* (see **ASPD** Vol. 1, No. 2, p.17 for more details). Bear this in mind when setting up your own

```
0330- 85 07      1830            STA POINTER+1    high byte and save it.
0332- A0 01      1840            LDY #$1          Save 2nd line's
0334- 91 67      1850            STA (TXTTAB),Y   high byte.
0336- 88         1860            DEY              Zero the Y-register.
0337- C8         1870 FINDEOL    INY              Look for the end
0338- B1 06      1880            LDA (POINTER),Y  of line marker
033A- D0 FB      1890            BNE FINDEOL      Keep looking.
033C- 98         1900            TYA              Found end of line.
033D- 18         1910            CLC              find value of
033E- 69 05      1920            ADC #$5          program start
0340- A0 00      1930            LDY #$0          low byte and
0342- 91 67      1940            STA (TXTTAB),Y   restore it.
                 1950 *
                 1960 *
                 1970 * This part of the program resets the
                 1980 * end of program pointers.
                 1990 *
0344- A5 67      2000            LDA TXTTAB       Store start of
0346- 85 06      2010            STA POINTER      program pointers
0348- A5 68      2020            LDA TXTTAB+1     in POINTER for
034A- 85 07      2030            STA POINTER+1    future use.
034C- A9 00      2040 LOOP2      LDA #$0          Initialize end of
034E- 85 08      2050            STA TESTBYT      program test byte.
0350- B1 06      2060 LOOP3      LDA (POINTER),Y  Start scanning
0352- C8         2070            INY              the program.
0353- D0 02      2080            BNE ZEROCHK      Page boundary?
0355- E6 07      2090            INC POINTER+1    Yes, increment the byte.
0357- C9 00      2100 ZEROCHK    CMP #$0          Does the accumulator=0?
0359- D0 F1      2110            BNE LOOP2        No, keep scanning.
035B- A5 08      2120            LDA TESTBYT      Yes, is it the
035D- C9 02      2130            CMP #2           end of the program?
035F- F0 04      2140            BEQ EXIT         Yes, finish up.
0361- E6 08      2150            INC TESTBYT      No, increment the test byte.
0363- D0 EB      2160            BNE LOOP3        Get the next byte.
0365- C8         2170 EXIT       INY              Adjust the byte
0366- 98         2180            TYA              count & see if
0367- D0 02      2190            BNE STORPTR      we have to increment
0369- E6 07      2200            INC POINTER+1    the high byte too.
036B- 85 69      2210 STORPTR    STA VARTAB       Store the low byte
036D- 85 6B      2220            STA ARYTAB       of the end of the program
036F- 85 6D      2230            STA STREND       in the appropriate
0371- 85 AF      2240            STA PRGEND       zero page locations.
0373- A5 07      2250            LDA POINTER+1    Store the high byte
0375- 85 6A      2260            STA VARTAB+1     of the end of the program
0377- 85 6C      2270            STA ARYTAB+1     in the appropriate
0379- 85 6E      2280            STA STREND+1     zero page
037B- 85 B0      2290            STA PRGEND+1     locations.
037D- 60         2300            RTS              Return.
                 2310 *
                 2320 *
                 2330 * This is where text for program title
                 2340 * and copyright notice are stored.
                 2350 *
037E- A6 D2 C5
0381- D3 D4 CF
0384- D2 C5      2360 TEXT       .AS -"&RESTORE"
0386- 8D 8D      2370            .HS 8D8D
0388- C2 D9 A0
038B- CA D5 CC
038E- C5 D3 A0
0391- C8 AE A0
0394- C7 C9 CC
0397- C4 C5 D2   2380            .AS -"BY JULES H. GILDER"
039A- 8D         2390            .HS 8D
039B- C3 CF D0
039E- D9 D2 C9
03A1- C7 C8 D4
03A4- A0 A8 C3
03A7- A9 A0 B1
03AA- B9 B8 B2   2400            .AS -"COPYRIGHT (C) 1982"
03AD- 8D         2410            .HS 8D
03AE- C1 CC CC
03B1- A0 D2 C9
03B4- C7 C8 D4
03B7- D3 A0 D2
03BA- C5 D3 C5
03BD- D2 D6 C5
03C0- C4         2420            .AS -"ALL RIGHTS RESERVED"
03C1- 8D 8D 8D   2430            .HS 8D8D8D
03C4- D2 C5 C1
03C7- C4 D9 AE   2440            .AS -"READY."
03CA- 8D 00      2450            .HS 8D00
```

protection schemes. Don't be lazy. Take the extra effort to include a wipeout feature in your protection schemes, if you really want to keep your programs from prying eyes.

For those of you who are interested in just how the &RESTORE program works, a detailed description of this assembly language program follows. For those of you who just want to use it, typing the accompanying BASIC program and it will install &RESTORE into memory for you and give you the option of saving the machine language program out to disk.

Redefining commands

In this program I'll also show you how you can use the existing set of key words and give them new functions to perform. In this case, as you've already guessed, we're going to use the **RESTORE** command. This command will still perform its usual function without any problems. But, when it is preceded by another command, the ampersand (&), it takes on an entirely new task.

The &RESTORE program begins, on line 1410, by setting up the ampersand jump vector to point to START and after that jumps to START2 (line 1470), skipping the code that checks for the presence of the word **RESTORE**. At line 1620, which is the ampersand entry point, the program loads the token for the word **RESTORE** (which is $AE) into the accumulator and then jumps to the syntax character checking routine (SYNCHR) to see if that token matches the information following the ampersand. If it doesn't, the subroutine prints out **SYNTAX ERROR** and stops execution of the main program. If it matches, the main program falls into the START2 routine.

It is not at all necessary to use the RESTORE command, but I thought you'd like to see how to do it. If you prefer to use just the & as the command, simply eliminate lines 1470, 1620 and 1630 and rename the label on line 1640 START. Once at line 1640, the program clears the screen and prints out the program's title, copyright notice and the word **READY**, indicating to the user that the program has already been restored. While the program has not yet been restored, the task is accomplished so quickly, that the user never realizes it.

The actual program restoration begins on line 1780 where the start of program pointer, TXTTAB, is used to produce another pointer (lines 1780 to 1830), called POINTER, which will skip the first four bytes of the line (these consist of the next line pointer and the line number). The reason we want to skip these bytes is that ultimately we want to find the end of the first line which is terminated with a zero. However, any of the first four bytes can legitimately contain a zero, which could result in premature termination of this program.

After POINTER has been calculated and stored, the high-byte of the start of program pointer is still in the accumulator and it is stored as the high byte of the pointer to the second line in the program (line 1850).

Now that the high-byte of the next line link to the second line has been restored, we have to find out where the first line ends in memory so that we can restore the low-byte. The routine that does this, FINDEOL, begins in line 1870. In lines 1870 and 1880, the Y-register is incremented and the contents of the location pointed to by both POINTER and the offset of the Y-register, are checked to see if they are zero. If not, the process is repeated until they are. If they are, the Y-register is transferred to the accumulator (line 1900), the carry bit is cleared in preparation for adding two numbers (line 1910) and 5 is added to the accumulator (line 1920). The five includes the four bytes that were skipped at the beginning, plus an additional byte so that the pointer will point not to the last character of the Applesoft line, but one past it, where the next line actually begins. This number is stored in the low byte of the next line pointer (line 1940).

If the program were to stop at this point, you would be able to list the program and it would appear as if it had all been restored. It hasn't, because if you saved it out to tape or disk and then loaded it back in, you'd find you had nothing, even though you were able to list it, and also run it. The program can be saved at this point only by listing it to an EXEC file. The reason the program will not save out properly is that we have not adjusted the end of program pointer, PRGEND, to point to the end of the program. This is what is done, starting at line 2000, where TXTTAB, the start of program pointer, is loaded into POINTER (lines 2000 to 2030).

In lines 2040 and 2050, a flag called TESTBYT is set to zero. This is going to be used to help us determine when the end of the program has been reached. A loop to scan the program is set up starting at line 2060, where POINTER and the Y-register are used to determine the next location from which a byte will be loaded and tested to see if it is equal to zero. After the byte is loaded, and before the test is performed, the Y-register is incremented (line 2070) and a check is made to see if a memory page boundary has been crossed (e.g. did we go from an address in the $800 range to an addresses in the $900 range). If no page boundary was crossed (line 2080) the program branches to ZEROCHK, otherwise, the high-byte of POINTER is incremented by one.

ZEROCHK is where the byte in the accumulator is tested to see if it is a zero (line 2100). If it's not, the program branches back to line 2040 where TESTBYT is reset to zero, and then checks the next byte. If it is a zero, we have to determine if this is the end of an Applesoft line or the end of the program. To do this we check TESTBYT and see if it is equal to two (lines 2120 and 2130). If it is (line 2140), this is the end of the program and the program branches to a routine that stores all of the pointers. If it's not equal to two, we increment TESTBYT by 1 and go back to check the next byte. As you see, TESTBYT is used to determine how many consecutive zeros we have encountered. The end of the program is indicated by three consecutive zeros; one for the end of line marker and two instead of the next line pointer.

The EXIT routine is where all of the Applesoft pointers are adjusted. These include the end of program pointer (PRGEND), the start of variable storage (VARTAB), the start of array storage (ARYTAB) and the end of string storage (STREND). In line 2170, the Y-register is incremented by one because we want to point to one past the three consecutive zero bytes. The Y-register is then transferred to the accumulator (line 2180) and the high-byte of POINTER is incremented if a page boundary is crossed (lines 2190 and 2200). All of the appropriate zero page pointers are updated in lines 2210 to 2290.

continued on page 6

In the Next Issue
THE ULTIMATE LINE HIDER

ASPD PROGRAM DISKETTES AVAILABLE FOR ONLY $15 EACH

Every month we will make a DOS 3.3 diskette available that contains all of the programs for the current issue of *Apple Software Protection Digest.*

Each diskette is available for only $15 each. Diskette 1 contains the programs from issues 1 and 2. There are currently 3 diskettes available.

To order send a check, money order or your credit card number and expiration date to:

REDLIG SYSTEMS, INC.
2068 - 79th Street
Brooklyn, New York 11214

REDLIG SYSTEMS, INC.
2068 79th Street
Brooklyn, New York 11214

BULK RATE
U.S. POSTAGE
PAID
BROOKLYN, NY
Permit No. 631

APPLE SOFTWARE PROTECTION DIGEST

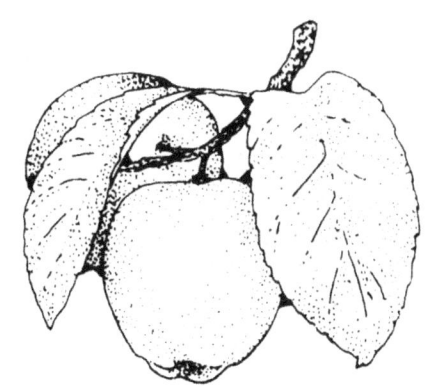

$3.00

Vol. 1, No. 5   1986

THE JUDGE WAS WRONG

Contents

Editorial 1
Cracks Wanted 2
Letters 2
Bugs 2
Crack Index 2
DOS 3.3: In the Back Door,
   Through the Drive Door...... 3
How to Crack It's the Pits....... 5
The Ultimate Line Hider 6
Coming Next Issue 10

Apple Software Protection Digest

Publisher & Editor, Jules H. Gilder; Contributing Editor, J. Scott Barrus. Copyright © 1986 by Redlig Systems, Inc., 2068 - 79th Street, Brooklyn, New York 11214. All rights reserved. No part of this publication may be reproduced, or electronically transmitted or stored without the publisher's written permission. Published monthly at $24 per year by Redlig Systems, Inc. (718) 232-8429. Reprints of prior issues available at $3 each. Printed in the U.S.A.

Apple is a registered trademark of Apple Computer Inc.

In late October, a federal court judge in San Francisco issued a ruling that could have disasterous results for the American software industry. In his ruling, Judge William H. Orrick upheld the right of a software developer to copyright the overall appearance, structure and sequence of screens used in a program.

The ruling came in a copyright infringement suit filed by both Broderbund Software and Pixellite Software against Unison World, Inc., and the programs involved in the suit were Broderbund's *Print Shop* and Unison's *Printmaster*. Broderbund's was the first of the two on the market and Unison's is functionally identical to it. What Unison apparently did was look at how the program operated and asked programmers to sit down and do the same thing, on their own, without stealing any code from Broderbund. Apparently they succeeded, because the suit did not charge Unison with "plagarism." Rather, it claims that the use of a similar (although clearly different) screen format and a similar sequence of screens violates the program's copyright. Unfortunately for all of us, the judge upheld their claim.

The public will suffer

If the decision is not appealed and overturned, all owners of personal computers will suffer for it. No longer will companies have to worry about producing a bug-free product. If they're the first to annoucnce what potentially could be a good product, all they have to do is foist it upon an unsuspecting public and prove to the world that they were out with it first. No one can compete head on with them, because of their "look and feel" copyright.

Not only will we see the quality of initial offerings drop, but we'll also see the prices of this inferior software skyrocket. With no competition, there would be no incentive for developers to keep prices low. Another unhappy result of this decision will be to stifle the development of better software. If company A comes out with a product and company B figures out a way to make a similar but far superior product, shouldn't they be allowed to do it? In commenting on the judge's ruling, Lindsey C. Kiang, Lotus Corp.'s (the maker of 1-2-3) lawyer said, "I don't buy the idea that progress in the industry depends on copying other people's work." Those are pretty high and mighty words, but where would Lotus be today if it didn't copy the spreadsheet idea from VisiCorp, manufacturers of VisiCalc, the original electronic spreadsheet?

Judge Orrick we feel your decision was dead wrong and hope it gets overturned.

Jules H. Gilder

Publisher & Editor

Cracks Wanted

Listed below are programs that our readers would like to unprotected. Anyone who comes up with a method of removing the protection from any of these programs will get a free three-month subscription, or extension to **ASPD**, so get those solutions in.

If you have a program that you'd like to see unprotected, please let us know, and we'll add it to our list so that some of our readers can try their hands at it.

1. Ace Writer II
2. Aztec
3. Bag of Tricks
4. Batter Up!
5. Blazing Paddles
6. Certificate Maker
7. Compress Software
8. Crush, Crumble & Chomp
9. Dazzle Draw
10. Disk-O-Check
11. Magic Memory
12. Newsroom
13. Sargon III
14. Sensible Speller - DOS
15. Sensible Speller - ProDOS
16. Success With Math
17. The Game Show
18. Wizardry
19. Word Handler

Bugs

Although we spend a lot of time testing and rechecking all the information we present here, every once in a while a problem will crop up. As soon as I find out about it, I'll let you know in this column. It is my sincere hope that this column will be missing from most issues, and be very short in those issues in which it is included.

Print Shop Companion

In Vol. 1, No. 2 we listed the COPYP parameters the you could use to make a backup copy of the *Print Shop Companion*. Unfortunately there was a bug in it which was corrected in Vol. 1, No. 4. While this bug allowed you to make backup copies of the program, it wouldn't always work. We have now come up with a sure-fire solution which will consistently produce good backup copies of *Print Shop Companion*. Simply add the following lines to your COPYP program (see Vol. 1, No. 2, p. 2).

```
72   POKE 863,34
1000 DATA 3,6,25,160,96
1010 DATA 3,6,26,0,64
```

Letters

Dear Editor:

My subscription to the **Apple Software Protection Digest** started with Vol. 1, No. 3 and it's just great. Your explanation of cracking techniques using Applewriter //e as an example suddenly clarified a whole bunch of things I've heard and read elsewhere, but couldn't quite grasp. Alas, I also discovered that Vol. 1, No. 2 apparently has some great stuff in it too, including a crack for the *Print Shop Companion*, for which I have been looking ever since last Christmas. Please send me a back issue of Vol. 1, No. 2, for which I am enclosing a check for $3.

Donald L. Martin
Santa Barbara, CA

I'm glad that you enjoyed our article on "How to Crack Applewriter". We try to put things in simple, nontechnical language so that you don't have to be a hacker to use the information. A new version of the Print Shop Companion crack is in this issue of **ASPD**. *A copy of Vol. 1, No. 2 has already been sent to you.*

Dear Editor:

Your publication has provided me with lots of information and ideas. Keep up the good work. Enclosed with this letter is a short article on a simple modification to normal DOS 3.3 that renders some protection schemes ineffective. I would like to have this included in one of your future issues. If accepted, please give authoring credit and extend my subscription as you offered.

David Stoll
Manitoba, CANADA

I'm glad you enjoy our newsletter David. Thanks for your article, Five Byte Disk Analyzer. *We've scheduled it for publication in the next issue of* **ASPD**. *Your subscription has been extended. Keep the articles coming.*

Crack Index

In order to make life just a little more convenient for you, each issue of **Apple Software Protection Digest** will contain a list of all the programs cracked so far, and what issues those cracks appeared in. This will save you from going through all past issues of the digest in order to find a particular program.

Applewriter //e - Vol. 1, No. 3, p. 3
Bookends - Vol. 1, No. 1, p. 7
Financial Cookbook - Vol. 1, No. 3, p. 6
Hayes Terminal Program - Vol. 1, No. 3, p. 11
Homeword - Vol. 1, No. 2, p. 9
Homeword Speller - Vol. 1, No. 2, p. 9
Microwave - Vol. 1, No. 3, p. 11
PFS PLAN - Vol. 1, No. 2, p. 9
PFS Series (ProDOS) - Vol. 1, No. 2, p. 7
Print Shop - Vol. 1, No. 1, p. 10
Print Shop Companion - Vol. 1, No.2, p. 6, Vol. 1, No. 5
Sensible Grammar - Vol. 1, No. 2, p. 7
Time Is Money - Vol. 1, No. 2, p. 9

DOS 3.3: IN THE BACK DOOR, THROUGH THE DRIVE DOOR

There is a little documented trap or error in DOS 3.3 that will often allow you to get into BASIC or the monitor without any hardware modification. To understand the trap, one needs to examine the way DOS works. In the boot process, normal DOS loads itself and then proceeds to run the HELLO program of the file type set when the diskette was initialized. DOS contains *vectors* or pointers which tell it many things, inculding where to go in the event of an error. The standard DOS error routine is set up to print error messages when appropriate and then return to BASIC. When a program is running, the ONERR flag traps the condition without interruption.

The weak link in this chain of activity is the small period of time between the loading of DOS and the loading and execution of the HELLO program. Try an experiment with a write-protected backup copy of a normal DOS 3.3 diskette—the System Master will do just fine. Boot the diskette. The moment you see the Applesoft BASIC prompt], open the door on the disk drive. DOS should be in the process of loading the HELLO program, and because it can no longer read data from the diskette, go immediately to the error handling routine which will print out a message saying that an I/O Error has occurred.

Now, close the door of the disk drive and type **CATALOG**. After a few moments of grinding sounds, during which time the disk drive is recalibrating the position of the head, you will see the catalog of files on the diskette. And, if you carefully examine the situation, you will find that you have complete access to all the normal DOS commands as well as the monitor. You can then load and examine programs at will. There is one thing you should be very careful about however, even though you have access to DOS and the monitor, you may find that the DOS that is loaded into memory may be a modified *protection* DOS. Part of this modification may take the form of renamed DOS commands, so you'll have to examine some DOS memory locations to determine if the commands have been changed or not. You can easily do this by entering the short Applesoft program, *DOS COMMAND COMPARER*, that is shown in the listing.

How the program works

The operation of this program is very simple. It looks in memory where that names of all the DOS commands are supposed to be stored—between locations 43140 and 43271—and takes the data stored there and converts it into a string (lines 50 to 70). In order to determine when the end of a particular command is reached, without having to waste an extra byte as a delimiter between commands (such as a space), the designers of DOS added 128 to the ASCII value of the last letter of each command. We can use this fact to determine where each command ends (line 40) and then set the string we've constructed equal to one of the elements in the A$(X) array (line 70). Now that we know what the commands are for the DOS we're examining, we can compare it to the standard set of DOS 3.3 commands by reading them in from the DATA statements in lines 180 to 240. This will produce a comparison listing on the screen. If you want a printed listing just include the following line to turn your printer on:

145 PR#1

and the next line to turn your printer off when the program is finished:

250 PR#0

Useful for old programs and new

This method of breaking out of a protected program is most useful for older programs where only minor modifications were made to standard DOS to make it difficult to copy the program. This technique is also useful on the newer *hidden bit* protection schemes, where information is hidden between

```
  1   REM DOS COMMAND COMPARER PROGRAM
  2   REM
 10   DIM A$(28)
 20   N = 1
 30   FOR X = 43140 TO 43271
 40     IF  PEEK (X) > 128 THEN 60
 50     A$ = A$ +  CHR$ ( PEEK (X) ): NEXT X
 60     A$ = A$ +  CHR$ ( PEEK (X) - 128 )
 70     A$(N) = A$
 80     A$ = ""
 90     N = N + 1
100   NEXT X
110   PRINT : PRINT "DOS COMMAND COMPARER"
120   PRINT : PRINT "STANDARD DOS","THIS VERSION OF DOS"
130   PRINT "============","===================="
140   PRINT
150   FOR X = 1 TO 28
160     READ T$: PRINT T$,A$(X)
170   NEXT
180   DATA INIT,LOAD,SAVE,RUN
190   DATA CHAIN,DELETE,LOCK,UNLOCK
200   DATA CLOSE,READ,EXEC,WRITE
210   DATA POSITION,OPEN,APPEND,RENAME
220   DATA CATALOG,MON,NOMON,PR#
230   DATA IN#,MAXFILES,FP,INT
240   DATA BSAVE,BLOAD,BRUN,VERIFY
```

bytes on a specific sector. In general, most software publishers try to maintain a high degree of similarity between their *protected DOS* and standard DOS 3.3 so they won't get caught off guard by hardware modifications by Apple that will make their software unusable.

Two examples of programs that this technique can be used on are *Font Downloader* by RAKWARE and *Smart Eyes* by Addison-Wesley. *Font Downloader* is an example of an older program which can be entered through the back door. After you break out of the boot process by opening the drive door and you fall into the Applesoft mode (where you'll see the] prompt displayed), you will be able to LOAD and BLOAD all of the program files except two configuration text files (the flags for those are in the BASIC programs and can be manipulated easily). Now, in order to transfer these files to an unprotected diskette, just place a previously initialized DOS 3.3 diskette into drive 2 (you can use drive 1 and swap diskettes if you don't have a second drive) and LOAD or BLOAD each file into RAM one at a time and then SAVE or BSAVE it to the DOS 3.3 diskette.

If you're using the BLOAD and BSAVE commands for binary (B) files, you'll have to determine the starting address (in hexadecimal) of the file by looking at locations $AA72 and $AA73. This gives you the address in reverse order, low-byte first. Next, look at locations $AA60 and $AA61 for the length of the file, again in hexadecimal and in reverse order. Don't forget to use this information when BSAVEing a file. To BSAVE a binary file called TEST after you've determined the starting address and length of the file you would enter:

BSAVE TEST, A$aaaa, L$bbbb

where **aaaa** is the hexadecimal value of the starting address and **bbbb** is the hexadecimal value of the length of the file. *Smart Eyes*, from Addison-Wesely, is an example of one of the newer programs that uses the *hidden bit* protection scheme. In addition to using the hidden bit technique, *Smart Eyes* also uses a nibble count routine for additional protection. This will have to be disabled. Instructions on how to do that follow.

Disable the nibble count

Smart Eyes has a HELLO program that BRUNs SMART.OBJ, which has a starting address of $4000 and a length of $5480. SMART.OBJ does some housekeeping on start up and then implements the nibble count protection scheme. Let's look at some of the code from the beginning of the program:

```
1. 4000- AD AD AD    LDA   $ADAD
2. 4003- A0 00       LDY   #$00
3. 4005- 99 63 08    STA   $0863,Y
4. 4008- 88          DEY
5. 4009- D0 FA       BNE   $4005
6. 400B- 20 63 93    JSR   $9363
7. 400E- A5 01       LDA   $01
8. 4010- D0 F9       BNE   $400B
9. 4012- AD 11 11    LDA   $1111
```

As you can seee from the partial listing above, I've added line numbers to what would normally be a simple disassembly produced by typing **4000L** from the monitor mode. The line numbers are only there to make it easy for me to reference specific lines during the discussion. The protection checking routine starts at location $400B (line 6) with a JSR $9363. When the program returns from this routine, a flag value will be stored in location $01 if everything is okay. The program then checks the contents of location $01 to see if it is any value but zero (lines 7 and 8). If it is, it continues to execute the program (line 9). Otherwise, it goes back and runs the check loop forever (line 8).

The check loop can easily be disabled by replacing the branching code in line 8 with NOP (no operation) instructions as shown below in the new lines 8 and 9. With these NOP instruction in place, it doesn't matter whether the diskette passes the "protection test" or not, the program just continues to go on operating. When unprotecting programs with nibble counts, you may find that the program contains more than one call to the nibble count routine, but in this case, the program only checks for the protection scheme once.

```
7. 400E- A5 01       LDA   $01
8. 4010- EA          NOP
9. 4011- EA          NOP
10. 4012- AD 11 11   LDA   $1111
```

Cracking it step-by-step

Now I'll give you step-by-step instructions on how to crack *Smart Eyes*.

STEP 1. To start off with, you'll need to make a copy of the original diskette. NEVER WORK ON THE ORIGINAL!!

STEP 2. After you have a copy of the program, boot it up and get into DOS via the back door as explained earlier.

STEP 3. BLOAD SMART.OBJ and change the two bytes at $4010 and $4011 to NOPs ($EAs) and then BSAVE the program back to the diskette.

That's all there is to it. You now have an unprotected copy of *Smart Eyes*. If you want to disable the nibble count on other programs you should look for a call to DOS' RWTS (Read and Write a Track and Sector) routine. Bear in mind that not all calls to RWTS will involve protection checking, especially if the program interacts with the disk a lot, but its a good place to start. To find this routine scan memory for a JSR $3D9, which would be represented by the byte sequence: 20 D9 03. I use the scanning program that S-C Software gives away on its *S-C Macro Assembler* diskette. It's short and easy to key in. A copy of it is listed in ASPD Vol. 1, No. 3, p. 4. Once you find the JSR, examine the four locations prior to it. These should contain an LDY instruction and an LDA instruction, which are used to setup the parameters for the RWTS routine. Once you've found that, look for a subroutine jump that goes to the RWTS setup code. In the case of *Smart Eyes*, the subroutine jump we want is located

(continued on page 10)

HOW TO CRACK IT'S THE PITS

by Philip Goetz
Ellicott City, MD

It's the Pits is a program produced by Cactus Computer Co, of Moscow, Idaho. It is a total-load program which doesn't do any disk accessing while the program is running. Therefore, it is possible to unprotect the program and store the whole thing as a single disk file. In order to unprotect this program you will need at least a 48K Apple with one disk drive, a DOS 3.3 initialized diskette with at least 105 sectors free the old Integer F8 ROM or some other way to get into the monitor and of course the *It's the Pits* program diskette.

Boot code tracing proved fruitless for me, so I installed my old F8 ROM, booted up, pressed RESET, and looked through memory. The program begins at $1800 and runs to $3FFF, with pictures on non-displayable hi-res pages 4 and 5 ($8000-BFFF). (Oddly enough, this program uses page 2 for display and page 3 as a background preserver. If you want to examine the shape generator which draws on the screen, it begins near $1900.) On bootup, the program loads these 2 pictures at $4000-7FFF and moves them to $8000-BFFF. We can do this too. A little experimenting reveals that the game starts at $185A. So we need our file to move 2 pictures to hi-res pages 4 and 5, set the reset vector to $185A, and clear the high score to zero. By setting a high score, pressing reset, and searching zero page, we see that it is kept at $63-65.

So, here are the steps to unlock *It's the Pits*. If you have an Integer BASIC Apple II, skip steps 2 and 3. Neither I nor Apple Software Protection Digest are responsible for any damage you do to your computer. The main danger is that you could break off pins while pulling the F8 ROM out or putting it in. If you are patient, you shouldn't have any problems.

STEP 1. Boot a normal disk with 105 free sectors and rename the HELLO program so it won't be loaded on bootup.

STEP 2. Open the Apple lid, touch the power supply to release any static electricity you may have, and carefully pry off the Applesoft F8 ROM. It is on the left-hand side of the motherboard in the middle between front and back with the words ROM-F8 in front of it. Note that there is some kind of mark on one end of the chip, consistent with marks on all the other chips. Whenever inserting a chip, use this mark to make sure that you put it in the right way. If you don't have a chip puller, pry the chip off by gently rocking it back and forth. Don't force it, and make sure you exert very little pressure so it doesn't come flying out and bend its pins.

STEP 3. Install an old Integer F8 ROM. You can buy these from most Apple dealers for about $15. Note that with the old ROM, you have the monitor Step and Trace functions, but cannot use the ESC-I,J,K, or M. You can use ESC-A,B,C, and D, but they are less convenient.

STEP 4. Boot *It's the Pits*. When the picture appears, press RESET. You should fall into the monitor and receive a * prompt.

STEP 5. Type **4000<8000.BFFFM**

STEP 6. Type the following startup code.

```
1828:A0 00 A9 00 85 42 85 3C
:A9 80 85 43 A9 40 85 3D
```

(continued on page 10)

```
  5  D$=CHR$(4)
 10  PRINT D$;"BLOAD IT'S THE PITS": HIMEM: 4096
 20  TEXT : HOME : PRINT   TAB( 15)"IT'S THE PITS"
 30  G =   PEEK (7209): PRINT : PRINT "1. GRIMPI : "G:SL =
       PEEK (7251) + 1: PRINT : PRINT "2. M STARTING LEVEL : "SL:
       PRINT : PRINT "3. N SPEEDS : ";: FOR C = 10976 TO 10981:
       PRINT    PEEK (C)",";: NEXT : PRINT    PEEK (10982)
 40  PRINT : PRINT "4. A SPEEDS : ";: FOR C = 10984 TO 10989:
       PRINT    PEEK (C)",";: NEXT : PRINT    PEEK (10990)
 50  U =   PEEK (7048) - 128:D =   PEEK (7064) - 128:L =   PEEK
       (7056) - 128:R =   PEEK (7072) - 128: PRINT : PRINT "5. UP "
       CHR$ (U): PRINT : PRINT "6. DOWN " CHR$ (D): PRINT :
       PRINT "7. LEFT " CHR$ (L): PRINT : PRINT "8. RIGHT " CHR$ (R)
 60  PRINT : PRINT "9. RUN PROGRAM": PRINT : PRINT "WHICH? ";:
       GET A$:C =   VAL (A$): IF   NOT C OR C < 0 THEN 20
 70  V = C * 2 + 1: VTAB V: ON C GOTO 90,110,130,150,170,180,190,200
 80  CALL 6184
 90  HTAB 13: GET A$:G =   VAL (A$): IF   NOT G OR G > 9 THEN 20
100  PRINT A$: POKE 7209,G: POKE 7229,G: POKE 7243,G: GOTO 20
110  HTAB 23: GET A$:SL =   VAL (A$): IF   NOT SL OR SL > 6 THEN 20
120  SL = SL - 1: PRINT A$: POKE 7251,SL: GOTO 20
130  HTAB 14: INPUT " ";C(0),C(1),C(2),C(3),C(4),C(5),C(6):
       FOR D = 0 TO 6: IF C(D) > 255 THEN 20
140  POKE 10976 + D,C(D): NEXT : GOTO 20
150  HTAB 14: INPUT " ";C(0),C(1),C(2),C(3),C(4),C(5),C(6):
       FOR D = 0 TO 6: IF C(D) > 255 THEN 20
160  POKE 10984 + D,C(D): NEXT : GOTO 20
170  HTAB 7: GET A$:U =   ASC (A$): POKE 7048,U + 128: GOTO 20
180  HTAB 9: GET A$:D =   ASC (A$): POKE 7064,D + 128: GOTO 20
190  HTAB 9: GET A$:L =   ASC (A$): POKE 7056,L + 128: GOTO 20
200  HTAB 10: GET A$:R =   ASC (A$): POKE 7072,R + 128: GOTO 20
```

THE ULTIMATE LINE HIDER PROGRAM

by Grant Stevens
Broad Brook, CT

When I first issued a challenge to **ASPD** readers to come up with a machine language program that would implement the line hiding technique that used the 5 colons (see **ASPD** Vol. 1, No.1) I had hoped that someone would come up with a complete program that would not only change the appropriate colon to a zero, but would also insert the colons automatically. But no one did, until recently when I received a program from Grant Stevens. Grant's program, which I call, "*The Ultimate Line Hider*" does that and more.

The program lets you protect a single line or a whole range of lines. In addition, Grant has made provision for allowing you to enter a four-character code which will be imbedded in each coded line. Finally, Grant has included a routine that will unprotect lines that were hidden with this technique. Since Grant implemented all of the features I originally specified in my challenge, I am giving him a free seven month extension to his subscription, even though his entry was late. You did a nice job Grant.

How it works

The Ultimate Line Hider program starts out by setting the ampersand (&) jump vector so that the computer will jump to the start of the program whenever the ampersand key is pressed. The sixteen bytes of code that are used to set this vector will only be run once, after that, they can be eliminated. For this reason, Grant has placed them in the last part of the input buffer, starting at $2F0, so if it is accidentally wiped out, it has no affect on the program.

The actual program starts on line 1610 where the processor status register is saved on the stack and a check is made to see if a number or a U follows the ampersand. If it is a digit, the pro-

```
             1000 *****************************
             1010 ***                       ***
             1020 ***  THE ULTIMATE LINE HIDER  ***
             1030 ***                       ***
             1040 ***      by Grant Stevens    ***
             1050 ***                       ***
             1060 *****************************
             1070 *
             1080 *
             1090 *
             1100 * SYNTAX: &[U] LNUM1 [- LNUM2] [STREXPR]
             1110 *
             1120 * RAM USAGE
             1130 *
0006-        1140 STRING     .EQ    $6
003C-        1150 A1L        .EQ    $3C
003D-        1160 A1H        .EQ    $3D
003E-        1170 A2L        .EQ    $3E
003F-        1180 A2H        .EQ    $3F
0042-        1190 A4L        .EQ    $42
0043-        1200 A4H        .EQ    $43
0050-        1210 LNUM       .EQ    $50
0069-        1220 LOMEM      .EQ    $69
0094-        1230 MOVEND     .EQ    $94
0096-        1240 MVSTART    .EQ    $96
009B-        1250 LINADRS    .EQ    $9B
009D-        1260 STRLEN     .EQ    $9D
009E-        1270 STRADR     .EQ    $9E
00AF-        1280 PGMEND     .EQ    $AF
00B1-        1290 CHRGET     .EQ    $B1
00B7-        1300 CHRGOT     .EQ    $B7
03F5-        1310 AMPVEC     .EQ    $3F5
             1320 *
             1330 * ROM USAGE
             1340 *
D39A-        1350 MOVEUP     .EQ    $D39A
D4F5-        1360 EXIT       .EQ    $D4F5
D61A-        1370 FINDLIN    .EQ    $D61A
D66C-        1380 CLEAR      .EQ    $D66C
DA0C-        1390 LINGET     .EQ    $DA0C
DD6C-        1400 STRCK      .EQ    $DD6C
DD7B-        1410 EVAL       .EQ    $DD7B
DEC0-        1420 SYNCHEK    .EQ    $DEC0
DEC9-        1430 SYNTAX     .EQ    $DEC9
FE2C-        1440 MOVDOWN    .EQ    $FE2C
             1450 *
             1460            .OR    $2F0
             1470 *
             1480 * Set up the ampersand (&) vector to jump to
             1490 * the start of the program.
             1500 *
02F0- A9 4C  1510            LDA    #$4C
02F2- 8D F5 03 1520          STA    AMPVEC
02F5- A9 00  1530            LDA    #START
02F7- 8D F6 03 1540          STA    AMPVEC+1
02FA- A9 03  1550            LDA    /START
02FC- 8D F7 03 1560          STA    AMPVEC+2
02FF- 60     1570            RTS
             1580 *
             1590 * Execution of the & begins here. Get the line number(s)
             1595 * and optional code string.
             1600 *
0300- 08     1610 START      PHP           Save Hide/Unhide selection.
0301- 90 11  1620            BCC    START.1  Branch if digit follows "&".
```

gram branches to line 1700 where the number is retrieved. If it's not a number, then the only other correct character is a capital U. In line 1630, a capital U is loaded into the accumulator and then a jump is made to the syntax checking routine in the Apple ROMs. If the character is a capital U the program returns from the syntax checking routine with the carry bit cleared and then a branch is made to line 1700 where the line number is retrieved. If the character is not the required U, then the carry bit is set and the program jumps to a routine in the Apple's ROMs that prints out the SYNTAX ERROR message (line 1660).

As was mentioned earlier, at line 1700, the number following the ampersand is retrieved here. The Apple's LINGET routine is used to do this. When it gets the number, it converts it to hexadecimal and stores it in zero page locations (LNUM) $50 and $51, low byte first. Next the accumulator is temporarily stored on the stack (line 1710) because the next routine that is called destroys the contents of the accumulator. This routine, also in the Apple ROMs, is called FINDLIN. It starts at the beginning of an Applesoft program and searches for the line number that is currently stored in LNUM and LNUM+1. If the line is found, its beginning address is stored in two other zero page locations called LINADRS and LINADRS +1 ($9B and $9C).

Upon returning from the FINDLIN routine, the program restores the accumulator by pulling the value it temporarily stored on the stack off (line 1730) and then checks it to see if there is supposed to be a second line number (line 1740). If there is, the program goes to line 1760 where an attempt is made to retrieve the number. If no number is found, a syntax error message is generated (line 1770). If a number is found, it is retrieved and converted to hexadecimal (line 1780). If there is not supposed to be a second line number, or if there is and it is successfully retrieved, control is passed to line 1790 where the buffer area that is used to store the four letter

```
0303- A9 55      1630             LDA  #$55          If not a digit, must be a "U".
0305- 20 C0 DE   1640             JSR  SYNCHEK
0308- 90 0A      1650             BCC  START.1       Error if no line number.
030A- 4C C9 DE   1660 SYNTAX1     JMP  SYNTAX        Print SYNTAX ERROR
                                                     message.
030D- 28         1670 DONE        PLP                Clear Hide/Unhide from stack.
030E- 20 6C D6   1680             JSR  CLEAR
0311- 4C F5 D4   1690             JMP  EXIT          End.
0314- 20 0C DA   1700 START.1     JSR  LINGET        Get the first line number.
0317- 48         1710             PHA
0318- 20 1A D6   1720             JSR  FINDLIN       Point to the selected line.
031B- 68         1730             PLA
031C- C9 C9      1740             CMP  #$C9          Is there a second line
                                                     number?
031E- D0 08      1750             BNE  NOLNUM        Branch if no.
0320- 20 B1 00   1760             JSR  CHRGET
0323- B0 E5      1770             BCS  SYNTAX1       Error—no line number found.
0325- 20 0C DA   1780             JSR  LINGET        Get second line number.
0328- A2 03      1790 NOLNUM      LDX  #$3           Get ready to clear the
032A- A9 A0      1800             LDA  #$A0          string storage area.
032C- 95 06      1810 INITSTR     STA  STRING,X      Clear it.
032E- CA         1820             DEX
032F- 10 FB      1830             BPL  INITSTR
0331- 20 B7 00   1840             JSR  CHRGOT        Is there a string expression?
0334- F0 18      1850             BEQ  SETLOM        No, set LOMEM.
0336- 20 7B DD   1860             JSR  EVAL          Yes, get it.
0339- 20 6C DD   1870             JSR  STRCK         Make sure it's a string.
033C- A4 9D      1880             LDY  STRLEN        Find out how long it is.
033E- C0 04      1890             CPY  #$4           Is it longer than 4 letters?
0340- 90 09      1900             BCC  NOTRUNC       No, it's okay, continue.
0342- A0 03      1910             LDY  #$3           Yes, truncate it.
0344- B1 9E      1920 MOVSTR      LDA  (STRADR),Y    Copy string to new area.
0346- 09 80      1930             ORA  #$80
0348- 99 9E 00   1940             STA  STRADR,Y
034B- 88         1950 NOTRUNC     DEY
034C- 10 F6      1960             BPL  MOVSTR
                 1970 *
                 1980 * Now, go through the selected range of line numbers
                 1990 * hiding or unhiding lines within the range.
                 2000 *
034E- A5 AF      2010 SETLOM      LDA  PGMEND        Set LOMEM to default value.
0350- 85 69      2020             STA  LOMEM         This is required by the
0352- A5 B0      2030             LDA  PGMEND+1      EXIT routine.
0354- 85 6A      2040             STA  LOMEM+1
                 2050 *
                 2060 * Process one line.
                 2070 *
0356- A0 01      2080 DOLINE      LDY  #$1
0358- B1 9B      2090             LDA  (LINADRS),Y   Have we reached end of
                                                     program?
035A- F0 B1      2100             BEQ  DONE          Yes, finish up.
035C- C8         2110             INY                No, do this line.
035D- A5 50      2120             LDA  LNUM          Get current line number
035F- D1 9B      2130             CMP  (LINADRS),Y   and see if it is within the
0361- C8         2140             INY                selected line limits.
0362- A5 51      2150             LDA  LNUM+1
0364- F1 9B      2160             SBC  (LINADRS),Y
0366- 90 A5      2170             BCC  DONE          It's not, finish up.
0368- 28         2180             PLP                Recall Hide/Unhide selection.
0369- 08         2190             PHP
036A- C8         2200             INY                Now Y=4.
036B- B1 9B      2210             LDA  (LINADRS),Y
036D- 90 27      2220             BCC  HIDELIN       Hide the line.
                 2230 *
                 2235 * Unhide one line.
                 2240 *
036F- D0 4E      2250             BNE  NEXTLIN       Don't unhide if not hidden.
```

code is blanked out. Then in line 1840, a check is made to see if the user entered a string that is to be hidden in each erased line. If there is none, the program jumps to line 2010. If there is, it is retrieved in line 1860.

Once the code data is retrieved, another of the Apple's ROM routines is used to verify that in fact the data is a string and not a number (line 1870). The routine that checks to see if a string was entered, also stores the length of the string in zero page location $9D. The program next retrieves the length of the string (line 1880) and checks to see if it is more than four characters long (line 1890). If it's not, the Y-register is decremented by one (line 1950) so that it will contain the proper count (3) to handle all four code characters. If the string is longer than four characters, the string is truncated by loading a 3 into the Y-register (line 1910). In either case, the program goes to line 1920 next where each character of the code is retrieved in turn and the high bit is set to zero (line 1930). The string is then stored in a new area (line 1940).

After the string has been moved, LOMEM is set to its default value (the end of the program) and the program then begins to process a single line (line 2080). The first thing that the line processor does is to check if the end of the program has been reached. If it has, control is passed to the routine labelled DONE (line 2100). If not, the Y-register is incremented so that it will be pointing to the low byte of the line number and the number of the current line is loaded into the accumulator (line 2120). It is then checked to see if the current line is within the range of the lines we are processing. If it's not, the program branches to the DONE routine and finishes up. If it is, the processor status byte is pulled off the stack to retrieve the Hide/Unhide selection, and stored back on the stack for use again later (lines 2180-2190).

Next, the Y-register is incremented to 4, so that it points to the fifth byte in the BASIC program line (remember we

```
0371— A5 69      2260            LDA    LOMEM
0373— 85 3E      2270            STA    A2L
0375— E9 05      2280            SBC    #$5          Carry is set.
0377— 85 69      2290            STA    LOMEM        Set up parameters for move.
0379— A5 6A      2300            LDA    LOMEM+1
037B— 85 3F      2310            STA    A2H
037D— E9 00      2320            SBC    #$0
037F— 85 6A      2330            STA    LOMEM+1
0381— A5 9B      2340            LDA    LINADRS
0383— 85 42      2350            STA    A4L
0385— 69 04      2360            ADC    #$4          +1 since carry is set.
0387— 85 3C      2370            STA    A1L
0389— A5 9C      2380            LDA    LINADRS+1
038B— 85 43      2390            STA    A4H
038D— 69 00      2400            ADC    #$0
038F— 85 3D      2410            STA    A1H
0391— 20 2C FE   2420            JSR    MOVDOWN      Note: Y=4
0394— B0 29      2430            BCS    NEXTLIN      (forced)
                 2440  *
                 2450  * Hide one line.
                 2460  *
0396— F0 17      2470  HIDELIN   BEQ    PUTSTR       Don't hide if already hidden.
0398— A5 69      2480            LDA    LOMEM
039A— 85 96      2490            STA    MVSTART
039C— 69 05      2500            ADC    #$5          Carry is clear.
039E— 85 94      2510            STA    MOVEND       Set up parameters for move.
03A0— 85 69      2520            STA    LOMEM
03A2— A5 6A      2530            LDA    LOMEM+1
03A4— 85 97      2540            STA    MVSTART+1
03A6— 69 00      2550            ADC    #$0
03A8— 85 95      2560            STA    MOVEND+1
03AA— 85 6A      2570            STA    LOMEM+1
03AC— 20 9A D3   2580            JSR    MOVEUP       Make room for 5 bytes.
03AF— A0 04      2590  PUTSTR    LDY    #$4          Get ready to hide the line.
03B1— A9 00      2600            LDA    #$0
03B3— 91 9B      2610            STA    (LINADRS),Y  Hide it.
03B5— C8         2620  PSTR.1    INY                 Point to next byte.
03B6— B9 01 00   2630            LDA    STRING-5,Y   Get character to hide.
03B9— 91 9B      2640            STA    (LINADRS),Y  Hide it in line.
03BB— C0 08      2650            CPY    #$8          Done yet?
03BD— 90 F6      2660            BCC    PSTR.1       No, get another character.
                 2670  *
                 2680  * Advance to next program line.
                 2690  *
03BF— C8         2700  NEXTLIN   INY
03C0— B1 9B      2710            LDA    (LINADRS),Y  Look for the end of the line.
03C2— D0 FB      2720            BNE    NEXTLIN      Didn't find it, keep looking.
03C4— 98         2730            TYA                 Found it, set up pointer so
03C5— 38         2740            SEC                 that it points to it.
03C6— 65 9B      2750            ADC    LINADRS
03C8— 85 9B      2760            STA    LINADRS      Point to next line.
03CA— 90 8A      2770            BCC    DOLINE
03CC— E6 9C      2780            INC    LINADRS+1
03CE— B0 86      2790            BCS    DOLINE
```

```
 1  REM BASIC PROGRAM TO INSTALL THE ULTIMATE LINE HIDER
 2  REM
10  TEXT : HOME
20  PRINT : PRINT : PRINT : PRINT
30  PRINT "INSTALLING THE ULTIMATE LINE HIDER..."
40  FOR X = 752 TO 975
50     READ Y
```

start with 0 so byte number 4 is actually the fifth byte). In line 2210 the fifth byte of the current BASIC line is loaded into the accumulator and then the carry bit from the processor status register is checked to see if the line is to be hidden or unhidden (line 2220). If it's to be hidden (the carry bit is clear), the program branches to HIDELN on line 2470.

The first thing the HIDELN routine does is to test the accumulator (which contains the value of the fifth byte) to see if it is already zero (line 2470). If it is, the line is already hidden and does not have to be re-hidden. If it's not hidden, then the program has to be moved up in memory by five bytes to make room for the data required to hide the line (lines 2480-2580). After the program has been moved in memory, a zero is stored in the fifth byte (lines 2590-2610) and the four character code (or four spaces) is added to the line (lines 2620-2660). Once the line has been hidden, the programs pointers are setup to point to the next line to be processed (lines 2700-2780) and then the program goes back to process another line (line 2790).

If the carry bit was set when it was tested in line 2220, the branch is not taken and processing continues with line 2250. This is where the unhide routine begins. The first thing this routine does is to check if the line was already hidden. If it wasn't, there's no need to unhide it and the next line is retrieved. If it was hidden, we simply have to move the BASIC program down in memory five bytes, thus wiping out the hide-a-line code. This is done in lines 2260-2420. The program then gets the next line (line 2430).

Using the program

Using the *Ultimate Line Hider* is easy, but you must make sure you use the correct syntax. You may hide or unhide a single line or a range of lines. If you are going to include a four-letter code in you hidden lines, it must be surrounded by quotation marks. Thus to hide lines you could type:

&10 (no code included)
&10"JHG" (3 letter code included)
&10-100
&10-100"ABCD"

To unhide lines you must type in a command line that looks something like one of these:

&U10
&U10-100

When specifying a range of lines, the starting and ending line numbers must be separated by a hyphen and not a comma. To hide or unhide an entire program, use the range 0-63999.

```
60    POKE X,Y
70    NEXT X
80    PRINT : PRINT : PRINT : PRINT "INSTALLATION COMPLETE."
90    PRINT : PRINT "TYPE 'CALL 752' TO RUN PROGRAM."
100   DATA 169,76,141,245,3,169,0,141
110   DATA 246,3,169,3,141,247,3,96
120   DATA 8,144,17,169,85,32,192,222
130   DATA 144,10,76,201,222,40,32,108
140   DATA 214,76,245,212,32,12,218,72
150   DATA 32,26,214,104,201,201,208,8
160   DATA 32,177,0,176,229,32,12,218
170   DATA 162,3,169,160,149,6,202,16
180   DATA 251,32,183,0,240,24,32,123
190   DATA 221,32,108,221,164,157,192,4
200   DATA 144,9,160,3,177,158,9,128
210   DATA 153,158,0,136,16,246,165,175
220   DATA 133,105,165,176,133,106,160,1
230   DATA 177,155,240,177,200,165,80,209
240   DATA 155,200,165,81,241,155,144,165
250   DATA 40,8,200,177,155,144,39,208
260   DATA 78,165,105,133,62,233,5,133
270   DATA 105,165,106,133,63,233,0,133
280   DATA 106,165,155,133,66,105,4,133
290   DATA 60,165,156,133,67,105,0,133
300   DATA 61,32,44,254,176,41,240,23
310   DATA 165,105,133,150,105,5,133,148
320   DATA 133,105,165,106,133,151,105,0
330   DATA 133,149,133,106,32,154,211,160
340   DATA 4,169,0,145,155,200,185,1
350   DATA 0,145,155,192,8,144,246,200
360   DATA 177,155,208,251,152,56,101,155
370   DATA 133,155,144,138,230,156,176,134
```

DON'T MISS A SINGLE ISSUE OF

Apple Software Protection Digest

SUBSCRIBE TODAY!

DOS 3.3: In the Back Door
(continued from page 4)

at $9373 where a JSR $93F9 can be found. The code at $93F9 looks like this:

```
93F9-   A9 94      LDA  #$94
93FB-   A0 05      LDY  #$05
93FD-   20 D9 03   JSR  $03D9
```

This is the so-called *smoking gun* and is the clue to search for when you're trying to disable code that checks the status of the diskette.

Locking the back door

Now that we've told you how to sneak into many programs through the back door, you're probably wondering why this technique won't work with all programs. The answer is easy, many people simply lock the back door. Locking the back door is not difficult. All you have to do is locate the DOS error handling routine and patch it so that instead of printing out an error message, it jumps to the code that reboots the disk. We'll show you how to do this in a future issue, but in the meantime think about it. You can use the book *Beneath Apple DOS* to find the necessary locations. If you come up with any interesting solutions, let us know.

How to Crack It's the Pits
(continued from page 5)

```
:A9 FF 85 3E A9 7F 85 3F
:20 2C FE A9 5A 8D F2 03
:A9 18 8D F3 03 49 A5 8D
:F4 03 A9 00 85 63 85 64
:85 65
```

STEP 7. If you press ESC when the game menu is displayed, you will get a flashing number congratulating you on your high score. The number that appears has no apparent function. It is stored at $1C5D, $1C61, and $1C65. To change it to zero, for instance, type:

```
1C5D: 0
1C61: 0
1C65: 0
```

STEP 8. Boot the normal disk with 105 free sectors with a **6 ctrl-P**.

STEP 9. Type: BSAVE IT'S THE PITS, A$1828, L$67D8

You can customize the game

If you have 5 more free sectors on the disk and want to gain some control over the program, type in the following program that runs the game. I saved it under the name *PITS*. All of the modifications possible with this program are self-explanatory except for the speed changes. The fastest speed is 0, while the slowest is 128.

Do not modify the program to allow higher values than it does (i.e. over 9 Grimpi) or the screen will fill up with garbage during the game. Also, make sure that you never have more than 9 Grimpi. If you are finishing the second, fourth, or sixth level and have 9 Grimpi left, kill one off or else you will gain a tenth Grimpi when you reach the third, fifth, or seventh level. When the game tries to draw the shape for the "digit" 10, it will fill up the screen with garbage.

COMING NEXT ISSUE

How to Crack DAZZLE DRAW
Unprotecting LOCKSMITH 5.0 Level F and the Fast Disk Backup Routine
Review: LOCKSMITH 6.0
Five Byte Disk Analyzer
Parameters for Backing Up THE HOBBIT, KARATE CHAMP and KUNG-FU MASTER

BECOME AN ASSEMBLY LANGUAGE PROGRAMMING WHIZ

You've spent a lot of time learning Apple assembly language and finally know the difference between BEQ and BCS. Now it's time to put your new-found knowledge to work. Time to throw away your Applesoft programming manual and write programs that make your Apple work like a super-charged, super-fast computer. Time to graduate from the Applesoft BASIC used by beginners, to the 6502 assembly language used by professionals.

To help make this transition, you need an experienced programmer to guide you. You need to develop a library of subroutines that make programming in assembly language as easy as programming in BASIC. You need to learn all the tricks that take experienced assembly language programmers years to acquire. Most important of all, you need the book, *"Now that You Know Apple Assembly Language: What Can You Do With It?"* because it contains all this information *and more.*

It shows you how, step-by-step

"Now That You Know Apple Assembly Language: What Can You Do With It?" will take you step-by-step through the assembly language programming experience. You'll delve into the mysteries of the 6502 stack and learn how to use it to increase the power and versatility of your programs. You'll also learn how to use the Apple's built-in routines to minimize the amount of coding you must do.

Control the output and the input

Frequently it's desirable to gain total control of the computer's output. This book shows you how to *steal control away from the Apple's normal output routines and redirect it to your own program.* Thus if you wanted, you could see the normally invisible control characters, display text on your screen as black on white instead of the normal white on black, format text sent to a printer into pages and much more.

Expand the power of your Apple by *stealing control away from the normal input routines.* Do things like adding a screen print capability, or *convert part of the normal keyboard into a numeric keypad.* It's even possible to *produce self-modifying programs* by EXECing in commands from RAM instead of from the disk drive. Think about the possibilities that offers for protecting your programs. When you want to go back to Applesoft programming, *you'll be able to do it faster with the aid of Applesoft Shorthand,* an assembly language program that types in one or more Applesoft commands at the press of a key, or use another program in the book to *automatically count the number of lines in your Applesoft program.*

With this book you'll also learn about *generating tones and how to figure out the frequency, producing sound effects, teaching your Apple to send Morse code, restoring accidentally erased Applesoft programs, adding new commands to Applesoft and running two Applesoft programs in memory together,* to name a few.

Everything is explained

Unlike other books that merely consist of a collection of programs, this one explains what's happening, where and why. You get detailed descriptions of how the programs work and detailed program listings with virtually every line of code explained. Nothing is left to chance or misinterpretation.

Order now, get 2 FREE gifts

The book costs only $19.95 plus $2 for shipping and handling. Order now and you'll also get a *FREE Programmer's Number Conversion System* that makes it easy to convert between binary, hexadecimal and decimal numbers. No calculators are required. You'll convert numbers almost instantly and wonder how you ever got along without it.

As an extra bonus for prompt ordering, you'll receive a *FREE coupon worth $5 off* the price of a disk with all the assembled programs on it or a disk that contains the source code. These disks normally sell for $15 each. We're offering these FREE gifts for a limited time only, so hurry! *Order today!*

Money-back guarantee*

We're so confident that you'll find this book invaluable and want it in your library, that we're offering a 10-day, no-questions-asked, money-back guarantee. Order the book. Read it and try the programs for ten days. At the end of ten days if you don't think it's worth every penny you paid for it, just send it back in resalable condition and we'll refund your money immediately, no questions asked.

Redlig Systems, Inc., Dept. A 97
2068—79th St., Brooklyn, NY 11214

Please rush me _____ copies of **"Now That You Know Apple Assembly Language: What Can You Do With It?"** at $19.95 each plus $2 shipping and handling. I understand that if I am not delighted with the book I may return it within 10 days for a prompt and courteous refund. In any case, the Programmer's Number Conversion System and $5 coupon are mine to keep.

☐ Enclosed is my check for $ _____

Please charge my credit card:
☐ American Express   ☐ MasterCard   ☐ Visa

Card No. _____ Exp. _____
Signature _____
Name _____
Address _____
City _____ State _____ Zip _____

---

*NOTE: Shipping and handling fees are not refundable.

ASPD PROGRAM DISKETTES AVAILABLE FOR ONLY $15 EACH

Every month we will make a DOS 3.3 diskette available that contains all of the programs for the current issue of *Apple Software Protection Digest*.

Each diskette is available for only $15 each. Diskette 1 contains the programs from issues 1 and 2. There are currently 4 diskettes available.

To order send a check, money order or your credit card number and expiration date to:

REDLIG SYSTEMS, INC.
2068 - 79th Street
Brooklyn, New York 11214

REDLIG SYSTEMS, INC.
2068 79th Street
Brooklyn, New York 11214

BULK RATE
U.S. POSTAGE
PAID
BROOKLYN, NY
Permit No. 631

APPLE SOFTWARE PROTECTION DIGEST

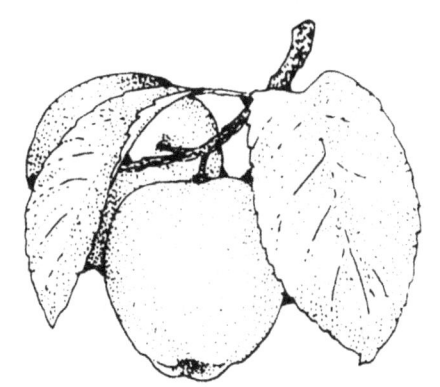

$3.00

Vol. 1, No. 6   1986

Contents

Editorial 1
Cracks Wanted 2
Letters 2
Next Issue 2
Crack Index 2
How to Crack Dazzle Draw 3
Five Byte Disk Analyzer 6
Unprotecting Locksmith 5.0 8
COPYP File Parameters 9
REVIEW: Locksmith 6.0 10

Apple Software Protection Digest

Publisher & Editor, Jules H. Gilder; Contributing Editor, J. Scott Barrus. Copyright © 1986 by Redlig Systems, Inc., 2068 - 79th Street, Brooklyn, New York 11214. All rights reserved. No part of this publication may be reproduced, or electronically transmitted or stored without the publisher's written permission. Published at $24 per year by Redlig Systems, Inc. (718) 232-8429. Reprints of prior issues available at $3 each. Printed in the U.S.A.

Apple is a registered trademark of Apple Computer Inc.

BETTER SOFTWARE WARRANTIES

After years of taking the customer for granted and sticking unsuspecting consumers with programs that have not even been properly tested and debugged, it looks like the software industry is about to make some changes. Forced into action by a proposed bill from California Assemblywoman Gloria Molina, the industry has apparently decided that they'd be better off coming up with their own warranty improvements than having even tougher ones imposed on them by law.

For years software publishers have been passing off disclaimers as limited warranties. Typically these insults to the consumers intelligence go something like this:

This program is provided "as is" without warranty of any kind, either express or implied, including, but not limited to the implied warranties of merchantability and fitness for a particular purpose. The entire risk as to the results and performance of the program is assumed by you. Should the program become defective, you (not the publisher or its dealer) assume the entire cost of all necessary servicing, repair and correction.

That's not a warranty, limited or otherwise. It's just a way of squeezing money out of the unsuspecting consumer withouth having to give him anything of value. To make things even worse, most companies that offer "warranties" such as the one above, also copy protect their programs so that even if you did want to correct their program, you couldn't.

Anyway, at least one legislator had the guts to come out and tell these guys off. Molinas proposed a bill in 1985 that would force publishers to stand behind their products. The bill is currently tabled and Adapso, a computer and software manufacturers organization and the Software Publishers Association are both encouraging their members to adopt a warranty that says the publisher would stand behind the claims made in advertisements, documentation and specification statements. At least 40 companies have improved their warranties so far and one, Micropro, is even offering a 90-day money-back guarantee. Another company, Hayes Microcomputer Products, offers a warranty that guarantees performance.

Software publishers are finally beginning to realize that it is the customer who keeps them afloat, and if they're going to keep their customers, they're going to have to treat them better. Thanks to you Ms. Molinas, you did a good job getting the ball rolling. Now if you could only convince publishers to remove copy protection.

Jules H. Gilder

Publisher & Editor

Cracks Wanted

Listed below are programs that our readers would like to unprotected. Anyone who comes up with a method of removing the protection from any of these programs will get a free three-month subscription, or extension to ASPD, so get those solutions in.

If you have a program that you'd like to see unprotected, please let us know, and we'll add it to our list.

1. Ace Writer II
2. Aztec
3. Bag of Tricks
4. Batter Up!
5. Blazing Paddles
6. Certificate Maker
7. Compress Software
8. Crossword Magic 4.0
9. Crush, Crumble & Chomp
10. Disk-O-Check
11. Magic Memory
12. Newsroom
13. Sargon III
14. Sensible Speller - DOS
15. Sensible Speller - ProDOS
16. Success With Math
17. The Game Show
18. Wizardry
19. Word Handler

Next Issue

The next issue will start to whittle down our list of Cracks Wanted. Among the articles that will be in that issue are:

1. How to Crack Newsroom
2. Unprotecting Sensible Speller (ProDOS)
3. Making a BRUNable Copy of Locksmith's Fast Disk Backup
4. How to Use Two CATALOG Tracks on One Diskette

Letters

Dear Editor:

The issues of your publication that I have received have been very informative, but I'm still learning and I don't have any contributions in the area of copy protection yet. I do have a few questions, however. How does a nibble count protection scheme work? What is bit insertion? How do I form two CATALOG tracks on one diskette? I look forward to hearing from you at your earliest convenience.

Rick A. Crawford
Denver, CO

Don't worry about your not having contributions for us now Rick, but if you come up with something that would be of interest to others, let us know. In the mean time, let's tackle your questions. A nibble count is actually a very simple thing. Generally, one track, usually 34 or 35 but it could be any track, is reserved for the nibble count. This track is specially formatted so that it has a starting header and the rest of the track contains sync bytes. These are special bytes that are 10 bits long and are more difficult to copy than 8-bit bytes. When this track is written, the speed of the drive that is used for writing is generally reduced so that more bytes can fit on the track. This means that drives working at the correct speed can't copy all of the bytes, even if a way is found to read and write the 10-bit bytes. Thus, when the routine that counts the bytes on this track is called, it finds that the wrong number of bytes is present, determines that the disk is a copy and crashes. Bit insertion is when more cycles are used to write a byte to the diskette than usual. This causes more bits to be used to write a byte. That's how we get 10-bit bytes. I'm preparing a tutorial article on both these subjects for a future issue of the digest. As for your last question, in the next Apple Software Protection Digest *there will be an article that will show you how to use two CATALOG tracks on one diskette.*

Crack Index

In order to make life just a little more convenient for you, each issue of **Apple Software Protection Digest** will contain a list of all the programs cracked so far, and what issues those cracks appeared in. This will save you from going through all past issues of the digest in order to find a particular program.

Applewriter //e - Vol. 1, No. 3, p. 3
Bookends - Vol. 1, No. 1, p. 7
Dazzle Draw - Vol. 1, No. 6, p. 3
Financial Cookbook - Vol. 1, No. 3, p. 6
Hayes Terminal Program - Vol. 1, No. 3, p. 11
Homeword - Vol. 1, No. 2, p. 9
Homeword Speller - Vol. 1, No. 2, p. 9
It's the Pits - Vol. 1, No. 5, p. 5
Locksmith 5.0 - Vol. 1, No. 6, p. 8
Karate Champ - Vol. 1, No. 6, p. 9
Microwave - Vol. 1, No. 3, p. 11
PFS PLAN - Vol. 1, No. 2, p. 9
PFS Series (ProDOS) - Vol. 1, No. 2, p. 7
Print Shop - Vol. 1, No. 1, p. 10
Print Shop Companion - Vol. 1, No.2, p. 6, Vol. 1, No. 5
Sensible Grammar - Vol. 1, No. 2, p. 7
Smart Eyes - Vol. 1, No. 5, p. 4
Time Is Money - Vol. 1, No. 2, p. 9

Don't miss a single issue SUBSCRIBE TODAY!

HOW TO CRACK DAZZLE DRAW

by The Executor & Byte Doc

One of the most popular and difficult programs to crack on the Apple is Broderbund's *Dazzle Draw*. This article will give you step-by-step instructions on how to crack this program. Because the protection techniques used on *Dazzle Draw* are more sophisticated than you find on many other programs, the instructions for cracking it will be a little more complicated as well. However, if you follow the step-by-step procedures slowly and carefully, you should be able to make your own unprotected backup copies of the program. We will try to keep the complicated technical information to a minimum to minimize confusion.

When *Dazzle Draw* is first booted up, at some point during the booting process, you'll hear some unusual sounds from the disk drive. Upon close examination of the disk while it was booting, we found that this occurs when the head is located over track 31 ($1F). Closer examination, with the aid of a nibble editor, revealed that this sound was probably an indicator of a nibble count routine that is used to protect the program. In addition to the nibble count routine, examination of the diskette revealed that Broderbund also made a change to the standard address marker that is written onto the diskette when it is formatted. While the normal address marker contains the bytes DE AA, Broderbund has changed the marker to DE FF. This change, which is both simple to make and easy to overcome, will prevent ordinary copy programs from duplicating the diskette.

In order to crack *Dazzle Draw* you are going to need to prepare a few things. First of all, you'll need either an Apple //c or //e with 128K of RAM. This is not asking too much, because *Dazzle Draw* will only work on one of these computers anyway. Of course, you'll also need an original copy of *Dazzle Draw*. Other tools that are required are a sector editor (we're going to modify *COPYP* so that we can use just the sector editor portion of it), one blank diskette, one diskette that has been initialized as a 48K slave (just type INIT HELLO on a 48K or larger system) DOS 3.3 diskette, Apple's ProDOS System (also called User's) diskette and the COPYP program (see ASPD, Vol. 1, No. 2, p. 2). Once you have assembled all of the things you'll need to crack this program, your ready to begin. *Remember, initialize your DOS 3.3 diskette before you begin*.

First copy it with COPYP

The first step of the cracking process is to make a backup copy of *Dazzle Draw* with *COPYP*. In order to do this however, we're going to have to add one line to *COPYP* and change another. The reason for these modifications is, as mentioned earlier, Broderbund has changed the normal address marker. Specifically, they've changed the last byte in the *address field epilog* (see ASPD, Vol. 1, No. 2, p. 20-22 for more details on address and data fields).

To accomodate the modification, we have to change line 910 in *COPYP* so that it reads:

910 DATA 222,255

This change will make it possible for *COPYP* to read information from Broderbund's specially formatted diskette and write that same information out to a diskette that has been formatted with the normal address field epilog byte.

When you use *COPYP* to backup the original *Dazzle Draw* diskette, use the blank, uninitialized diskette as your target diskette. (From now on, we will refer to the *COPYP* produced version of *Dazzle Draw* as the backup copy of *Dazzle Draw*. This is not to be confused with the backup copy that *Dazzle Draw* itself permits you to make.) *COPYP* will automatically initialize the blank diskette as a normal diskette. Save the DOS 3.3 diskette that you already initialized for use later on.

Before you run *COPYP* There are a few more things that you are going to have to do. The first is, you're going to have to add a line to the program that will cause it to only copy the first 31 tracks (Track 30 is the last track we're going to copy, but remember, our first track is track 0, which is how we get 31 tracks even though the last one is track 30). As mentioned earlier, track 31 contains nibble counting information. Since we're going to eliminate the need for the nibble counting routine, and this track would normally be very difficult to copy anyway, we won't need it. The tracks beyond 31 are not used. To make track 30 the last one we copy, all we have to do is add line 76 listed below:

76 POKE 863,30

We've said that tracks 31 to 34 are not used. The way the diskette is currently configured, however, the operating system thinks these tracks are used and thus unavailable. We can change that by doing some sector edits to the diskette's Volume Table Of Contents (VTOC). *Dazzle Draw* is a ProDOS-based diskette, and as such, its VTOC is located on track 0, sector 3. If we change bytes 31 to 34 ($1F to $22) in this sector to $FFs, we can make those tracks available to Pro-DOS. To do that, the following lines should be added to the *COPYP* program:

1000 DATA 0,3,31,0,255
1010 DATA 0,3,32,0,255
1020 DATA 0,3,33,0,255
1030 DATA 0,3,34,0,255

With these final additions made to the *COPYP* program, you are now ready to make your backup copy of *Dazzle Draw*.

After the copy is made, label it and set it aside for a moment. Now, take your ProDOS system diskette and reboot your computer. Exit to BASIC if you're not already there when the boot ends. Now, we're going to create a dummy file with the name PRODOS on our backup copy of *Dazzle Draw*. It is necessary to put this file on the diskette so that we don't get the "UNABLE TO LOAD PRODOS" error message when our copy is booted. To create this dummy file, remove the ProDOS user's diskette from the disk drive and insert your backup copy of *Dazzle Draw*. Now, type the following line:

CREATE PRODOS,TSYS

This should create a new entry in the ProDOS directory on the diskette, with the name of PRODOS.

Now that we've created the dummy file, we have to make some changes to it. To do this we're going to need a sector editor. You can go out and buy one, or, you can use *COPYP* as a sector editor. To do that, all we have to do is disable the copy portion of the program. This is done by adding line 89 below, which causes a jump to the sector editor. The jump is made at line 89 in order to assure that all of the DATA statements that precede the sector edit data are read and program is ready to read the sector editting data. By typing the number 70 (below) and then pressing the RETURN key, we delete line 70 from the *COPYP* program. It's not absolutely necessary to do this, but since we're not copying anything, there's no need to load in the machine language portion of the copy program. The other lines that are listed below, contain the sector editing information.

```
70
89  GOTO 400
1000 DATA 0,11,238,22,38
1010 DATA 0,11,255,248,9
```

We're going to need to use *COPYP* one more time. Reload the program from your disk so that you start with a copy of the original version and not the one we've just modified. Once again we're going to use only the sector editing capabilities of the program. This time however, we're going to copy an entire sector from the ProDOS system master to our backup copy of *Dazzle Draw*. This gets rid of the strange boot sequence used by the original *Dazzle Draw* diskette and in the process eliminates the check for the copy-protected diskette. Modify the fresh copy of *COPYP* by typing in the following lines:

```
70
89  GOTO 400
460 TK=0: SE=0
470
490 PRINT: PRINT"REMOVE THE
    PRODOS SYSTEM DISK"
500 PRINT"INSERT THE BACKUP
    DAZZLE DRAW DISK"
505 INPUT"PRESS <RETURN>
    WHEN YOU'RE READY";Z$
520 GOTO 550
```

Once these lines have been added to the *COPYP* program, place your ProDOS system diskette in drive 1 and run *COPYP*. When the program tells you to, remove the ProDOS system diskette from the drive and replace it with your backup copy of *Dazzle Draw*. Then press RETURN. The boot sector from your ProDOS system diskette will then be transferred to the diskette containing the unprotected version of *Dazzle Draw* that we are creating.

Capturing the program

We have now finished most of the work that is required to produce an unprotected copy of *Dazzle Draw*. The only thing left for us to do now is to capture the startup program and save it out to disk. Do not confuse this with the STARTUP program on the ProDOS system diskette.

In order to capture the startup program, and at the same time eliminate the need for the protection checking subroutines, we're going to have to boot the original program several times and interrupt it at specific points. This part of the *crack* may be the most confusing to you, but if you follow each step exactly, you should have no problems.

To cause the boot to stop exactly where we want it to, we're going to move program code that handles the booting process from it place in ROM (on the disk controller card) into RAM so that we can modify it.

STEP 1. Turn on your Apple //e or //c and press RESET (or CTRL-RESET if your keyboard is setup that way) to turn the disk drive off.

STEP 2. Enter the monitor mode by typing: **CALL -151**

STEP 3. Move the disk controller ROM code to RAM and modify it so that it jumps to the monitor mode by typing the following two line:

8600<C600.C6FFM
86F9:59 FF

STEP 4. Insert your original *Dazzle Draw* diskette in drive 1 and execute a partial boot by typing:

8600G

STEP 5. Your Apple will beep and a monitor prompt (*) will appear. Type in the following lines to turn off the disk drive, modify the next stage of the booting process and reboot the program.

C0E8
843:59 FF
86F9:01 08
8659:50
8600G

STEP 6. When you type the 8600G in STEP 5, your drive will reboot and in a moment the Apple will beep and the monitor prompt will appear. Now let's turn the drive off again and make a few more modifications:

C0E8
602B:0F
843:00 60
850:40

STEP 7. Now, type in this short *capture* routine to save everything in memory from $0000 through $08FF and store it from $8000 through $88FF:

F00:8D FC 0F 8E FD 0F 8C FE
F08:0F BA 8E FF 0F A2 00 BD
F10:00 00 9D 00 80 E8 D0 F7
F18:EE 11 0F EE 14 0F AD 11
F20:0F C9 09 D0 E8 4C 59 FF

STEP 8. Execute this by typing:

8600G

STEP 9. The disk drive will reboot again and in a moment, your Apple will beep and the monitor prompt will appear. At this point, turn off the drive and examine what was in the 6502 registers when the program jumped to the monitor by typing in the following lines:

C0E8
FFC.FFF

STEP 10. Make a note of the values returned for locations $FFC to $FFF. You'll need them later. The contents of $FFC = Accumulator, $FFD = X-register, $FFE = Y-register and $FFF = Stack pointer.

STEP 11. Next, disable the configuration save option by typing:

75C5:A7 7B

STEP 12. Now, take the DOS 3.3 diskette that you initialized earlier and insert it into drive 1, after removing the original *Dazzle Draw* diskette. Boot the DOS 3.3 diskette by typing **C600G** and then save the memory pieces that we've just assembled through this series of partial boots. Saving the file at this point is just a precaution so that you won't have to go through the entire series of partial boots again in case something goes wrong in the following steps. Type in the following lines:

C600G
BSAVE DD,A$6000,L$2900

STEP 13. Enter the monitor and move the program code down to $2100 where it belongs by typing:

CALL -151
2100<6000.88FFM

STEP 14. Type in this routine which reconstructs the memory:

2000:A2 00 BD 00 41 9D 00 00
2008:BD 00 21 9D 00 60 E8 D0
2010:F1 EE 04 20 EE 07 20 EE
2018:0A 20 EE 0D 20 AD 0A 20
2020:C9 41 90 DE 20 9A 61 AD
2028:E9 C0 A2 FF 9A A0 00 A2
2030:60 AD 10 C0 A9 BA 4C 00
2038:64

STEP 15. Now enter the values you wrote down for the four 6502 registers as follows:

2035:xx   (value of the Accumulator)
2030:xx   (value of the X-register)
202E:xx   (value of the Y-register)
202B:xx   (value of the Stack pointer)

STEP 16. Save the whole *Dazzle Draw* startup program by typing in the following line:

BSAVE DAZZLE.SYSTEM,A$2000, L$2A00

STEP 17. Put the DOS 3.3 diskette with the DAZZLE.SYSTEM file on it aside now and boot up the ProDOS system diskette. Execute the DOS converter program by typing:

—CONVERT

STEP 18. If you have a two-drive computer system skip down to STEP 24. If you have a one-drive system, go to STEP 19.

STEP 19. Set the prefix by pathname by pressing **P** twice and type in the pathname **/RAM**.

STEP 20. Insert the DOS 3.3 diskette that has the startup file on it. Transfer the DAZZLE.SYSTEM file from the DOS 3.3 diskette to the internal RAM disk by pressing **T** and then typing the name **DAZZLE.SYSTEM** when the program asks which DOS 3.3 file you want to convert.

STEP 21. Next, insert the ProDOS system disk and type **Q** to quit. When the program asks you for a file name type in:

/USERS.DISK/BASIC.SYSTEM

STEP 22. Without shutting off the computer, startup the ProDOS file transfer program by typing **F**.

STEP 23. Move DAZZLE.SYSTEM from your RAM disk to your backup copy of *Dazzle Draw* by pressing **F**, **C** and using **/RAM/=** and **/DD/=** as pathnames respectively. Go to STEP 26.

STEP 24. Set the prefix by pathname by pressing **P** twice and type in the pathname **/DD**.

STEP 25. Insert the DOS 3.3 diskette that has the startup file on it into drive 2 and the backup copy of *Dazzle Draw* into drive 1. Transfer the DAZZLE.SYSTEM file from the DOS 3.3 diskette to the backup diskette by

(continued on page 9)

FIVE BYTE DISK ANALYZER

by **David Stoll**
Manitoba, CANADA

While this article does not describe a crack for a specific program, it does describe a simple modification to normal DOS 3.3 that renders some protection schemes ineffective. All that is required to implement this modification to DOS is to change just five bytes of code. The changes to the five bytes are implemented via a short BASIC program, which also allows you to scan each track of the diskette and locate the CATALOG track.

I'd like to point out that this modification to DOS does not remove the copy protection from the programs it is used with. It simply makes it possible for the usual DOS commands to access any of the files on the protected disk. In many instances, this is all you need to do to make a backup copy of the protected program.

While this technique will not work with the new sophisticated protection techniques being used, there are still enough programs out that can use this techniques to make it useful. Programs that are particularly susceptible to this technique are those that alter the address field, data field or checksum and those that relocate the diskette's directory to a different track.

Using the program

To use the *Five Byte Disk Analyzer*, you should begin with a normally initialized DOS 3.3 diskette. Once the diskette is initialized, enter the BASIC program listing shown and save it to the diskette.

To check a protected diskette, boot up the *Five Byte Disk Analyzer* program. When the message, "INSERT PROTECTED DISK" is displayed, remove the *Five Byte Disk Analyzer* diskette and insert the copy-protected diskette. Then press any key when you're ready, and the program will attempt to CATALOG the diskette. *(Editor's Note: David originally used the CATALOG command in lines 40 and 140. I replaced it with the CALL 42350).* The CATALOG command is implemented by directly calling the machine language routine that handles it because some protection schemes change the names of the DOS commands to make life tougher on the user.

If the diskette's catalog is located on track 17 ($11) it will be displayed. You can then quit the program and try the conventional DOS commands to see if they work. If they do, fine, if not, you might want to run the *DOS Command Comparer* program that appeared in the last issue of *ASPD* on page 3, to find out what the new commands are. Even if you get a catalog listing right off the bat, you might want to use the program's scan option anyway because some protection schemes use two catalog tracks and switch back and forth between them.

If the program does not display the diskette's catalog right away, you're presented with a two-choice menu. You can either quit, or scan all of the tracks on the diskette, looking for the catalog track. The program starts scanning from track 1 (track 0 is the boot track and you can't have a catalog there) and goes up to track 34. You could probably safely start scanning from track 3, because tracks 1 and 2 are generally used to store DOS. If you find that most of the diskettes you scan have relocated directories on higher numbered tracks, you can change line 110 so that scanning will start with track 34 and work its way down. To do that, type in the following line:

110 FOR X = 34 TO ST STEP -1

If you suspect that the diskette you're examining has more than 35 tracks on it and that the catalog is on one of these extra tracks, you'll have to make some more changes to DOS. For more information on adding extra tracks to your diskette or moving the catalog to another track see ASPD Vol. 1, No. 1, p. 8 or Vol. 1, No. 3, p. 9.

```
10   REM FIVE BYTE DISK ANALYZER
20   POKE 47405,24 : POKE 47406,96 : POKE 47497,24 : POKE 47498,96
30   HOME : VTAB 7 : CALL -958 : PRINT TAB(10); "REMOVE DISK" :
     PRINT TAB(10); "INSERT PROTECTED DISK" : VTAB 10 : PRINT
     TAB(10); "PRESS ANY KEY WHEN READY"; : GET AN$
40   CALL 42350
50   PRINT : PRINT : PRINT TAB(6); "(S)CAN DISK FOR CATALOG
     TRACK" : PRINT TAB(6); "(Q)UIT" : PRINT TAB(6); "SELECT S OR Q";
60   GET AN$ : IF AN$ = "Q" OR AN$ = "q" THEN 180
70   IF AN$ = "S" OR AN$ = "s" THEN 90
80   GOTO 60
90   ST = 1
100  ONERR GOTO 170
110  FOR X = ST TO 34
120     HOME : PRINT "TRACK = "; X
130     POKE 44033,X
140     CALL 42350
150     VTAB 24 : CALL -958 : PRINT "PRESS A KEY FOR NEXT TRACK
        (Q = QUIT)"; GET AN$ : IF AN$ = "Q" OR AN$ = "q" THEN 180
160  NEXT X
170  POKE 216,0 : ST = X + 1 : IF B < 35 THEN 100
180  POKE 44033,17 : END
```

Noise and caution

As the program tries to CATALOG each track it is scanning, it will make a lot of noise. Do not be concerned. That's what happens when it tries to read a nonexistant directory on a track. After it tries each track, you will be given the option to quit, or continue the scanning.

When using this program there are two things you should be aware of. First, do not exit the track scanning routine by using the RESET key or turning the power off while the disk drive is running. The possible head bounce or transient currents generated by exiting in this manner may have undesireable results on your original disk. Always use the **Q** key to quit and avoid any damage. Quitting via the **Q** key also resets DOS to its normal value for the catalog track.

The second thing you must realize is that this method of searching for the catalog track that is used here, though simple, is crude. The errors and disk drive noises that occur, do so when the file manager routine in DOS checks sector zero of each track for the Volume Table of Contents (VTOC). Bytes 1 and 2 of the VTOC sector point to the starting track and sector of the directory entries. Since these bytes on nondirectory tracks are *dead ends* (but DOS does not know it) the disk drive arm moves, or tries to move, to this destination even if such a track does not exist on the diskette. Assuming you know what a VTOC sector should look like, a track dump program, such as the one found in Worth and Lechner's *Beneath Apple DOS* book, can be used first to see if a particular track is a catalog track.

How the program works

The simplest change made by this program, was the one that allows us to catalog any track we want. The DOS code from $ABDC to $AC05 initializes DOS's File Manager work area and sets it up to CATALOG the diskette. At location $AC01 (44033) the directory track value is assigned. To catalog a different track, only this one byte has to be changed. By changing this value inside a loop that runs from 1 to 34 and then issuing the CATALOG command (or its equivalent CALL 42350), it is possible to uncover a relocated directory track. In the worst case, this technique should produce 34 errors and one success.

The second part of the *Five Byte Disk Analyzer* defeats some types of protection by changing four bytes of DOS. The routine at $B944 to $B99F reads the address field of a track and is called by the File Manager in response to a CATALOG command. The routine checks for the presence of the address field prologue bytes $D5, $AA and $96 so that it can locate the start of a track. It also saves the volume number, track, sector and checksum, verifies the checksum and finally locates the epilogue bytes $DE and $AA. In an unmodified DOS, if any of these steps fails, the 6502's Carry Flag is set at $B942 and control is handed back to the File Manager. If the File Manager finds the Carry Flag set, the CATALOG command is terminated and an error message is displayed.

Fooling the File Manager

If we insert a clear carry (CLC) instruction and a return form subroutine (RTS) instruction before the checksum and the epilogue are checked, we can fool the File Manager into thinking that everything is okay and have it continue reading from the diskette. To make this change we must modify the bytes at locations $B989 (47497) and $B98A (47498). This is done by the last two POKEs on line 20 of the BASIC program listing.

A similar change is also made in the routine that reads a sector from the diskette. This routine is located from $B8DC to $B943. The sector read routine checks for the first two bytes of the address field ($D5 and $AA) but not the third byte. It then reads the sector data and stores the 256 bytes in a buffer in high memory. As all the sector data is now in RAM, a similar clear carry and return from subroutine modification can be inserted in this subroutine, at $B92D (47405) and $B92E (47406). This is done by the first two POKEs of line 20, and the File Manager is once again fooled into thinking that no errors exist.

If the protected diskette can be CATALOGed at this point, then individual files can be accessed and transferred one by one to a previously initialized, DOS 3.3 diskette. If the directory is still located on track 17 ($11), then at this point you can BRUN FID and transfer the files much more easily than doing it one at a time. If the directory is located on a track other than 17, you'll have to transfer the file to RAM, POKE 44033,17, transfer the file from RAM to an unprotected diskette and then rePOKE the relocated directory track into DOS so that you can access the next file on the protected diskette.

Some diskettes that appear to CATALOG correctly but only display garbage may have their program set up to look and act like DOS. In other words, on booting, the program is loaded and executed as an addition to, or in place of DOS.

If this program has allowed you to access programs on a protected diskette, you may or may not have overcome the protection scheme. It's very possible that there is still some code buried in the program that checks to see if the program is on its original protected diskette. Run the program to find out.

UNPROTECTING LOCKSMITH 5.0

by Brian A. Troha

This article was received from one of our readers without a letter or return address. We would like to give the author credit and a subscription extension and if he contacts us we will.

By now, most of you are probably well aware of the value of backing up your software. Now that most software is protected, however, this task is much tougher, hence the popularity of publications such as **Apple Software Protection Digest** and bit copier programs. One of the first commercial bit copiers that was available was *Locksmith 2.0*, which has gone through ten updates to revision 6.0. From version 2.0 up through version 5.0 level F, all were copy protected.

Bit slip protection used

Version 5.0 level F of *Locksmith* was protected with a form of the bit-insertion technique that is called *bit slip* protection. It works this way. The disk drive controller reads a special series of bytes from the diskette once, recording the values as it reads them. Then it reads this series of bits again. Due to hardware limitations (and the added zero bits) the values will *not* match up each time. When a copy is made, the bits will be "cleaned up" and thus each time these special bits are read, they will match up. When that happens, the program decides that the disk it is reading must be an illegal copy, and thus refuses to boot.

Of course, it is possible to make a bit copy of *Locksmith 5.0* with *Copy][Plus* (using the sector copy) and *Essential Data Duplicator* version 3 or 4 (with parameter changes), but the copies you make will still be protected. You can also make a nonworking copy of the program with any copier, including *COPYA* and the fast disk backup routine of *Locksmith*. When a working copy of the program is run, location $A9 in the zero page gets loaded with a $60 (the code for a return from a subroutine). On a bad (nonworking) copy, you will find that location $A9 gets loaded with the value $12. During the check to see if the disk is an original or a copy, the program does a jump to location $A9. If the copy is good, it will encounter the return code and continue execution. But, if the copy is bad, it will encounter a $12 and crash. Interrupting the program with a RESET will also scramble the code at $A9, so you won't be able to restart it easily.

How to make a good copy

Since there is no unusual formatting of the diskette with *Locksmith* it is possible to make a "bad" copy of the program with any copy program. We will use *COPYP*, because as you will see in a few minutes, only a one-byte change, accomplished with the aid of the sector editor in *COPYP*, is necessary to convert a bad copy into a good copy.

Once you've made a copy of the *Locksmith* diskette, you could try to break it by scanning the diskette for a series of bytes such as **4C A9 00** for the JMP $00A9 instruction or you could search for the code that stores a $12 in location $A9 when a bad copy is made and change it. The bytes you'd look for in this case would be **A9 12 85 A9**. Either search would be in vain, however, because the data on the diskette are encoded. The encoding method used is to EOR (exclusively OR) the data by the value of its location on a page of memory. In the case of the value $12 which is stored when a bad copy is made, the $12 is EORed with the value of its location, which is $70. The result is $62. If you know where to look on the diskette (and I'll tell you in a minute) you can find that value.

You can get a better understanding of what's going on by booting up *Locksmith* and once the main menu appears, getting into the monitor by pressing RESET if you have an old F8 ROM installed or using the *Wild Card* (from Central Point Software). Once you're in the monitor, you can try to search for the byte sequences mentioned earlier with a memory searching program, such as the one that appeared in ASPD Vol. 1. No. 3, p. 4. Doing this, you should find the **4C A9 00** code at $1446 and the **A9 12 85 A9** code at $196F. Taking a closer look, we find three segments of code that are of interest:

```
A) 1446-  4C A9 00    JMP $00A9
   1449-  60          RTS

B) 196F-  A9 12       LDA #$12
   1971-  85 A9       STA $A9
   1973-  60          RTS

C) 1B19-  4C 46 14    JMP $1446
```

Several cracks possible

A crack for this diskette can be implemented by modifying the code in anyone of the three segments shown above. In case A, we have a a very short subroutine whose whole purpose is to jump to location $A9. If the diskette is a good copy, this location will contain a $60, and control will return immediately to the subroutine listed in A, where control is returned to the caller and the program continues to execute. A crack that deals with this segment of code would be to replace the three bytes of the jump code with three NOP bytes ($EAs).

In case B, we have the actual culprit, the code that is executed to inform the program that a bad copy is in fact bad. In this segment of code a $12 is loaded into the accumulator and then stored in location $A9, where it waits until it is time to cause the copy to crash. The *Locksmith* protection scheme can be cracked by modifying the code in segment B in any one of three ways.

1. The first byte of code segment B (the $A9) can be replaced with a $60, which is the code for a return from subroutine, so that this subroutine is essentially bypassed and ignored.
2. The $12 can be changed to a $60 so that the correct value (to indicated a good copy) is always stored in $A9.
3. The code that stores the $12 can be replaced with NOP instructions.

Finally, in case C, we can crack the program by making sure that the program never jumps to subroutine that checks the protection in the first place. This would be done by replacing the three bytes of the JMP $1446 instruction with NOP codes.

Undoubtly, the meticulous cracker could find several additional ways of cracking this program as well, but these are the most obvious. The best way to crack *Locksmith* is to always store the right value, no matter what happens. This prevents crashes caused by other possibly undetected routines that check to see if the copy is good.

A single sector edit is all that is required to convert a bad copy into a good copy. We want to make sure that a $60 is stored in $A9. Once the program is loaded into memory, the value of $60 would be found at location $70 of the page of memory it's located in. Earlier we said that the byte is encoded by EORing the value with the page location or $60 EOR $70, which equals $10. So if we're going to make the bad copy good, we'll have to store a $10 at the right spot on the diskette. To find the right spot on the diskette, we have to EOR each byte in case B with its page location (e.g. A9 EOR 6F, 12 EOR 70, 85 EOR 71, A9 EOR 72). If you do this, the byte sequence you wind up with is **C6 62 F4 DB**. If you search your "bad" copy of *Locksmith* for this byte sequence (using *Copy][Plus* or some other diskette scanner), you'll find the sequence on track $0F, sector $0E. As we said earlier, the byte we want to change is byte $70.

Since we now know where the change has to be made, we can use *COPYP* to do it as it makes the copy to begin with. We do that by simply adding the following line to the *COPYP* program:

1000 DATA 15,14,112,98,16

That's all there is to it. You now have an unprotected copy of *Locksmith*. Next month we'll show you how to strip *Locksmith's* Fast Backup utility of the diskette and convert it into a BRUNable file.

How to Crack Dazzle Draw
(continued from page 5)

pressing **T** and then typing the name **DAZZLE.SYSTEM** when the program asks which DOS 3.3 file you want to convert.

STEP 26. DAZZLE.SYSTEM is now on our ProDOS backup diskette as a binary (BIN) file and must now be converted to a system (SYS) file. We can do this by typing in the following series of lines:

BLOAD DAZZLE.SYSTEM,A$2000
DELETE DAZZLE.SYSTEM
CREATE DAZZLE.SYSTEM,TSYS
BSAVE DAZZLE.SYSTEM,A$2000, L$2A00,TSYS

That's all there is to it. You now have an unprotected copy of *Dazzle Draw* that boots up just like the original. You can make additional copies of this program by using any standard copy program such as COPYA.

COPYP FILE PARAMETERS

Listed below are several parameter files for use with the *COPYP* program that was presented in ASPD Vol. 1, No. 2. You can key these lines in directly or you can do what I do and create text files that contain these lines. Then you can load *COPYP* and EXEC in the appropriate file for the program you want to copy.

The following parameters were submitted by Brian A. Troha of Stoughton, WI. Thanks Brian, we're going to add an extra month onto your subscription for your contribution.

Karate Champ

Brian says that the *Karate Champ* crack started out when a friend asked him to make a backup copy of his original. He says he used *Copy][Plus*, but the diskette that resulted didn't work. He then checked the reset vector at $3F2 and found the address $BE93 (3F2- 93 BE), so he searched the diskette for these values and located the protection routine on the diskette. The following lines when added to *COPYP* will let it copy *Karate Champ*.

1000 DATA 0,3,190,32,234
1010 DATA 0,3,191,0,234
1020 DATA 0,3,192,191,234
1030 DATA 0,3,193,144,234
1040 DATA 0,3,194,3,234
1050 DATA 0,3,195,76,234
1060 DATA 0,3,196,147,234
1070 DATA 0,3,197,190,234

REVIEW: Locksmith 6.0

by Scott Barrus

As you may recall from my review of *Locksmith 5.0 Level G* from an earlier issue of **ASPD** (Vol.1, No. 2), I have been anxiously looking forward to receiving the new version of Locksmith. It finally arrived, and I was very excited about some of the new features that it offers. Included in this new version of the program is an Auto Boot Tracer/Debugger, a fast copy utility that recognizes the presence of a Ramworks II card and uses that extra memory to speed up the copying process, a RAM card utilities section and last but certainly not least, easier-to-use parameters. The program still contains many of the good features from its predecessor too.

There are many difference between the new Locksmith and the old one. The first of these is in the manual. Compared to the 140-page manual that accompanied the previous version, the new 75-page manual for Version 6.0 is kind of skimpy. The new manual skims over some of the technical information and operating instructions have been cut to a bare minimum, and sometimes even below that. For example, the section on the Fast Disk Backup (FDB) states that "...FDB will automatically recognize any RAM cards in your Apple, whether they are in slots 0 - 7 or in the auxilliary slot of the Apple //e." The section on the Auto Boot Tracer (ABT) states,"...ABT will prompt you for the slot number of the RAM card. Key in digit from 0 to 7." Upon close examination we see that the memory in auxilliary slot 3 is not mentioned. The words *RAM card* seem to refer only to slot RAM cards and not Ramworks II style cards. When I tried to load the Auto Boot Tracer onto a Ramworks II card located in the auxilliary slot, it would not work, so I called Alpha Logic Business Systems. They said that a sofware technician would contact me to help straigten out the situation. So far, no one has returned my call. I guess we can safely say that customer support is not one of the key features of this program.

Among some of the new and interesting features that are included in the new Locksmith program are:

- Disk, nibble, memory and track/sector editor for protected diskettes
- Framing bit analyzer
- RAM card utilities
- Automatic Boot Tracer/Debugger
- DOS 3.3 utilities
- Advanced disk recovery.

The disk, nibble and memory editor (formerly the nibble editor on L.S. 5.) can be used to manually read, search, change and rewrite information either in sector or nibble format. It can also edit ProDOS or DOS 3.3 files, or modify data on any RAM card that is installed in an Apple. Unfortunately, specific information on how to access RAM card data isn't in the manual.

The framing bit analyzer is actually a part of the disk, nibble and memory editor. It performs statistical analysis using precise timing loops and reports the timing relationship of the nibbles.

RAM card utilities are used to test RAM cards in the Apple. The utilities are somewhat limited however in that they cannot test any auxilliary memory found in the Apple //e or //c computers. In addition to testing slot-based RAM cards, the utilities can also dump the contents of any 16K RAM bank into main memory.

Boot tracer is nice, but...

One of the most effective ways of overcoming copy protection schemes is to trace the action of the program as it boots up. The problem with *boot code tracing*, as it is commonly called, is that it can be complicated. Alpha Logic has attempted to simplify this process by including an automatic boot code tracer in this new version of Locksmith. and it works nicely, as far as it goes. But there are some problems with it, which lead us back once more to the program's ability, or should I say lack of it, to interface with all popular RAM cards. Although the program is supposed to be able to work with *any* RAM card, I could not get it to load onto the Ramworks II card or even into the back 64K of a 128K Apple //e or //c. It would only load into the top 16K. This causes some problems, mostly with ProDOS based software since this top 16K is where ProDOS resides. Thus it is not possible to use the automatic boot tracer to trace any ProDOS-based programs.

The DOS 3.3 utilities that are included with the program can come in very handy. You can use them to alphabetize a catalog, undelete a file, load a DOS file into memory for examination by the disk editor, display a disk free space map, correct catalogs and VTOCs and remove DOS from a diskette so that you'll have more room to store programs and data.

In addition, the program contains some advanced disk recovery utilities that can read partially clobbered diskettes and write out a good copy to another diskette. The disk recovery utilities can even recover data from a diskette that was writtin to while it was inserted into the disk drive off-center.

Parameters are easier to use

The programmers who produced this new version of Locksmith did their homework as far as the copy parameters are concerned. They've made them much easier to use. The same Locksmith Programming Language (LPL) is used in this version of the program as in previous ones, and the parameters are the same too. But, unlike earlier versions, which loaded parameters in from a file based on the first letter of the parameter and then searching for the exact match, this version presents a list of parameter names. By moving the cursor to the correct name and pressing the RETURN key, you can get the parameters you need.

It makes fast copies

One of the nicest features of this program is its Fast Disk Copy routine. If you have a 128K Apple //e or //c, the routine will copy an unprotected diskette in only two passes. However, if you have a Ramworks or compatible memory expansion card with more memory (I have 512K), a diskette can be copied in only *one* pass!

This new version of Locksmith seems to work much better than its predecessor and it is definitely worth getting. There are however a few areas where the program can stand improvement. To begin with, it would be nice if the program were setup so that it could be used from a hard disk. Currently the program is automatically loaded in with the operating system and no separate file exists that can be transferred to a hard disk. The other major objection I have to the program is its poor manual. More time and effort should have been put into producing a complete, informative and useful manual. If you're willing to put up with these drawbacks, however, you'll find this program to be a useful addition to your anti-copy protection arsenal.

Source: Alpha Logic Business Systems, 4119 North Union Rd., Woodstock, IL 60098. **Call:** (815) 568-5166.

BECOME AN ASSEMBLY LANGUAGE PROGRAMMING WHIZ

"Now That You Know Apple Assembly Language: What Can You Do With It?" will take you step-by-step through the assembly language programming experience. You'll delve into the mysteries of the 6502 stack and learn how to use it to increase the power and versatility of your programs. You'll also learn how to use the Apple's built-in routines to minimize the amount of coding you must do.

Control the output and the input

Frequently it's desirable to gain total control of the computer's output. This book shows you how to *steal control away from the Apple's normal output routines and redirect it to your own pro-*

*NOTE: Shipping and handling fees are not refundable.

Redlig Systems, Inc., Dept. A 9783
2068—79th St., Brooklyn, NY 11214

Please rush me _____ copies of "**Now That You Know Apple Assembly Language: What Can You Do With It?**" at $19.95 each plus $2 shipping and handling. I understand that if I am not delighted with the book I may return it within 10 days for a prompt and courteous refund. In any case, the Programmer's Number Conversion System and $5 coupon are mine to keep.

☐ Enclosed is my check for $ _____

Please charge my credit card:
☐ American Express ☐ MasterCard ☐ Visa

Card No. _____ Exp. _____
Signature _____
Name _____
Address _____
City _____ State _____ Zip _____

---

gram. Thus if you wanted, you could see the normally invisible control characters, display text on your screen as black on white instead of the normal white on black, format text sent to a printer into pages and much more.

Expand the power of your Apple by *stealing control away from the normal input routines.* Do things like adding a screen print capability, or *convert part of the normal keyboard into a numeric keypad.* It's even possible to *produce self-modifying programs* by EXECing in commands from RAM instead of from the disk drive. Think about the possibilities that offers for protecting your programs. When you want to go back to Applesoft programming, *you'll be able to do it faster with the aid of Applesoft Shorthand*, an assembly language program that types in one or more Applesoft commands at the press of a key, or use another program in the book to *automatically count the number of lines in your Applesoft program.*

With this book you'll also learn about *generating tones and how to figure out the frequency, producing sound effects, teaching your Apple to send Morse code, restoring accidentally erased Applesoft programs, adding new commands to Applesoft and running two Applesoft programs in memory together,* to name a few.

As an extra bonus for prompt ordering, you'll receive a *FREE coupon worth $5 off* the price of a disk with all the assembled programs on it or a disk that contains the source code. These disks normally sell for $15 each. We're offering these FREE gifts for a limited time only, so hurry! *Order today!*

Money-back guarantee*

We're so confident that you'll find this book invaluable and want it in your library, that we're offering a 10-day, no-questions-asked, money-back guarantee. Order the book. Read it and try the programs for ten days. At the end of ten days if you don't think it's worth every penny you paid for it, just send it back in resalable condition and we'll refund your money immediately, no questions asked.

ASPD PROGRAM DISKETTES AVAILABLE FOR ONLY $15 EACH

Every month we will make a DOS 3.3 diskette available that contains all of the programs for the current issue of *Apple Software Protection Digest*.

Each diskette is available for only $15 each. Diskette 1 contains the programs from issues 1 and 2. There are currently 4 diskettes available.

To order send a check, money order or your credit card number and expiration date to:

>   REDLIG SYSTEMS, INC.
>   2068 - 79th Street
>   Brooklyn, New York 11214

REDLIG SYSTEMS, INC.
2068 79th Street
Brooklyn, New York 11214

BULK RATE
U.S. POSTAGE
PAID
BROOKLYN, NY
Permit No. 631

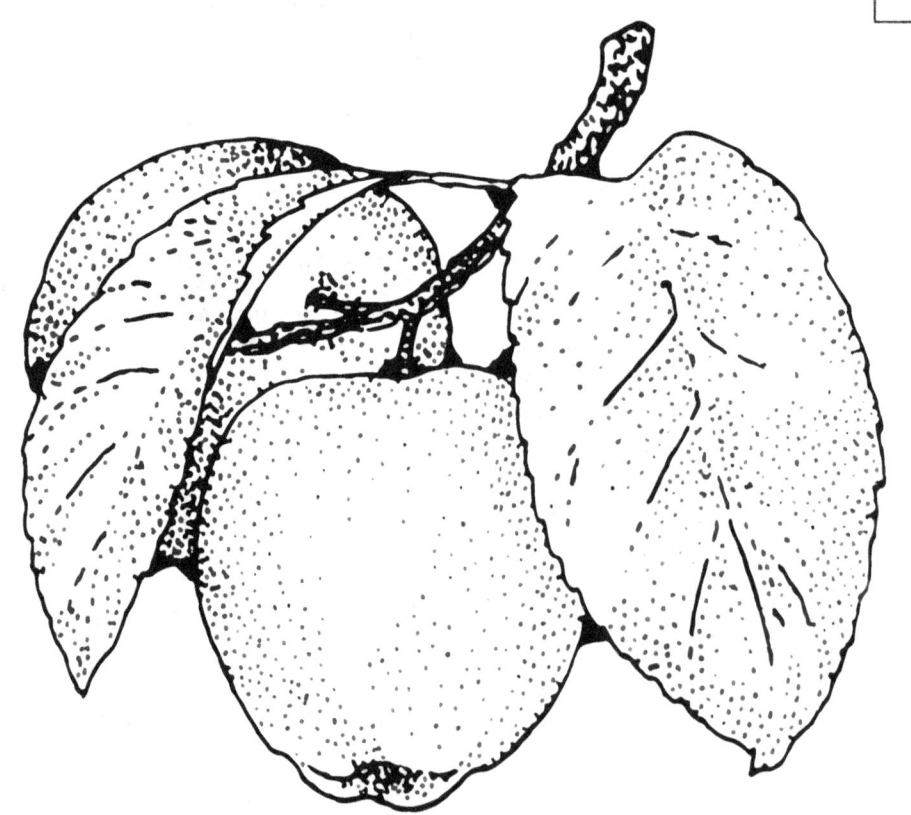

www.ingramcontent.com/pod-product-compliance
Lightning Source LLC
Chambersburg PA
CBHW081450220526
45466CB00008B/2582